# THE RIVALS

ERIN SWANN

This book is a work of fiction. The names, characters, businesses, and events portrayed in this book are fictitious. Any similarity to real persons, living or dead, businesses, or events is coincidental and not intended by the author.

Copyright © 2021 by Swann Publications

All rights reserved.

No part of this book may be reproduced, stored in a retrieval system, or transmitted in any form or by any means, electronic, mechanical, photocopying, recording, or otherwise, without the express written permission of the publisher. Reasonable portions may be quoted for review purposes.

The author acknowledges the trademarked status and trademark owners of various products referenced in this work of fiction, which have been used without permission. The publication/use of these trademarks is not authorized, associated with, or sponsored by the trademark owners.

Cover images licensed from shutterstock.com, depositphotos.com

Cover design by Swann Publications

ISBN: 979-8533547161

Edited by Jessica Royer Ocken

Proofreaders: My Brother's Editor, Donna Hokanson

Typohunter Extraordinaire: Michelle

The following story is intended for mature readers. It contains mature themes, strong language, and sexual situations. All characters are 18+ years of age, and all sexual acts are consensual.

**Want to hear about new releases and sales?**

If you would like to hear about Erin's **new releases** and sales, join the newsletter HERE. We only email about sales or new releases, and we never share your information.

Erin can be found on the web at https://www.erinswann.com

✽ Created with Vellum

## ALSO BY ERIN SWANN

Why romance? Because we all need a chance to escape doing the next load of laundry.

We deserve a chance to enjoy love, laughs, intrigue, and yes, fear, heartbreak, and tears, all without having to leave the house.

If you can read my books without feeling any of these then I haven't done my job right.

**Covington Billionaires Series:**

**The Billionaire's Trust** - Available on Amazon, also in AUDIOBOOK

(Bill and Lauren's story) He needed to save the company. He needed her. He couldn't have both. The wedding proposal in front of hundreds was like a fairy tale come true—Until she uncovered his darkest secret.

**The Youngest Billionaire** - Available on Amazon, also in AUDIOBOOK

(Steven and Emma's story) The youngest of the Covington clan, Steven, avoided the family business to become a rarity, an honest lawyer. He didn't suspect that pursuing Emma could destroy his career. She didn't know what trusting him could cost her.

**The Secret Billionaire** – Available on Amazon, also in AUDIOBOOK

(Patrick and Elizabeth's story) Women naturally circled the flame of wealth and power, and his is brighter than most. Does she love him? Does she not? There's no way to know. When Pat stopped to help her, Liz mistook him for a carpenter. Maybe this time he'd know. Everything was perfect. Until the day she left.

**The Billionaire's Hope** - Available on Amazon, also in AUDIOBOOK

(Nick and Katie's story) They came from different worlds. Katie hadn't seen him since the day he broke her brother's nose. Her family retaliated by destroying Nick's life. She never suspected where accepting a ride from him today would take her. They said they could do casual. They lied.

Previously titled: Protecting the Billionaire

**Picked by the Billionaire** – Available on Amazon, also in AUDIOBOOK

(Liam and Amy's story) A night she wouldn't forget. An offer she couldn't refuse. He alone could save her, and she held the key to his survival. If only they could pass the test together.

**Saved by the Billionaire** – Available on Amazon, also in AUDIOBOOK

(Ryan and Natalie's story) The FBI and the cartel were both after her for the same thing: information she didn't have. First, the FBI took everything, and then the cartel came for her. She trusted Ryan with her safety, but could she trust him with her heart?

**Caught by the Billionaire** – Available on Amazon, also in AUDIOBOOK

(Vincent and Ashley's story) Ashley's undercover assignment was simple enough: nail the crooked billionaire. The surprise came when she opened the folder, and the target was her one-time high school sweetheart, Vincent. What will happen when an unknown foe makes a move to checkmate?

**The Driven Billionaire** – Available on Amazon

(Zachary and Brittney's story) Rule number one: hands off your best friend's sister. With nowhere to turn when she returns from upstate, Brittney accepts Zach's offer of a room. Mutual attraction quickly blurs the rules. When she comes under attack, pulling Brittney closer is the only way to keep her safe. But, the truth of why she left town in the first place will threaten to destroy them both.

**Nailing the Billionaire** – Available on Amazon

(Dennis and Jennifer's story) Jennifer knew he destroyed her family. Now she is close to finding the records that will bring Dennis down. When a corporate shakeup forces her to work with him, anger and desire compete. Vengeance was supposed to be simple, swift, and sweet. It was none of those things.

**Undercover Billionaire** – Available on Amazon

(Adam and Kelly's story) Their wealthy families have been at war forever. When Kelly receives a chilling note, the FBI assigns Adam to protect her. Family histories and desire soon collide, questioning old truths. Keeping ahead of the threat won't be their only challenge.

**Trapped with the Billionaire** – Available on Amazon

(Josh and Nicole's story) Nicole returns from vacation to find her company has been sold to Josh's family. Being assigned to work for the new CEO is only the first of her problems. Competing visions of how to run things and mutual passion create a volatile mix. The reappearance of a killer from years ago soon threatens everything.

**Saving Debbie** – Available on Amazon

(Luke and Debbie's story) On the run from her family and the cops, Debbie finds the only person she can trust is Luke, the ex-con who patched up her injuries. Old lies haunt her, and the only way to unravel them is to talk with Josh, the boy who lived through the nightmare with her years ago.

**Return to London** – Available on Amazon

(Ethan and Rebecca's story) Rebecca looks forward to the most important case of her career. Until, she is paired with Ethan, the man she knew years ago. Mutual attraction and old secrets combine to complicate everything. What could have been a second chance results in an impossible choice.

**The Rivals** – Available on Amazon

(Charlie and Danielle's story) He was her first crush. That ended when their families had a falling out. Now, they are forced to work together on a complicated acquisition. Mutual attraction is complicated by distrust as things go wrong around them. A second chance turns into an impossible choice.

**Clear Lake Series:** The Clear Lake books follow the Bensons of Clear Lake as they deal with a disappearance in town which shatters the tranquility of their community and puts them in the cross-hairs of the local police chief.

**Temptation at the Lake** – Available on Amazon

(Casey and Jordan's story) Shot in the line of duty and on temporary disability, Jordan leaves the city for Clear Lake to recuperate. Getting back to one hundred percent was supposed to be hard, but she didn't count on the irresistible Casey becoming the devil pushing her to the breaking point. A fling with this devil becomes complicated when she gets pulled into the dangerous town feud.

**Desire at the Lake** – Available on Amazon

(Waylon and Anna's story) Things quickly spiral out of control for Anna when her boss disappears. Suddenly out of a job and with no place to stay, her only refuge becomes Waylon's garage. The undeniable chemistry between them explodes. Everything changes when Waylon is arrested for her ex-boss's murder.

# CHAPTER 1

*Charles*

On Monday morning, the farther I walked from my downtown Boston hotel, the more the streets and the nature of the neighborhood deteriorated. The overnight rain hadn't cleansed the air of the smell from the garbage bins I passed.

A crow cawed at me from its perch on a pole, reminding me that this was his country, not mine. My hand in my pocket clutched the warm mobile phone—a device I couldn't do without and dared not trust. I slowed to navigate the puddles of the poorly maintained road. The store ahead would be remote enough for my purpose.

The same thin man as before had followed me from the hotel this morning, but I'd lost him by entering a breakfast restaurant on my way here and exiting through the back door. It would have been exhilarating if there wasn't so much on the line.

After all the turns I'd taken since, I didn't think I'd been followed. But I still took a casual look both ways—a lady with a child, a teenaged couple, and a woman with grocery bags in both arms.

The coast was clear.

I pulled open the cold door handle. A chime sounded as I passed inside to the musty interior.

The girl behind the counter looked up. A crinkle at the corner of her eye said she didn't judge me to be from this part of town. "What can I help you with?"

"I'd like to purchase a mobile—sorry, a cell phone." I had to remember my American English.

A smile appeared, and she pointed to my right. "Over here."

I followed her and peered into the counter display.

"You're British?" she asked.

I nodded. "London, nearabouts. Is that okay?" The accent gave me away.

"Sure, so long as you have American money." She stroked her hair behind her ear. "Calling home?"

"Me mum." I didn't say any more than that. Already I was making more of an impression than I cared to. Memorable could be bad.

"A lot of people like this one." She pointed out a simple smartphone.

"If you say so. I'll also need a card—let's say fifty dollars."

That earned me a smile as she pulled the box from under the glass.

She totaled it up, and I paid with bills instead of my card.

"Would it be okay if I unboxed it and set it up here?"

She shrugged. "Be two dollars for the trash."

I reached for my wallet again.

"Just kidding ya." She laughed. "Here." She handed me scissors to attack the packaging.

Ten minutes later, I walked out with the phantom mobile in one pocket and the charger in the other.

A block away, I dialed Dad with the new device.

He didn't pick up. It went to voicemail.

"Dad, it's Charlie," I told him. "I've picked up a fresh mobile for security. Call me back on this number when you get the message."

Dad's return call rang two blocks later.

"What's this about a new number?" he asked as soon as I answered.

"I think we're being bugged."

He was silent for a moment. "Why do you say that?"

"We moved up our offer last night, and another offer arrived at the same time, but one-tenth higher. It was if they *knew* what we were going to bid."

"That could be a lucky guess on their part."

"The first time might have been a coincidence, but this is the second time it's happened. And I've also seen someone following me."

"Following you? Perhaps this is a good precaution."

"This process of theirs is all so strange. Are you sure this is worth pursuing?" I asked.

Sellers always held the meetings on their home turf, in an environment comfortable for them, and sometimes intentionally uncomfortable for us—but not Hawker Technologies. They'd picked the hotel I was staying at and insisted on meeting there.

Dad and I had agreed it was part of their insistence on keeping the competing buyers from knowing who else was in the bidding.

Acquisitions, by their very nature, could be secretive affairs. The selling company often didn't want its employees, or a hostile competitor, to know it was on the market. And the person on the other side, such as us, didn't want the negotiations to be known either.

Having it come out in public before the signatures were in place always worsened the situation. Speculators upped the price, and a competitor could even come in to steal the deal. There was a lot to keep track of.

"Beyond being outbid yesterday, what else do we know?" Dad asked.

I stayed silent for a moment as I passed an old man. "They told us the fourth party had dropped out." The number of bidders had never been a secret, only the identities.

"Nice of them to tell us. That makes it a little easier, I suppose. My information is that Wentworth is likely one of the others. Any clue on your end as to who else may be in the mix?"

"No idea at all." It was time to talk strategy. "How much higher do you want to go? This is no longer a bargain, and frankly, I think at the current level, it's becoming too big a bite as well."

"Let's go up another three percent, but ask for a more detailed plan for the next two fiscal years. The delay would be good. Eagerness is not rewarded."

We would be nearing the endgame soon. "Is three percent as far as you want to go?"

"I want this company. That's it for this round."

"Okay." I rang off and pocketed the mobile again.

Being determined to win regardless of price was uncharacteristic for Dad, but it was his prerogative.

The chance to buy a conglomerate with a jet-engine subsidiary was the only thing rare about Hawker. In the final analysis, the products they made were just an intermediate step to getting paid. Making money is what a company is all about, and it could be done as easily with hair dryers as aircraft engines or anything else.

Dad's agreement that I'd get the chance to run the Berlin office was all that motivated me about this particular deal. Getting into operations would mean I wouldn't be living out of a suitcase for a change—that and cutting the marionette strings a bit. If this deal didn't come through, I'd have to wait for the next one.

I pulled up the map app on the mobile to find the most direct route back to the restaurant. Getting back before Thin Man figured out I'd left through the back was the plan.

Twenty minutes later, I exited through the front door of the eating establishment with a growling stomach and turned right.

I spotted Thin Man again a block back as I approached the hotel. Skipping the meal had been worth it to procure the mobile without alerting him. Now I had an advantage he wasn't aware of—him and whoever he worked for.

~

### Danielle

My phone beeped with a reminder to leave for Daddy's weekly staff meeting. Being the boss's daughter came with responsibilities. One of those was to always be early.

Outside we had the normal London overcast. I pulled up the weather in Paris. Sunshine. That's what I had to look forward to, eventually.

My phone rang as I walked up to the conference room for Daddy's meeting. It was my brother, John. Dispatched to Boston to represent the Wentworth interests in a potential acquisition, his weather was likely better as well.

"For once you have your mobile on you," he said by way of greeting.

He'd switched to calling a cell phone a *mobile* in deference to our London officemates. He'd even picked up the accent of a local, slightly.

I stuck to the American terms of *phone* or *cell* since I'd gotten my first cell phone as a young child in the States. "Hey, big brother, find any cute babes out there?" I asked in my American accent. Having grown up there, and moved here later, I could switch it on and off.

He'd been gone over a week now on the latest deal our Daddy was pursuing, and it was a big one.

"Very funny, Dani. I need you to talk to Dad about calling off this deal."

"You're the one he listens to."

"I'm serious. This doesn't feel right, and I don't think we should do it, but he's not hearing me."

As I passed by, the copy room was empty, so I ducked in there and closed the door. The faint smell of machine oil from Daddy's industrial-strength shredder filled the air. I opened my day planner on top of a copier to take notes. "What's the problem? And what can I do about it? He didn't want me to go along with you on this."

Our father hadn't let me participate in any of our merger deals—yet.

"This negotiation process smells to high heaven, and I don't trust them. Maybe you can ask Dad a few questions and get him thinking about it. When I talk to him, he's not listening. His sole focus is winning."

The last few times I'd asked Daddy if I could join John on one of these trips, his answers had ranged from *"it's rather technical"* to *"you're needed here."* But I knew my time would come, if I kept at it. I was only a year younger than John, and Dad knew my goal.

I wanted to run one of our Paris subsidiaries. I dreamed about having everybody in the building working for me, and seeing the Eiffel Tower out my window.

Dad had been clear that "doing deals," as he called it, was the step to running one of the subsidiaries. It made sense that John would get the opportunity before me, as he was older, but that didn't mean I wanted to wait to get started.

"Okay, if you think it will help," I told my brother.

He sucked in a loud breath. "I appreciate it."

"The staff meeting's about to start. I'll talk to him after that."

"Thanks."

We hung up.

When I entered the conference room, Dad hadn't arrived yet, and my brother John's normal seat on Dad's right was empty, so I claimed the power chair.

Ellis Wyman, who Daddy often sent out to take charge of our acquisitions in the early months, entered the conference room next.

I nodded. "Ellis."

He returned the greeting and, unfortunately, chose the chair next to me.

His last name was prophetic, as almost every time I asked him to do something for me, his reply was *why?* I was growing tired of justifying myself.

Ellis opened his laptop.

I opened my day planner. A pen and paper were my preference.

The room quickly filled, with the other arrivals electing to sit farther from my end of the table, probably to avoid the occasional lightning bolts that emanated from my father when he was displeased with somebody's weekly report.

Dad arrived promptly at ten and started the meeting. Punctuality was one of his qualities.

The sales VP started off, and I was next up with marketing. The two of us got the least grilling, and there was only one question across my three pages of presentation.

Most of the group considered it either impolite or dangerous to question the boss's daughter too aggressively. I could never tell which.

When the next speaker started, I zoned out and considered my conversation with John. It wasn't like him to panic, so what had him so ruffled?

I smiled to myself when I realized this meant I wasn't the only one being ignored when it came to giving Dad advice. If John trusted me to help convince our father of something, that had to be good.

Ellis looked over, and his eyes narrowed.

I schooled my face back to impassive and returned my gaze to the presentation.

∽

AFTER THE MEETING, I PREPARED A CUP OF TEA BEFORE HEADING TO DADDY'S office.

He looked up from his desk as I reached the door. He had the desk phone to his ear.

When he finished the call, I entered and closed the door behind me. "Are you sure this deal John's working on is worth the worry and effort?"

Dad lifted his chin with a knowing smirk. "He talked to you too."

I laid out my brother's message as plainly as I could. "Daddy, John has a bad feeling about this."

He steepled his hands and nodded. "This is a difficult one."

"Maybe I could go out and help him. Two heads are better than one." The two heads saying was one of his favorites.

"He has it handled for now. I have faith in him." He didn't add whether he had faith in me or not.

I stood and walked to the door. With my hand on the handle, I turned. "If you have complete faith in him…" I opened the door. "Why ignore his advice to drop this one?"

The door closed behind me before he had a chance to answer. Mission accomplished. John's message had been reinforced, and Daddy could stew on his own words.

# CHAPTER 2

*Charles*

This afternoon, I was done being passive.

It was time to be proactive, and the best thing I could think to do was figure out who the other bidders were.

I'd loaded my secret phone with the few numbers I'd need to make contact back in London, then added one more number here in the States that I hadn't used in five years—Bill Covington in California.

He was the cousin nobody except Dad and my brother knew about. We'd agreed to keep the relationship between our families secret, for both our sakes. Nobody gained by having it become known that my grandfather had strayed, or that Bill's father was the result.

Downstairs, I entered the hotel fitness center. A gentleman was on one of the treadmills. I took the other and started a jog.

He left shortly after, and I stopped my machine.

I dialed Bill Covington's number on my spare mobile. This room wouldn't be bugged.

"Hello?" the voice from years ago answered.

"Bill, this is Charlie Blakewell. Do you have a few minutes?"

"Sure, hold a second." He spoke to someone else on his end. "Can you give me a minute? Family business. Thanks." The sound of a door closing came through the phone. "Yes, cuz, it's been a long time. What can I do for you?"

I walked toward the window. "I'm in a bit of a bind, and I need your help."

"Sure. Anything for family. What do you need?"

I breathed easier. Calling him had been taking a chance, and I'd hoped he would help, but hadn't known what his reaction would be. "I'm in Boston, and I need someone who can check for bugs."

"I've got a top-notch firm out here, but for resources there, you should ask Vincent Benson. He's in town."

I wasn't keen on involving anyone outside the family. "I'm not sure—"

"Don't worry. The Bensons are close friends of the family. I'll send you his contact info. He owes me. Tell him you're a friend of mine, and he'll fix you up with someone you can trust."

I looked out the window. Somewhere out there was the enemy. "Thanks, Bill. I appreciate it."

"No thanks necessary. It's what we do for family."

We rang off after I assured him he could count on me for anything he needed in the UK.

The contact information for Vincent Benson arrived a moment later, with the message that I should wait a few minutes before calling.

I checked my watch and looked up Vincent Benson online while I waited. He turned out to be an executive at Covington Enterprises here in Boston. I dialed after the requisite time had elapsed.

"Benson," he answered.

"My name is Charlie Blakewell," I began. "Bill Covington referred me to you."

"Guys, can you give me a minute? I need to take this," I heard him say, followed by the sound of a door closing. "Bill said you might call. How can I help?"

"I know I'm being watched, and I suspect I'm being listened to."

"Is this line secure?" he asked.

"Yes. I just purchased this mobile. I need someone who can check for bugs in my hotel room."

"Give me the hotel and room number. I'll send over Ben Murdoch, our director of security. He'll be able to take care of you."

"Thanks." I gave him the details he needed.

"And," he said, "don't hesitate to call if there's anything else I can do for you."

"I won't. Thank you." I'd always thought having Bill Covington as a cousin was a liability to be hidden, but today it was paying off.

I sent Bill a thank-you text.

MURDOCH ARRIVED FORTY MINUTES LATER WITH A FINGER TO HIS LIPS. HE HELD out a card that read:

Hallway—close the door behind you

I did.

Vincent Benson's director of security looked the part: small eyes, a head of hair—if you could call it that—trimmed to a quarter inch, and a scar through one eyebrow.

Once the door was closed, Ben introduced his helper, Milosh Nikolic, who carried a small suitcase.

"You're a friend of the Covingtons?" Ben asked.

I gave him half a nod. "Yes."

"They're good people. Keycard," he said, obviously a man of few words.

I handed it over.

"Make yourself scarce. I'll text you when we're done."

After wandering downstairs and out to the street, I purchased a cup of Earl Grey from the Starbucks on the other side of the road.

The text he'd promised arrived before the tea was cool enough for my first sip.

When I returned, they stood outside the door. Milosh carried the aluminum suitcase, same as before, and Ben had a sheet of paper in his hand.

"No video, but three audio devices," he told me, pointing to one of several red Xs on his hand-drawn map of my hotel suite. "One under the nightstand to the left of the bed." He moved to the next X. "One next to the couch, here, and another under the desk." He looked up. "How do you want to proceed?"

"Pardon?"

"We can either remove them, which I don't recommend because it alerts the other side." This was all a game to him. "Or just feed them what you want, and only say the rest outside in the open."

"What about my mobile phone?"

He scrolled his phone and turned it to show me a picture. "This is one of the devices in there. It's first-rate stuff, not dime-store crap. These guys will be using software to listen to your cell phone almost guaranteed. Unless you want to invest in encrypted phones on both ends, just get yourself a burner they don't know about, and that's that."

I pulled my second mobile from my pocket. "Already done."

He handed me the piece of paper, a business card, and a cardkey. "I've already cleared it with Mr. Benson. The address at the bottom is a condo on Tremont across from the Common, one floor below Mr. Benson's unit. The place is secure, and you can use it as long as you like. This cardkey will get you in. The doorman is named Carl. He knows you're a guest of Mr. Benson, and he'll get you anything you need. Mr. Benson said you think you have a tail. Do you have a picture of him?"

I hadn't thought of that. "No."

"Get me one, when you have a chance, and call any time, day or night, if you need anything else. Any questions?"

I shook my head, and they were gone a second after I thanked them.

I reentered the suite and put the paper down. I looked over at the hotel phone on the desk. I'd used it to call Dad. A listening device there explained a lot.

I still had this afternoon's session with Hawker to look forward to. Thanks to my cousin Bill's help, I'd leveled the playing field somewhat.

I LEFT THE MEETING WITH THE HAWKER PEOPLE LATE IN THE DAY, AND IT HAD not gone well.

I dialed Dad on my secret mobile once I reached the street. When he answered, I gave him the bad news. "Whoever the third bidder is just upped the stakes ten percent."

I'd already increased our bid to the maximum Dad had authorized this round. This would put us out of the running, and I'd be coming back empty-handed.

"That's not good," he said.

"Do you want me to withdraw or keep our offer in play to see if the other guy fails somehow?"

He sighed audibly through the phone. "I don't want to let this one go, and there is one other alternative. I'll be in touch tomorrow morning."

"What other alternative?" I dreaded that he might suggest additional borrowing.

"I have to make a call. I'll let you know."

We rang off, and I decided on some exercise in the fitness center, followed by a late dinner.

~

## Danielle

The delicious aroma of fresh-baked scones greeted me as I entered the kitchen. Alicia's brow rose as she sipped her morning tea. "Your tea is on the counter. Do you think he's going to ask you soon?"

That was not a question I'd expected this morning from my third stepmother.

We got along well, but Alicia was every bit a busybody and definitely of the a-woman-should-get-married-and-prioritize-the-home camp. She graded each of my boyfriends on her own marriage-material scale.

Gerald, the man I was currently seeing, rated highly in her eyes as stable and reliable. It was hard to fault her for those observations; he was both of those things.

I plated a scone and retrieved the tea she'd made me. "We're not at that stage." With Gerald it was hard to gauge exactly what step we were on, but it wasn't engagement territory. He hadn't suggested I move in with him yet, and that conversation would certainly come first.

"Sometimes they can surprise you," she said.

I settled at the table and turned the page of the newspaper. "Uh-huh." I wasn't even in a hurry to move in with a man for the first time. The thought scared me.

My brother had called me a commitment-phobe once, but he was dead wrong. I was merely cautious about who I shared a toothbrush and laundry with, and for good reason. It was a big and difficult-to-reverse step, so it made sense to be extra certain about it. So far, I hadn't found the right man— or he hadn't found me. It seemed logical that it would take time, because my standards were high.

Things with Gerald were comfortable as they were, and he might turn out to be the one. Time would tell.

For now, Daddy was beginning to take me seriously at the company. That meant I was getting closer to my goal of replacing Aunt Emily in the Paris office. That was the important thing in my life today.

"I see that smile," she said. "You're thinking about it."

"Actually, I was thinking about my eventual move to Paris."

"I'm sure your father will send you when the time is right."

That was the perpetual question. When would he judge me ready, and when would the time be right?

My phone rang. I held the screen up for her to see. "Speak of the devil. It's Gerald."

She smiled brightly as I rose from the table.

"Hi," I answered.

"Hey, Sugarplum. I miss you."

I walked to the window. "Miss you too." I hadn't seen him since he'd left for the continent last week on business.

"Don't forget dinner tonight. Dunbar's at five thirty."

It was a good thing he'd called to remind me. "Right, Dunbar's."

"See you there, Sugarplum."

"Okay, five thirty." We normally ate later.

After I hung up, Alicia eyed me. "Forget again?"

I shrugged. "We set it up over a week ago."

"What does that tell you?"

"That I need to set better reminders on my phone."

She shook her head. "No, I mean that he scheduled dinner ahead of time at a very expensive restaurant?"

It *was* a little out of character for Gerald. Our normal dinners were at simple, local places without crowds or leather-bound menus. "It's probably because he forgot our anniversary." We'd been going out for just over a year now.

I hadn't said anything about it until two days later.

*"It seems like just yesterday you accepted my first invitation to a date, Sugarplum,"* he'd said. A sweet thought, two days late.

"You should dress up," Alicia said.

"I always do."

Daddy strode in. "Always do what?" He leaned over to give me a kiss on the top of my head. "Good morning, Precious."

"I always dress appropriately," I answered.

Daddy leaned over and traded a brief kiss on the lips with Alicia. "And a double good morning to you, darling."

A blush rose in Alicia's cheeks. They were sweet together.

When Natalia had become stepmother number two ten years ago, I'd learned to accept that one of Dad's faults was his inability to make a marriage last.

Alicia was wife number four, having replaced Natalia almost five years ago.

Daddy's taste in women had always been good. While the stereotypical replacement wife was a pretty young thing who was dumber than a rock, none of his had been. Like Alicia, the others had been gorgeous, but also smart and very nice. Somehow Daddy always picked kind women—so kind, in fact, that we all got together at the holidays—all except Mom. We lost her to a skiing accident years ago. Why things never worked long term for Daddy was one of the mysteries of the universe, but animosity was never the result.

Faults be damned, he was my daddy, and I was his little Precious—and apparently doomed to stay that in his mind.

~

THAT EVENING, MY CAB PULLED UP IN FRONT OF DUNBAR'S A FEW MINUTES early.

I stepped out after paying.

A man beside me yelled out a name, and the couple at the door of the restaurant turned to look.

Two cameras flashed, catching the blonde's smile and the man's surprise.

*"Dress up,"* Alicia had said.

I smoothed down the black dress I'd chosen for tonight. Although it was dressy by my standards, it wasn't when I compared myself to the blonde at the door. Everything I owned was work attire, and none of it could compete with what she wore.

Inside, I didn't see my boyfriend anywhere, so I waited against the wall. There was no message on my phone when I checked it.

"Hey, Sugarplum," Gerald said ten minutes later when he arrived.

I smiled and leaned in for my peck on the cheek.

"You look beautiful tonight," he said.

"Thank you." I followed him to the maître d's podium.

We were shown to a table near a window, looking onto the back courtyard.

The waiter was on us immediately, and Gerald sent him away with an order for a bottle of cabernet.

"How was your trip to Paris?" I asked. It had been his first, and mentally

I had my fingers crossed for a good outcome. All his previous trips had been everywhere else—Belgium, Germany, Italy, Spain, and at least a dozen other EU countries, but not the closest one.

"Good. Well, as good as a trip to the continent can be."

"I thought you liked the travel."

"The travel, yes, but not the bloody French. The day clerk at the hotel didn't speak a word of English. You'd think with all the tourist business they get he'd spend a few minutes learning the most rudimentary phrases."

We'd been over this before, and at least part of the problem revolved around Gerald not wanting to make the effort to learn other languages. This was a case of two immovable objects.

"I'm staying at a different hotel on my next trip." He shook his head. "If I ever go back."

The wine arrived.

"Damned French," he muttered as he poured. He raised his glass to me. "To the most beautiful girl in this restaurant."

I blushed and raised my glass to his.

As we sipped, he talked a little more about his Paris trip—complaints mostly. When we'd ordered our meals, the conversation came back to my work a bit while we ate.

"How is John?"

Asking about my family was one of Gerald's nicer qualities.

"In the States," I told him. "Working on an acquisition."

He cut a piece of his meat. "Hawker?"

"I'm not sure." I shouldn't have let the details slip earlier.

Gerald's brows creased. "Sugarplum, you can tell me anything."

"It doesn't matter."

"It does too matter. You should be able to tell me anything and everything."

I nodded. "You're right." This wasn't worth the argument.

I still didn't say much about John's trip, except that he was in Boston. But it felt good to have a man who cared about my family.

A little while later, I cut into the last of my fish when Gerald surprised me. "I have a little trip planned for us." He laid two airline ticket folders on the table.

My phone rang with Dad and Alicia's ringtone.

I ignored it for the moment.

"To the States. Las Vegas."

It vibrated, and a text showed on the screen.

ALICIA: 9 9 9

That was her signal for something urgent. I looked up. *Oh my fucking God.*

Gerald had a box in his hand. Our eyes met. "Sugarplum, that can wait."

I wasn't ready for this, so I shook my head, opening my phone. "This is an emergency." I called Alicia back.

"Sugarplum," Gerald pleaded.

Blinking back tears, I looked at the box. I wasn't ready for an invitation to move in with him, much less what might be lurking in that box.

Alicia answered. "There you are. John has been in an accident, and your father is in the air, on his way to Hong Kong."

I sat up in my chair. "What happened? Where is he?" She wouldn't be calling unless John was hurt.

"Auto accident, in Boston."

"Is he okay?"

"He'll pull through, it appears, but he's in serious condition right now. It seems he broke a lot of bones, probably going too fast."

Alicia always complained about how fast John drove.

My heart was beating way too fast. I blew out a deep breath, trying to calm myself. "I'll leave for the airport right now and be in touch with you as soon as I can," I told her. I didn't need to be asked. "I'll take care of him."

"Thank you. I'll be waiting to hear—any time, day or night."

We hung up, and I checked my watch. I had enough time to make the eight o'clock last flight out of Heathrow to Boston. I'd memorized the schedules, having made the trip three times this year.

"What is it?" Gerald asked.

"John's been in an accident. I have to go."

"Now?" his face fell.

"Yes. Now. Didn't you hear me? My brother's in the hospital."

He didn't get up. He merely pocketed the box he'd brought out. "Sure. That comes first."

I didn't wait for Gerald to settle the tab. I left and grabbed a cab. I gave the driver my work address to pick up my bag and wondered what had been in Gerald's box. *Earrings? Necklace? Ring?*

Had I just walked out on my engagement? Of course not. There were progressions to these things. Dinner dates preceded going to bed with someone, just as moving in together preceded a proposal. Everyone knew that.

I hadn't treated Gerald very well. Maybe I should have held the cab for him so we could have talked on the way to the airport.

No. My first priority had to be my brother. I could call Gerald after I reached John. We could talk another time. Anyway, maybe it was only a nice necklace from Paris. Yes, that would be like Gerald.

˜

Just in time for the last flight of the day, I pulled my small, emergency roller bag through Heathrow. It contained enough for three days on the road and had come in handy several times already.

I left a voicemail for Jenny at the office. "I'm on the way to Boston. Pass any emergencies to Carlson. I'll be in touch when I can."

In the cab on the way here, I'd called and managed to snag the last first-class seat on the flight. Another call had gotten me a room at the Park Plaza, my usual accommodations in Boston. I didn't add a rental car since Alicia's text after we'd gotten off had told me John was at Mercy General, which was close to the hotel.

Without any information to go on, my brain spun scenarios, and I quickly decided the most likely reason for John to have been in an accident was his not being used to the American insistence on driving on the right-hand side of the road.

I'd warned him on his last trip, but had he listened? No way. His male ego demanded that he drive himself.

˜

## Danielle

My plane arrived just before eleven in the evening, Boston time.

Although I'd used my US passport to get through emigration, I flashed my UK one as I tried one more time to get past the nurse blocking my way at the hospital. I hoped she'd take pity on the befuddled foreigner.

"Visiting hours ended at nine o'clock," Nurse Beatrice repeated.

"But, Beatrice, I couldn't get here earlier. I just flew in from London."

"The only exception is end-of-life care, and your brother is not in that situation. You can come back tomorrow morning at eight."

Bureaucracy sucked.

"I'd like to see your supervisor."

She rolled her eyes. "I *am* the supervisor on this shift. If you don't turn around and let me get back to my patients, I'll be forced to call security."

I let out a heavy sigh. "No need. Please take good care of him."

"We do that for all our patients."

I turned rather than piss her off further. "Thank you, Beatrice."

Once downstairs, I called Alicia to give her the quick status, but I got voicemail.

"They won't let me see him until tomorrow. I'll call you after that."

Then I sent her a text as well.

ME: Can't see John until tomorrow - will call after I do

Then it was off to the hotel to check in and get some sleep, seeing as it was now five in the morning, London time.

# CHAPTER 3

*Charles*

Dad's call came the next morning before I made it to breakfast.

"We're going to do this as a collaboration," he said.

We didn't do joint ventures. I stopped walking and leaned against the wall to listen. "I don't understand." I'd expected him to say something about increased leverage, maybe allowing the Hawkers to maintain board seats and a minority position. Derek Hawker, Jr., the current COO, might not mind —he'd seemed to have an understandable attachment to the company.

His father, though, wouldn't go for it. He'd been clear about wanting a clean break. He intended to move on, to be out of Hawker Technologies with certainty.

"I was right about Wentworth," Dad said.

I dreaded what he might say next. Losing to them would put Dad in a bad mood for a month.

"I talked with Jarrod, and he and I have agreed that this deal is too big for either of us alone, so we're going to do it together—and screw whoever that third bidder is."

His sentence blew up my whole understanding of the dynamics here. Our family had once been close to the Wentworths—even vacationing together. But all that had changed one day, and we'd been fierce rivals for over a decade now.

"I'm not sure I heard you correctly," I ventured. Nothing could have surprised me more than working *with* instead of *against* the Wentworths.

Dad laughed. "Yes, I surprised him as well when I suggested it. But it's time to heal the rift. Neither of us wants to pass on this deal, and this is the only way to get it done. You and his son, John, are going to put together a joint offer."

"But—"

"No argument." He barked. "On second thought, tell me what you think."

That was a welcome turnaround. "I don't like the idea of doing a deal with the Wentworths."

"I thought your complaint before was that this was too big a bite to take."

"Yes, it was, but—"

"This solves that issue, does it not?"

"Yes, but it introduces a new one." At least this time I got it out without being interrupted.

"Which is?"

How was I supposed to explain that I didn't trust John Wentworth? Talia had already broken up with me when I saw them together, so it wasn't as if I could prove he'd intentionally stolen her away. Yet somehow I knew he'd meant to cause it. The episode still ate at me.

"Well?" Dad asked.

"I don't trust Jarrod Wentworth." Making it John's father instead of John in particular would certainly get an agreement from Dad.

"I haven't in the past either, but this is about putting all that behind us."

I slumped. If I couldn't appeal to his distrust of the elder Wentworth, I was sunk.

Dad coughed. "In the meantime, I have you to keep them in line. You draw up the contract properly, and we shouldn't have any vulnerabilities. Or should I send Ellis over to handle this?"

"No. I'll take care of it." Ellis was okay in certain situations, but he tended to miss a lot of the details that could turn into gotchas. And since he was on the same polo team as John Wentworth, I didn't trust him to be firm enough in insisting on safeguards for us.

"Good. Jarrod and I agreed on this. We'll leave it to you two to work out the details together."

"Are you certain?"

"Absolutely. Even half of Hawker is better than walking away. Just get this done." Once Dad made up his mind, he didn't look back.

A moment after we rang off, he sent John Wentworth's contact information.

My finger hovered over the call button for a second before I put the mobile down. I'd let John make the first move. If he didn't call by lunchtime, then I'd call him.

This joint-offer agreement between Dad and Jarrod Wentworth did clear up one thing: the people bugging us weren't the Wentworths. It had to be the other bidder.

∽

The morning had gone by slowly as I waited for John's call.

It didn't come, so after lunch I dialed him.

No answer. *Lazy bugger.*

I left a message and my number. This was like a bad version of who should call whom first in the dating world.

By three in the afternoon, when I still hadn't heard from him, I decided it was time to act. I called the Hawker people to tell them I needed a two-day delay to put together another proposal. I didn't let on how different it would be.

If Wentworth didn't get back to me by tomorrow, I'd know Dad's idea had died the horrible death it deserved. If the Wentworths couldn't manage to return a phone call, how could anything more complicated between us work out?

"For Dad," I repeated to myself. And, if we did do this deal together, I'd only have to put up with John for maybe a few weeks.

# CHAPTER 4

*DANIELLE*

THE NEXT MORNING, I RETURNED TO THE HOSPITAL JUST BEFORE EIGHT AFTER A restless night with little sleep, only some of which I could blame on jet lag.

Upstairs, I switched off my cell phone as the sign instructed.

Evil Nurse Beatrice was gone, and in her place was a cute nurse by the name of Wendy with a much better attitude.

When I entered the room, I had trouble swallowing the lump in my throat.

More machines than I'd ever seen in one place beeped. Dozens of wires and hoses snaked their way to my brother. It was all a bit Frankenstein-like. A bruise covered one side of his face, and I couldn't see much of the rest of him.

I'd thought the movies would have prepared me for the scene. They hadn't. The sounds of the machines, the jagged line on the heart monitor, the antiseptic smell in the air—it all made the room seem a dangerous, mechanical place, devoid of life.

I approached him slowly. "John, I came as quickly as I could." I reached for his hand. It was cold.

He didn't respond to my words or my touch.

"Don't," the nurse said, pulling me back. "He only just got to sleep and desperately needs the rest. He'll wake up soon enough, and you can talk to him then."

"Can I stay?" I asked.

She motioned to the chair in the corner. "Until the end of visiting hours, if you like."

I backed away from the bed. "What are his injuries?"

"He has a broken left leg, pelvis, ribs, collarbone, and left arm. Also, he has a back problem you'll need to talk with the doctor about."

The bad scenarios running through my brain quickly gave way to worse ones. "A broken back?"

"It's a disc issue, but as I said, you'll need to discuss it with the doctor. From the condition of the car, they tell me he's lucky to be alive."

I wiped a tear from my eye. How could this be happening?

She moved to the door. "The doctor should be by in a half hour or so, and you can discuss the treatment options with him."

I tipped my chin toward John. "Will he be able to talk?"

"Yes, but he'll have substantial pain."

I waited in the corner and listened to the beeps and chirps from the machines.

After a few somber minutes, Dr. Chen arrived even earlier than Wendy had predicted and introduced himself.

"He is stable this morning," he said after examining the chart that hung on the end of John's bed. "The good news is he doesn't seem to have suffered any head trauma."

"How long does he need to be here?" I asked.

John hated hospitals. He was convinced they were where people went to die.

"If he keeps on this track, probably another two days to be safe before we move him downstairs." He laughed. "With as many broken bones as he suffered, he'll be quite immobile and will need to be heavily medicated for a while. Luckily, no internal injuries means his prognosis for a full recovery is excellent."

"And his back?"

"That is a question mark at this point. He could end up needing anything from physical therapy to spinal fusion. He'll need to be seen by a specialist to answer that."

"Can you tell me what happened?"

He shook his head. "Car accident is all I know. For more details, you'd need to talk to the police about the accident report."

John was still asleep when the doctor left.

I settled into the chair and reclined it. Now that I knew John would be okay, I'd be better able to rest. When I opened my phone, several messages appeared.

ANDRINA: How was dinner? Did he ask you to move in? You totally should

MENA: Same here

ANDRINA: Live a little. Get out of that shell of yours

I typed out my reply in the group text with my two best friends from college. Texting made it easy to keep in touch, and I was so glad we'd kept it up. Usually I had to be careful of the time zone issues—with them still being in America and me in the UK now—but for once, that would be easy. Texting was also better for us because of all the incoming calls Mena had to juggle at work.

ME: Sorry - emergency trip to Boston - check in later

There were also a half dozen work emails that I forwarded to Carlson before dialing the office.

"Good morning, Ms. Wentworth's line," Jenny answered.

"Jenny, it's me."

"And who is me?" she asked. She was constantly trying to break me of my bad habit of not adding my name. Rude, she called it.

I blurted it all out. "I'm in Boston. John's in the hospital, and I don't know how long I'll be."

"My goodness, dear. That's terrible. I do hope he'll be all right. What happened?"

"Me too. An auto accident. I just talked to the doctor, and he was optimistic." I avoided the issue of his back.

"Well, dear. You're where you should be."

"I am," I agreed. And I'd stay as long as necessary. "Can you please put me through to Carlson?"

"No, dear."

I wasn't sure how to respond to that. Before I could decide, she continued.

"Now go take care of your brother. Don't you worry about Carlson. I'll see that he keeps everything running smoothly while you're out."

"Thank you. I will." As I hung up, I wished I had more employees like her.

I should have looked forward to the next call, but after the jewelry-box debacle before my departure, I was hesitant. But after a moment, I dialed anyway.

"Hello, Danielle," he answered.

No *Hey, Sugarplum* this time.

"Hi."

"You walked out on me."

The words were a cold slap in the face, given the condition my brother was in.

My blood boiled. "I told you, John's in the hospital. It's bad. I need to be here with him." I bit back any harsher words.

"You're right," he said after a moment, in a more caring tone. "We can reschedule. Let me know ahead of time when you're coming back so I can get a dinner reservation." He'd pivoted, and once again the box loomed in my future.

"I don't know—"

"I've got a call on the other line, Sugarplum. Miss you."

"Miss you too," I said before realizing the phone line was already dead. "Yes, I'll give John your regards," I added. My fist clenched involuntarily. I took a cleansing breath. I'd screwed up his big evening, *our* big evening.

I put the box and Gerald out of my mind while I dialed Alicia to give her the update on John. John came first.

We talked long enough to settle her fears, and she promised to relay it all to Daddy when she could reach him.

As I leaned back in the chair, the machines beeped. John's chest rose and fell. I closed my eyes.

∽

JOHN'S VOICE WOKE ME. "WHAT?"

Prying my eyes open, it took a second to realize where I was.

"What the hell?" John said. He held a hand up, trying to focus on the attached tubes and wires. "Where?"

One of the machines screeched annoyingly.

"What the hell?" John said again weakly.

I pulled my stiff body out of the chair, grasped my brother's hand, and squeezed. "John, I'm here. You're in the hospital."

He closed his eyes and opened them again. "Dani?"

"It's me."

Nurse Wendy rushed in.

"He just woke up," I told her.

She repositioned an apparatus on the end of his finger, and the noisy machine quieted. "You can't go yanking things off."

"I can't move my leg," my brother said.

"That's normal. You've had a nerve block. Otherwise, how is your pain level?"

"It hurts to breathe, but I've been worse."

A normal response from my brother. He epitomized stoic.

"I can up the pain medication for you," she said.

"No. Move it down. Things are fuzzy, and I need a clear head."

"Your choice." She punched buttons on a machine. After a minute of checking things, she stopped at the door and wagged her finger. "Be good now. If you pull anything else off, I'll be forced to tie you down."

John nodded. His breathing was irregular as he looked around the room. Normally, with a girl like her, he would have made a joke about tying *her* up instead—or something else totally suggestive and equally inappropriate.

"Do you remember anything about the accident?" I asked.

"They ran me off the road." His words were slightly slurred.

That brought me fully awake. "They what? Who?"

"How did you get here?" he asked through hazy eyes.

"Never mind. Tell me about the accident."

"What accident? Why are you here?"

"I heard you were in a hospital surrounded by cute nurses, and since I had nothing better to do, I flew over to save them."

He winced. "Cute?"

"That last one was."

"Which one?"

He already didn't remember Wendy. "You need your rest."

His eyes fluttered half closed. "Why are you here?"

"Somebody had to see if you were going to live."

"And you had nothing better to do, I guess."

"Actually, I was in the middle of getting a proposal of sorts." That would shock him awake.

His eyes closed. "Huh?"

"I think maybe Gerald was going to ask me to move in with him."

His eyes blinked open, and he winced as he tried to sit up. "No. Dani, you can't bloody do that. Not him." He reached for me and gripped my wrist with surprising strength. "I'm on my deathbed. You have to promise me. Not him." The machines started chattering loudly.

I pulled at his hand to get free. "He's not that bad."

His eyes were fully open now, and filled with fierce determination. "That wanker's not worth the rope it would take to hang him."

I was done being treated like a baby by the men in my family. Wrenching my arm loose, I backed away. "I'm old enough to make my own decisions." I didn't feel ready for that step, but it wasn't his place to decide for me.

Nurse Wendy raced in and checked the monitors.

"Promise me," John pleaded. "You'll wait to accept anything until I'm better and we can talk."

"John, you need to rest now," the nurse announced. She punched a button on one of the drip machines. "I'm giving you something to help you sleep."

"Promise me," John repeated.

Wendy glared at me. "Promise the man."

She didn't even know what we were talking about.

"Okay, already. I promise," I said. Why was it two against one? And now I couldn't even accept a nice pair of earrings without going through John first. I took a deep breath. My brother was worth that restriction, so not a big deal.

John's mouth curled into a slight smile before his eyes fluttered closed.

Wendy turned to me after checking the machines again. "I don't care what you have to promise him to make him calm down. In this stage of his recovery, we can't have spikes in his blood pressure."

I nodded. "I understand." I settled back into the chair.

"If you get him excited again, you'll have to leave," she added sternly. "Do we understand each other?"

"Yes. I'll be careful," I assured her.

"WHAT DAY IS IT?" JOHN ASKED.

I sat up and checked the time. He'd been asleep for a few hours. "Tuesday, but don't worry about that. You need your rest."

"Tuesday?" He looked confused as he blinked and looked around the room. "Hospital?"

I nodded. "You were in an accident."

"Tuesday." He squeezed his eyes shut and open again. "Tuesday." Then, something clicked for him. "Find my mobile. I have to call Dad."

"No way. You need to rest—doctor's orders." The machines weren't throwing the fit they had earlier, thank God.

"My phone. The deal. I need to call Dad."

*Work, work, work.* It never ended with him.

"Stay calm. It can wait. You have to get better first."

"I am calm," he hissed. "My fucking mobile. I need to call Dad."

The beeping of his heart monitor accelerated.

"He's in Hong Kong by now," I told him. "I'll call and tell him how you're doing."

"Now," he said firmly. "I hope it's not too late."

He was getting aggravated enough that I risked being kicked out by the nurse.

"Hold on." Extracting my phone from my purse and powering it on revealed almost a dozen missed calls from Alicia and Daddy.

I started by returning Dad's call.

After listening to my status update on John's condition, Dad asked, "And you think that hospital is up to par?"

Daddy was always evaluating alternatives. "Certainly."

"Then put John on."

I put it on speaker.

"John, boy, you should do a better job of keeping on the road."

John rolled his eyes at Daddy's attempt at humor. "I will."

I was surprised John didn't mention that he'd been attacked, so I decided to. "Actually, Daddy—" The finger John raised to his lips halted me.

My brother shook his head, staring me down.

I mouthed a silent *Why not?* to him.

"What, Precious?"

Warned to not mention the truth, I blurted out, "I think we should take his car keys away."

"Alicia already suggested that."

John gritted his teeth. "Forget my driving. We need to talk about Hawker."

It was my turn to shake my head in disapproval.

"Not until you tell me how you're feeling," Daddy replied.

John took in a labored breath. "Like a lorry ran over me."

"I'll bet. Now, you get well soon. That's an order. I need you back here for something else I'm working on."

"The nurses here are cute," John joked. "So it might be a while."

Dad laughed. "That's the spirit. I'll send Ellis to finish up that Hawker business. I assume you set up things with young Blakewell."

"No. Not yet." John smiled in my direction. "Dani can deal with it."

"No, I'll send Ellis over," Daddy said.

My father's attitude didn't surprise me.

John grunted out a breath. "I don't trust Ellis with this. Dani is who we need."

Daddy was silent.

"Ellis is wrong for this," John repeated. "I trust Dani, and so should you."

My heart sped up. My brother was going to bat for me.

Daddy was quiet for a second. "Okay, until you're ready to get back into things." He was still reluctant to give me a chance. "Precious, I have to go. John will fill you in."

A second later, he was off the line.

"So what's going on?" I asked. "Why didn't you tell him about the other car?"

"I don't want him to worry."

I crinkled my brow. *What the hell does that mean?*

"What you need to know is we're going in together with the Blakewells to get Hawker done."

My expression must have shown my surprise. "But Daddy hates them."

"I had the same reaction, but Dad insists it's what he wants to do. He told me just before I was in the accident. You need to call and meet up with Charles Blakewell right away. His number's in my mobile."

The lump in my throat threatened my breathing. "Charlie Blakewell?"

"Right away."

I hadn't seen Charlie Blakewell since the summer I was sixteen. I'd barely survived the crush I'd had on him. "Okay. But first I need to get up to speed on this deal."

He smiled. "You gotta find my clothes. I didn't know how long this would go, so I rented a flat." John hated being confined to a hotel room. "It's off Boylston. The key is in my pants pocket, and the address is on the tag."

"So you don't forget it?"

"Something like that."

I tried the small cupboard door, and was in luck. A plastic bag held his clothes—bloody clothes. I located the apartment key.

"Found it." I also pulled out his phone. It still had a small charge.

John unlocked it and started typing. "I'll set up a meeting for tonight, which should give you time to get ready. Now it's all up to you." He put the phone down.

I grasped his hand lightly. "Thanks." I got a squeeze back.

My phone vibrated as his message came in.

JOHN: Dinner mtg tonight 7pm Renatto's to discuss

The message had also gone to another number—one in England, clearly Charlie Blakewell's number. I swallowed and added it as a contact just in time for another text to arrive.

CHARLIE: Holmby's is quieter

John typed a response.

JOHN: Fine

"I'm also forwarding you the contacts you'll need," he told me.

Messages arrived with contact information for Derek Hawker, Sr., Derek Junior, Stanfield Whitaker, Maurice Roth, and Abby Denton.

"Who are the last three?" I asked.

"Abby is Hawker's assistant, nice lady. She'll be coordinating meetings and the like. Whitaker is their chief financial officer, and Roth is the lawyer. Those five are the only ones who might call. I'll let Abby know you're the contact from here on. Now get out of here. You have a folder to study."

His phone rang. He checked the screen and silenced it. "It's Blakewell. I won't take his calls. It's entirely in your hands now. Call me after the dinner and let me know if you think it'll work with them or if we have to pull the plug."

My chest swelled with pride. He trusted me. "And how long before we can close the transaction?"

"Another week, maybe two to finalize things. And then another few weeks to two months of due-diligence checking. I'd put it at four to eight weeks that you'll get to stay in this beautiful city."

I was absolutely going to need more clothes than what I'd brought. "I can handle that." But I did have a question. "You wanted me to talk Dad out of this. So why are you now pushing to finish it?"

"I thought it was too big a bite, but with the Blakewells taking half, it's digestible. That's not a problem anymore."

"So just like that, you're behind it?"

"Dad wants it, so it's my job to want it. Now it's in your hands. Go get it done."

I felt the weight of the responsibility land squarely on me. I'd wanted this, I'd asked for it, and now I had to prove myself worthy—of John's trust and Daddy's.

"And that's all the advice you have?" Normally John had a way of saying something I already knew and making it sound only slightly belittling.

"Don't let your crush on Blakewell influence your judgment."

"I don't have a crush on him," I insisted.

"You used to."

"Past tense."

"Good. Don't trust him any farther than you can toss him."

As expected, I already knew that, but I was on my way now. Soon I'd have this deal under my belt and nothing would keep me from my Paris destiny.

I turned at the door. "Anything more useful?"

"Dress sexy."

"No way." The words left my mouth in less than a nanosecond. I'd invested a lot in being professional at all times on the job. That meant appropriate attire—nothing that had even a remote relationship with the word *sexy*.

"It'll give you an advantage with him."

"But—"

"Trust me on this. Last month you said you wanted me to tell you something you didn't already know. This is it. Go shopping before tonight."

I walked out of the hospital contemplating his words. *"Dress sexy. It'll give you an advantage."* I'd asked for advice, and that's what I got?

I hailed the first cab I saw with a woman driver and climbed in. "I need to go shopping."

On the way, I dialed Alicia to fill her in. Messages to Andrina and Mena would come next. What a bonus to be in their time zone for a change.

## CHARLES

JUST LIKE HIS FATHER, JOHN WENTWORTH WANTED TO PUSH THE ENVELOPE.

After an entire day of no communication from him, his message about meeting for dinner had come in just as I was considering calling Dad.

I'd steered him toward a quiet, more suitable restaurant, but what a wanker. And why wait until this evening at seven? He probably agreed with me that our families collaborating on this was crazy and was trying to sabotage the deal rather than confront the issue.

But since he hadn't answered my call, I'd have to wait until this evening to tell him myself what I thought of his weakness. He needed motivation, and I had a plan for that.

When I met with him tonight, I'd let him know our deadline was tomorrow morning. That would either light a fire under him, or it would blow up Dad's proposal to do a joint deal with their family—one or the other.

God, I hoped he'd back out like the coward he was.

I dialed Abigail at Hawker to set the time for the meeting tomorrow morning. Whether it included lazy John Wentworth or not would be up to him.

At the end of the call, I sat back, surprised. The meeting would be at the Hawker building for a change, and I was to bring my best and final offer. Since it would look pretty stupid to talk about a joint offer with the Wentworths and then not show up with one, I hadn't mentioned it.

Meeting at their building also meant I'd probably also find out who the third bidder was, either because I saw him, or because I checked the visitor log.

Now the pressure was on.

# CHAPTER 5

*Charles*

HOLMBY'S GRILL, A QUINTESSENTIAL AMERICAN STEAKHOUSE, WAS ONE I'D found quite nice on my earlier visits to Boston.

I'd slipped out the back exit of the hotel and hadn't seen Thin Man. With several folders in hand, I walked toward the restaurant a full fifteen minutes early. Being late wasn't for me.

Before leaving my hotel, I'd trolled the Internet for recent information on John Wentworth, just to be prepared. There wasn't much I didn't already know, and no mention of Talia, or any pictures of them together when I did an image search. She was probably out of both our lives now.

I wasn't obsessed, just being thorough. And, noting that his polo club had won their last three matches, and that he'd scored in each, I now had at least a starting point for conversation.

After another quick check of the street for Thin Man, I pulled open the heavy, oak door to the establishment and passed into the cool, dry air of the dark interior. The smell—a mixture of leather and wood polish—was not as strong as in a new car, but equally pleasing.

It was quiet, as restaurants went, with only muffled, indistinct conversation. Secluded booths along the back would allow a private conversation.

Dark, wood-lined walls and a long bar on one side with a brass footrail made it look a lot like a scene out of a thirties noir mystery movie.

A quick scan of the entry area showed I'd beaten Wentworth here, which meant I could pick the table. I approached the young hostess. "I'm meeting a gentleman here. Do you have a reservation under Wentworth?"

She scanned her book. "What time?"

"Seven o'clock."

Her eyes lifted from the book. "I'm sorry, sir. I don't have a Wentworth. Could it be under a different name?"

"How about John?"

She shook her head. "No."

Peering over to look upside down at her list, I was surprised to find my name. "How about Blakewell?"

She giggled. "I knew we'd figure it out."

I pointed. "Would it be possible to be seated in the corner booth along the back?"

She checked her seating chart and marked an X through the corner table. "Certainly." She picked up two menus and started off.

I followed her through the crowded room, past several pairs of businessmen whose voices halted as we passed. Those and a few couples where the man was in a suit and the younger woman decked out with expensive jewelry marked this as *the* place for the powerful in this city to dine.

At the booth, I chose the side facing the room, with the better view of those approaching, or nearby.

The waiter arrived, introducing himself as Leo, with a bread basket and a water. "Will a special guest be joining you?"

"That's the plan. Could we please get him a water?"

When he brought it, I was still alone, still counting down until seven o'clock. Several more guests had arrived, none of them John Wentworth. Pulling out my phone confirmed I hadn't missed a message.

Then a striking woman followed the cheery little hostess toward my booth.

I checked my phone again.

"It's been a long time," the woman said.

I looked up and was awestruck.

A voluptuous beauty in a short black dress stood in front of me with her hand extended. "Hi, Charlie."

By instinct, I shook with her and raised up off the seat, but the table prevented me from standing.

"No need to stand." She pulled back her hand and slid into the booth across from me. "John won't be coming tonight. I'll be handling the purchase negotiation for our family."

"I'm sorry…" I was obviously a mile behind this conversation.

"Dani Wentworth. We used to—"

"Summer together," I filled in as it came back to me. "It's been a long time." The girl I'd known had been a teenager when I'd last seen her—a stick of a girl compared to this woman. To say she'd filled out nicely would be a monstrous understatement.

"Yes, that's right." She smiled.

Keeping my eyes from drifting down to her cleavage again was a difficult chore with her plunging neckline. Her blond locks were the same as I remembered, and the more I took in her face, the more the green of her eyes did remind me of that young girl.

Not a girl anymore, and what was she doing here?

"Why not John?" I asked, her cleavage scrambling my brain. Luckily I didn't say *Lazy John*.

∼

## Danielle

John had been right that "*dressing sexy*," as he'd put it, gave me an advantage. Charlie hadn't managed four coherent words since I'd arrived. The short, tight dress, push-up bra, and deep neckline had done the trick. His eyes had scanned me head to toe as I walked up, and he'd checked out my cleavage five times already. I'd counted. Score one for the little black dress. Guys could be so easy.

"You're staring," I told him. The way his eyes devoured me as I bounced in my seat was titillating.

He blinked and cast his gaze down to the table before returning to my eyes. "Uh, sorry. You surprised me. I was expecting your brother. I didn't recognize you. How have you been?"

But rather than small talk, I seized the initiative. "We'll have time for that later. Since we have a meeting tomorrow, why don't we get started on the reason we're here."

"Of course." Charlie's face still showed a hint of confusion.

John had been right that Abby would reach out, and she'd scheduled me to meet the Hawker people tomorrow at noon, which didn't give us much time to prepare.

A waiter arrived, asking if we'd like to start with cocktails.

I deferred to Charlie.

"Sauvignon blanc," he said.

"Yes, Mr. Blakewell." The waiter turned to me.

"Pellegrino for me, please. I need to keep a clear head."

Just the slightest crease showed at the corner of Charlie's eyes. "I changed my mind," he told the waiter. "The same for me."

"We'll need about a half hour before ordering," I told the waiter.

He nodded to me after only a cursory glance toward Charlie. "As you wish."

I'd settled who was in charge, at least for now, and I pulled the first file from my bag. "I've brought a starting term sheet for us to go over."

He accepted the paper I slid across, but not without looking me up and down again.

My phone vibrated on the table, and the screen showed a call from Gerald. I should have turned it off. Talking to him in front of Charlie would ruin everything.

He glanced at the noisy phone. "Do you need to get that?"

"No." I shut down the device.

"Are you sure?" he asked.

"No—I mean yes." I didn't need to explain myself.

He read for a minute before glancing at the phone again. "Father?"

*Why does he assume I have to be in constant contact with Daddy?*

I huffed. "No. My... My boyfriend." Why had I told him that? He didn't need that detail.

Charlie didn't look up. "And he doesn't know we're having dinner together?"

That was rude of him to ask. "It's not relevant."

"Of course not. What's his name?"

"Why?"

"So I can congratulate him when I meet him. You're quite the catch."

His response sent heat to my cheeks. Even backhanded, it was still a compliment. "Gerald. Now can we get back to work?" Alternating between charming and rude, he had me confused about the real Charlie Blakewell.

He went back to the documents. "Wimpy name," he mumbled.

"What was that?"

He looked up. "Simple name, Gerald—easy to remember."

I didn't call him on the lie.

As he read, he asked questions, and it was my turn to observe him. I'd looked up pictures of him online before coming over, so I'd recognize him. He'd changed a lot from the boy of eighteen I'd known before.

I decided for the moment that the rudeness might be an act. He'd grown to be quite the male specimen. The photos hadn't done him justice—strong jawline, broad shoulders, piercing gray eyes. He was a mesmerizing package in person. Those eyes had a life to them that didn't show on the computer screen. Too bad he seemed to enjoy being rude, and was a Blakewell.

"This is all quite thorough," he said.

There it was—another compliment. The Jekyll-and-Hyde routine creeped me out. Which was the facade, and which was real?

"You sound surprised," I noted.

His eyes held mine for a second in a grip I couldn't break, and his face was a blank mask I couldn't read.

"I meant it as a compliment." His baritone conveyed his sincerity.

I couldn't help but smile. "Then thank you. Thank you very much." Maybe I shouldn't have added that last *thank you*. Being overly gracious was a failing of mine, or so John had said on occasion.

"Can I ask a personal question?" Charlie asked.

The waiter interrupted the awkwardness and prevented me from being forced to answer.

Charlie didn't pick up his menu.

I left mine on the table as well while I waited for him to order his Kona-coffee-crusted New York strip steak, medium. "Swordfish," I told the waiter when he turned to me. "And the field greens salad, please."

That crinkle at the corner of Charlie's eye returned, but only for a second. Take that, Charlie Blakewell—score two for preparation.

"You've eaten here before?" I asked.

He nodded. "Yes, and I can assure you the food is exceptional."

A minute later we were alone, and I placed my finger on the term sheet. "As you see, we think we can go as short as four weeks on the due-diligence phase."

He ignored the paper in front of him, and his eyes locked with mine. "Not that I don't enjoy your company."

I felt heat rising in my cheeks.

"But I'd been told to expect John," he said.

I controlled my shiver. I'd screwed up in assuming he knew John's situation. "John is in the hospital."

Charlie's face fell. "That's terrible. Will he be okay?"

"Yes. He was in a car accident." I emphasized the paper by tapping my finger on the item again. "Back to the due-diligence time period."

Charlie was quiet for a second before extending his hand across the table to rest on mine. "What happened?"

The spark from his touch surprised me, but I left my hand in place. I couldn't let him see that he'd shaken me. *Be strong*, I repeated in my head. I took in a breath of courage. "I don't know the particulars, but he'll recover."

It wasn't entirely a lie. I knew the crash wasn't an accident, but I wouldn't be repeating that, and John would recover.

"That explains why he didn't return my calls. How bad was it?"

The concern in his eyes surprised me again. Did he actually care? I was pretty good at this, and I judged that he did. He continued to be hard to quantify.

As the heat of his hand over mine grew, my traitorous lady bits took notice. "I'm sorry, I should have explained." I uncrossed and recrossed my legs while my eyes tried to keep his from invading my brain. "He was pretty banged up. He has some broken bones that will take a while to heal, which is why I'm here."

"Well, give him my best when you talk to him next." He pulled his hand back.

I looked down to break the mind meld he'd attempted. "Sure." Had I just seen the real Charlie Blakewell or the deal-making actor?

Our waiter arrived with our salads, and as we ate, we got back to the issues of the business deal in front of us. I set my planner on the table and retrieved my list of issues.

I stole glances at Charlie between bites, trying to decipher his reactions to my points as I made them. No, that wasn't entirely it. There was something about the man that intrigued me beyond this business deal. I swallowed and lifted another bite of salad to my mouth, determined to be more focused.

In due course, our dinners arrived. The waiter hovered.

Having missed lunch, I abandoned decorum and quickly liberated a forkful of my fish from the plate. It melted in my mouth. "This is delicious." To make amends for my rush, I added a compliment as I pointed my fork at my dinner partner. "You picked a nice place."

That blank mask of Charlie's returned. "Yes."

"Will you be needing anything else?" our waiter asked.

I raised a finger for a pause while I chewed. I wanted to ask for more water before he disappeared.

Charlie cut into his steak. His blank mask took on a darker tone. He pushed the plate to the side so fast water spilled out of his glass. "This won't do."

I used my napkin to stop the water, just in time to keep it from spilling in my lap. *Note to self: Confirm rude on his list of attributes.*

"Is there a problem?" the waiter asked.

"I asked for medium well, not medium rare," Charlie said loudly.

*Okay, change attributes to flaws, change rude to super rude, and add a line for arrogant asshole to the list. Scratch that, give asshole its own line.*

The man at a neighboring table sent an annoyed glance our way.

The waiter picked up the plate. "I'll get this fixed right away, sir." He scurried off.

"You didn't handle that very well," I said softly across the table. I didn't need to embarrass him by saying it as loudly as he'd spoken.

"He's the one who got it wrong," Charlie complained.

∾

CHARLES

"LIKE YOU'VE NEVER MADE A MISTAKE," DANI SHOT BACK. "YOU WERE RUDE."

Her boyfriend, whoever he was, was probably some pansy who accepted mistakes. I looked her in the eye. "I apologize, then."

Her eyes flicked toward the kitchen. "He's the one you should apologize to."

She might be right, but backing down wasn't my style. "He screwed up."

"As I said, you've never made a mistake?"

"I try to keep it to one a day. Underestimating you was today's mistake." The pretty face and even better body had thrown me off kilter—and that dress. Holy fuck. I blinked to get that distracting-as-hell neckline out of my thoughts. She had a boyfriend. "But you calling me out on that was exactly correct."

A quizzical look crossed her face. "That's your idea of a test?"

"No, but you stood up to me, as you should have." Speaking up would be necessary in the negotiation we were embarking on.

The baffled look remained on her face, and a blush augmented it.

"If we're going to work together, I need you to evaluate the situation and not be intimidated by anyone, me included—even if I'm right and you're wrong."

Her countenance softened a bit. "You don't intimidate me, Mr. Blakewell. Disgust me maybe, but intimidate me? No."

I moved a hand to my heart. "Ouch."

"And you failed. You made another mistake tonight. You ordered medium, but complained that it wasn't medium well."

"What can I say? I'm fallible."

Leo returned and placed my plate in front of me. The meat had obviously been replaced, as this steak hadn't been sliced open.

I cut into it to find just the right amount of pink. "Perfect. Thank you very much."

He smiled. "Can I get you anything else?"

"Another water, please," Dani said.

I nodded. "Leo, Danielle—" I raised my chin toward her. "—was concerned that I hurt your feelings."

Dani's mouth dropped slightly.

"No need, ma'am. Mr. Blakewell tips well."

Her head tilted, and she turned toward me as soon as Leo left. "A little money doesn't excuse you acting like a jerk."

I nodded. "True enough, but who said anything about a little?"

She blew out a sigh and gave up the battle.

"I prefer being direct, and I always mean what I say."

"Too direct can come across as rude."

I nodded. "I guess." Her answer wouldn't be a surprise, but I asked the question anyway as I cut into my steak. "How many of the Wentworth deals have you been part of?"

Her mouth firmed into a line as she looked down and cut her food. "This is the first."

I brought the bite of meat to my lips. "We can talk while we eat." I chewed and spoke at the same time. "You're in the big leagues now, and we have a meeting tomorrow morning."

She gave in and cut another bite of her dinner. "Can we cut the theatrics?"

"Absolutely, but let's be clear. I don't do things halfway—not ever. I'm all in on this deal. If you aren't, we should call it off right now and not waste time."

She straightened, with a clenched jaw. "If you're asking whether I'm committed to making this a success, the answer is *completely*. If the question is am I willing to listen to your overinflated opinion of your prowess, the answer is yes, but it doesn't mean I have to believe you. If your question is will I follow all of your advice, the answer is it depends on what you have to say." Her mouth turned up in the hint of a smile.

"Good enough." My eyes rose to meet hers and saw true pride in their depths. "But this is your one chance to back out." I laid it out as clearly as I could. "I won't judge if you have better things to do with your time, but once you commit, there is no turning back."

Her gaze turned steely. "I'm in."

She seemed serious enough.

With that finished, I began in earnest. "This negotiation will be more about reading people's reactions to our proposal than it is the numbers. I need your honest interpretation of the situation after we meet with them."

"Is that all?"

"It's important."

"I can do that." Her words were hesitant, but her posture gave her away. She was all ears. "And you know this because?"

I finished another bite before answering. "Because I've been doing this longer than you have."

She set her jaw with determination. "Then enlighten me."

"Let's go over your list again, but this time with an eye to how things will play with the sellers' expectations."

Her head bobbed slowly as she positioned the paper in front of her. "You mean desires and motivations, right?"

"No, I mean expectations. Very simply, they're motivated to sell or we wouldn't be here. They expect us to come back with a certain set of demands and at a certain price. We need to meet or exceed the price and not go overboard on the demands."

"Not everything is about money," she said.

"It's always about money, sex, or power. The only one of those in play here is money. The price is always paramount."

Her shoulder lifted in a shrug. "If you say so." She didn't sound convinced as she held her pen over the planner.

"Put that away. We're discussing, not planning. Can't you do anything spontaneous?"

She put down the pen and lifted her water glass. "Would throwing this at you qualify?"

My only defense was a nod. "Not what I had in mind, but yes."

She put the water down and closed the damned planner.

I'd won this round.

It was a half hour later that the surprise came in the form of a call on my mobile from Derek Hawker, Jr. I angled the screen so Dani could see the name before I answered the call. "Hello, Edwin."

He'd told me he preferred Edwin, his middle name, to being called some form of Junior.

"Charles, Dad isn't willing to delay any longer, and quite frankly, his minimum has been met." It was odd that he'd tell me that. "Tomorrow morning we'll be accepting final bids, and we'll go with the best of the three offers. You each have a two-hour time slot and no more."

"So, no more rounds after tomorrow?" I asked to confirm.

"That's right. Dad isn't interested in spending any more time."

Derek, Sr., had been clear from the beginning that he considered time to be critical.

"Understood. I'll be prepared."

"Good. See you in the morning. Ten a.m. at our building," he said and hung up.

I set the phone down. "Junior said tomorrow's meeting is the last round, so we need to be clear about everything—most importantly the price."

"They told me twelve o'clock."

"He just told me ten. Two-hour time slots is tight. We'll go in together at the ten o'clock slot. If we need it, we'll run over into your slot. Having four hours available will give us an advantage."

"So what's the plan?" Her pen hovered over the day planner she'd opened again.

"No plan. They've changed the scenario. This is reading them and reacting to get to the right price."

"We still need a plan," she countered.

I could see the problem and pointed at it. "You probably have your whole life planned in that little book, don't you?"

She closed the planner, and her brow furrowed. "It helps to be organized."

"Some things in life can't be planned, or shouldn't be planned. You need to know when to let events dictate the course of things. Tomorrow's meeting will be one of those."

# CHAPTER 6

*Danielle*

We were staying in different hotels and had taken separate rides back from the restaurant.

Charlie hadn't offered to travel with me and see me safely back to my hotel. It shouldn't have bothered me. I was a modern, grown woman and didn't need a man to help me to get around the city. So why had I thought of it? As a business associate, he didn't owe me a ride back to my place, did he? The answer to that was certainly no.

Had I tried to put him in a different category than business associate? The question didn't really have an answer.

Upstairs in my room, I quickly ditched the heels, which were meant more for show than for walking, and padded over to the mirror with my phone and took several photos. This look needed to be memorialized for all time. I wasn't likely to repeat it.

I hadn't drunk anything except water at dinner. My claim that I'd wanted to keep a clear head was the truth. But now it was time to change that.

Opening the minibar, I pulled out two little bottles of liquor. Pouring the first one into a plastic cup I found next to the coffee maker, I added some ginger ale from the door of the small fridge. After downing that, I poured another.

Dad had wanted me to call regardless of the time, so I did. He halted my recounting of the meeting with Charlie after two sentences. "Tell me what conclusion you came to on the bidding."

I gulped because the numbers were so astronomical. "He suggested we'd need to be at two-point-seven to have a reasonable chance."

Daddy's answer was immediate. "That amount is okay with me. You can handle all the miscellaneous details with Blakewell. If you need advice, check with John."

He rang off, and just like that, we were done.

I spent a minute being amazed at how short my conversation with Daddy had been over such a large amount of money. Then I put down my glass.

After slipping out of the expensive dress I probably wouldn't have another use for in my lifetime, I contemplated the evening with Charlie and started on the second drink.

His breadth of knowledge was impressive, but his wooden personality was likely to cause a problem with the other side.

Thinking back, I hadn't seen a single smile out of the man. *Was that right? Not one?*

Had he just been trying to toughen me up and test me, as he'd said, or was the neutral, nice-guy part of his routine the fake part, and the arrogant ass the real Charlie? It was hard to figure out. He seemed to slip from one to the other with ease.

I pulled up Gerald's info to send him a message. It was too late in London to call.

ME: In a work meeting earlier. Couldn't talk

With that done, I turned my attention to the two people I could interact with at this time of night, Andrina and Mena.

I'd needed to study before dinner and hadn't had a chance to send the girls a picture of how the dress had turned out. Flipping through the photos I'd just taken, I decided on two and attached both to the message.

ME: How does this look?

After knocking back the last of my drink, I hit send. There was nothing to be ashamed of. It was just a little teasing.

ANDRINA: rockin girl

MENA: Which bra did you go with?

ME: The red

I'd originally chosen black to go with the color of the dress, but they'd both argued for red instead. I'd bought both, just in case.

MENA: What was the count?

ME: Five

Mena had bet on five stolen glances in the first half-minute, and Andrina had expected even more.

MENA: How long did that take?

ANDRINA: It doesn't matter

MENA: Yes it does

ME: About twenty seconds

The girls had been the ones to suggest calling him on his staring at my cleavage after a few times. They had absolutely agreed with John that dressing sexy would be the way to gain the upper hand with Charlie.

ANDRINA: So he's not a robot

MENA: Is he hot?

ME: This was a business meeting

MENA: With a side of dress sexy

She had a point there. It had been intentional to force his hormones to override his brain cells.

ME: It was just for distraction

And it had worked.

ANDRINA: Answer the question—is he hot?

MENA: Hot or not?

ANDRINA: Does he have a beard?

MENA: I prefer stubble to a beard

ANDRINA: You're not answering us

I typed a Y before erasing it. Charlie was hot with a capital H, but I wasn't admitting it to the girls. That would lead down a rabbit hole I wasn't interested in pursuing. Besides, Gerald was waiting for me back in the UK.

This assignment was my chance to prove myself to Daddy. I typed out an appropriately vague response.

ME: He is normal looking

ANDRINA: Send a pic

ME: I don't have one. This was a business meeting

MENA: You could still sneak a picture

ME: Not very professional

ANDRINA: And after dinner?

ME: I went back to the hotel

MENA: You never told us what the Gerald dinner was about?

ANDRINA: I think we should stick with Charlie dude

ME: I told you – I don't know I got the call about John and had to run

At least that was partly true. I wasn't saying anything about the box because they would go nuts assuming it was a ring and want to talk about yes or no. I was not going there.

MENA: Liar! The Blakewell guy is too hot

ANDRINA: How do you know?

MENA: Check him out online

I had to stop the hot-or-not banter. I had a boyfriend, not that a thing like that ever stopped Andrina from being provocative.

ANDRINA: You should have gone for drinks

That was always her suggestion.

MENA: She's going out with boring Gerald

ME: Right

ANDRINA: So?

Nothing like that had ever stopped Andrina before.

MENA: She's not you

My response was a little bit mean, but I sent it anyway.

ME: And proud of it

ANDRINA: You did lie about him. I just found the online pics of Charlie dude

MENA: Why are you lying to us?

ANDRINA: Yeah he's definitely hot

ME: If you go for his kind

ANDRINA: I'd definitely have drinks with him

MENA: Me too and I wouldn't make him wait

ME: This is business. There's nothing to make him wait for, and our families hate each other

ANDRINA: In denial much?

MENA: Sounds like it to me

ME: Cut it out. I said this is business

ANDRINA: Isn't that how it started with Gerald?

MENA: That's the way I remember it.

ME: I have to go to bed. Tomorrow is important

After the Gerald comment, I had to cut this off. Walking out on a proposal—if that's what the dinner had been meant to be—was an all-time low. I just wasn't anywhere ready for that. Maybe it had only been earrings. Probably.

MENA: Are you going to make it down here?

ANDRINA: Yeah your turn to buy

I didn't remember it that way, but it didn't matter. Getting together with these two was better than lying on a blanket on a sunny day. It recharged me.

ME: Probably a few weeks. I can't tell yet

ANDRINA: You could call him to get tucked in

Andrina wasn't letting go of the Charlie topic. And that tuck-in ploy was always another of her suggestions. She said it had worked for her, but

Andrina had always been the type to allow herself more than one man at a time. She was open about it with her dates, but it still wasn't for me.

MENA: Or offer to tuck him in

ANDRINA: The studies do show sex leads to better sleep

ME: Goodnight. I do need to sleep

ANDRINA: Did he call?

I sighed. It would have felt nice, but Charlie had just left me on the street outside the restaurant.

MENA: She's not answering. That means he did

ANDRINA: That's a good sign

ME: No he didn't

MENA: I still think you could text him

ME: Goodnight. I have a big day tomorrow

ANDRINA: Nite

MENA: Good luck tomorrow

After washing up, I pulled out my laptop and composed an email telling John I'd met with Charlie, we'd discussed the term sheet, and we were ready for the meeting tomorrow with Hawker.

As I put the machine away, my phone rang. My heart sped up when the screen showed Charlie Blakewell as the caller.

"Hello?"

"Hi, Dani. This is Charlie."

"I know. The caller ID gives it away." I regretted the snark as soon as I said it.

"Oh, yeah. I just wanted to check that you made it home all right. I mean, back to the hotel safely."

"I did. How about you?" That was lame of me.

"Yeah, of course."

In the awkward gap that followed, I thought about Andrina's suggestion, but I didn't ask him to tuck me in. I wasn't Andrina.

"I'll pick you up downstairs tomorrow at eight fifteen," he said.

We'd agreed on that before leaving dinner.

"I'll be ready."

"Okay. Goodnight then."

"Goodnight." After a second, I added, "Thank you for calling."

*He'd called.*

~

## Charles

I HUNG UP THE PHONE.

Dani had proved to be an intoxicating vixen this evening. I'd had to watch carefully for when her gaze shifted to her plate, so I could steal a glance. She had a boyfriend, after all.

All during dinner, I'd been tempted to put the papers away and turn the evening into something more social.

This was bad. Maybe I had to think of Dani as Danielle. Maybe that would allow me to keep my mind on the work instead of her. I'd expected John Wentworth to be a problem for me, but not by substituting his sister for himself.

After dinner I'd been careful to extract myself from the situation and not join her in the taxi to her hotel. My dick had argued the opposite, but my big brain had won out.

I'd caught a whiff of strawberry as I escorted her out. It was faint enough that I hadn't noticed it across the table from her. Just the memory of that got my dick's attention again.

I had to remind myself that her family was the enemy—had been for years. Although since we were doing a deal with them now, Dad seemed to have changed those rules. I unfolded the papers she'd brought to dinner and laid them out in front of me. One thing was clear. The woman was a lot more than a pretty face—and nice tits, and a nice arse, and nice legs, and nice eyes, and a nice smile. That was wrong. She had a beautiful smile, and the tits were more than nice.

*Cut it out, jerkwad. Business only, remember?*

Tomorrow was another day. And around a conference table, I was sure I could do better. I grabbed my phone and dialed her again.

"Hi again," she answered.

"One more thought for tomorrow."

"Yes?"

This was going to be difficult to broach. "Maybe we should adjust the wardrobe a little bit."

For a moment she didn't answer, and I wondered if I'd crossed a line. In today's environment, men weren't supposed to advise women about clothing choices in the workplace, but she was inexperienced at this, and it was a big deal.

"I'm not sure I understand," she said.

I refused to be drawn into her trap. "Maybe lower heels would be more appropriate tomorrow in case we have to negotiate some stairs."

She laughed. "And who said we shouldn't be intimidated by each other? And we should be honest? Why don't you say what you really mean?"

"You got me on that. To avoid giving Derek, Sr., a heart attack tomorrow, maybe you should try to dress more business casual than evening out." I added something even more honest. "He's old school."

"What? You didn't like the way I dressed this evening?"

Now she was just messing with me.

I didn't rise to the bait. "I'll swing by the hotel to pick you up at eight fifteen."

"I can get myself there, if you give me the address."

Why did she have to make this difficult? "Lobby at eight fifteen. Goodnight, Danielle."

"Goodnight, Charles."

At least she'd stopped arguing. After hanging up, I tried to concentrate on the term sheet in front of me. *Without success.*

The good news? I only had to endure her attitude for a couple of weeks.

# CHAPTER 7

*CHARLES*

I approached the lobby of her hotel at eight fifteen the next morning, and pushed through the door.

She waited just inside. "Good morning."

She wore a welcoming smile and, more importantly, an appropriate business suit with sensible heels. She'd need those this morning.

I waved her toward the street.

As she passed me for the door, I got a short whiff of strawberry—her strawberry scent. My cock took notice.

*Down, boy.*

With the crowd gathered outside the door, I didn't open my mouth until we reached the sidewalk. "Good morning."

"What's got you in a grouchy mood?" she asked.

I pointed down the street. "This way."

Instead, she went to the curb. "Let's take a cab."

I urged her along the sidewalk. "We walk." When she didn't start, I pulled at her elbow. "This way. We need the exercise."

"Speak for yourself."

I urged her once more with a head nod. "Now."

She came along with a huff. "Did you miss your breakfast or something?"

I waited until we were away from the crowd before answering. "This way we can talk without being overheard."

Her look shifted to concern.

"I've been under surveillance, and it's possible that now you are too."

She stopped mid-stride and faced me. "Are you kidding?" she asked quietly.

I pulled out the paper I'd gotten from the security guy, Murdoch, and handed it to her. "Listening devices were found in all these locations in my hotel room on Monday."

Her eyes widened. "Is this normal?"

"Let's walk."

We crossed the intersection. She stayed close.

Every time I looked over at her, I got an eyeful. The suit wasn't tight, but her curves were still evident. After seeing them on display last night, I could imagine them in vivid detail this morning.

I put a hand in my pocket to adjust big willy, because he was taking too much interest in Dani this morning.

Once we were away from others again, I spoke. "I don't think it's normal, no. But I haven't had a security team sweep my room before." I put a quick finger to my lips as a man approached from the other way. When he'd passed, I added, "For right now, it would be safest to assume that your room has been bugged as well."

Her eyes widened. "Who would do something like that?"

The question answered itself, in my opinion.

"Somebody who wants an advantage in the negotiation." I stopped us at the side of a building and pulled the second spare mobile I'd purchased from my pocket. I handed it over. "We'll use these to communicate when we don't want anybody listening. But only in private."

She slid the mobile into her purse. "Like spies?"

I made the mistake of watching her lips as she spoke instead of her eyes. Her eyes were expressive, but her lips drew me in and made me wonder what they'd feel like if I kissed her senseless. No, *when* I kissed her senseless.

*Where had that come from?* Sure, she was moderately good-looking. Okay, beautiful, if I had to be honest. But she was still a Wentworth, which meant she was part snake. Since when did snakes have jubblies like hers?

"You're staring again," she said.

"Uh... I was concentrating on what you were saying. Anything less would be disrespectful, don't you think?" I lifted a hand for us to continue. "Shall we?"

She seemed to accept my lame explanation. A few steps later, she drew my eyes over by touching my arm. "You're right. Sorry if I'm a little sensitive."

From this angle, the bare skin of her open collar brought my thoughts back to her glorious cleavage from last night. "I can understand your sensitivity to staring. You're a very beautiful girl."

Shit. Had I lost all control of my mouth?

"Why, Charles Blakewell," she said. "Did you just compliment me for the first time?"

*Was I that awful?* I shrugged as another group passed us. "It's possible. I have been known to say something nice on occasion. Right turn here."

After we were clear of people, I got back to the matter at hand. "Each of our last bids has been beaten by a small margin by the other bidder—and not you. My father talked to your father. So, if we believe each other, it has to be the third bidder, since number four dropped out."

She and I were quiet until we reached the next block.

"You're sure about this?" she asked.

"Yes."

She pulled me to a stop midblock. "Then we use it against them today."

She was obviously smarter than I'd given her credit for, but I was only mildly surprised. "My thoughts as well."

With narrowed eyes, her head tilted just slightly. "You didn't expect me to suggest that, did you?"

She'd called me on my shit again.

"I thought it might take you a little longer to get up to speed is all." It was the squishiest way I could agree with her.

"So you're a believer in the conservation of B?"

Probably an Americanism. "Pardon?"

"A woman can only have so much B—boobs and brains have to trade off with each other."

I had to laugh. "You're not dragging me into that discussion." I raised an arm. "Shall we?" We started off again. "Our last bid was two-point-six, and someone came in at two-point-six-five on the same day."

"And the last one John submitted on our behalf," she said, "was two-point-five-five. Last night you suggested we needed to be at two-point-seven to win. I take it you have a plan—even though you claimed otherwise last night."

We passed another group before I answered. "I do."

She listened intently.

"I discussed two-point-seven with my father last night, and he agreed."

"And you think they heard?"

I nodded as another group passed. "Undoubtedly. So a little later, I called Dad back on the secure mobile and got the go-ahead for up to two-point-nine."

∽

## Danielle

Had I heard him right?

"Another..." I paused as a couple passed us. "Two hundred million, just like that?"

He nodded, but he didn't look me in the eye, and couldn't tell if he was joking. "It's only one hundred from our side." Then he dropped the bombshell. "That is, if your father is willing to match it. Or, we could stop at two-point-eight with the extra point-one from our side and adjust the equity."

I narrowed my eyes. I could see where this would lead now, and Daddy wouldn't like it. This was a ploy to give them more than half and a controlling interest.

"It's up to you," he said flatly, "whether it's two-point-eight or you can call for authority to go to two-point-nine." His expression didn't show a preference.

I pulled out my phone as we approached a closed jewelry store with a recessed entrance. "I'll make the call." I startled when he grabbed my forearm for a second.

"Other mobile." He backed away. "Just in case."

Switching phones, I stepped into the alcove and dialed.

"Hello?" Daddy said in greeting. There was considerable crowd noise in the background.

"Daddy, it's me."

"Give me a moment to get somewhere quieter." A few seconds later, the noise diminished. "I don't recognize this number. Would that be my daughter, Precious me?"

"Stop it, Daddy. It's Dani." I refused to say Precious out loud at my age. "Charlie is concerned that our phones might be compromised."

Daddy laughed. "A secret spy phone, eh? Young Charles has you believing his conspiracy theory, does he?"

"Better to be safe, don't you think?"

"Carter believes his son." This was the first time I'd heard Daddy use Charlie's father's first name. "Says he used a friend of that young William Covington chap to confirm it, so I suppose so. Did I tell you I knew young William's father quite well?"

Anyone without mostly gray hair was young in Daddy's estimation. He'd obviously been drinking. His sentences expanded when he did.

"No, you didn't tell me that. I'm calling about the deal."

"Yes, Carter mentioned you might." Clearly there had been communication I wasn't included in. "What's the question?"

Maybe it had been less communication than I feared.

"They want to add two hundred to the total bid—or one hundred if you don't want to go any higher."

"Hmmm... Which are you in favor of?"

"It's up to you. Do you want it that badly?"

"I'm not sure about an extra two hundred. Sometimes these things are less about money than they seem. But if we have to, an extra one hundred from us is okay, I guess. The one thing we can't do is allow the shares between our families to be uneven."

Charlie sent a glance my way that I couldn't read, probably annoyed that I was taking this long.

I waved an acknowledgment at Charlie. "I'll be certain of that."

He kept staring. Always the staring. I turned away.

"Of course you will," Daddy said. "Ask Derek how his arm is doing. We were fishing in Cabo a long time ago, and he got a nasty cut."

"I will."

"Now, I must get back inside. They're feeding me some sea creature that looks like it came from another planet. Not fish and chips, I tell you."

I rolled my eyes, and when I hung up, Charlie was waiting for me, checking his watch to make it obvious what he thought.

"So?" he asked as we started walking again.

"I'm supposed to use my judgment."

Instead of asking more about that, he was quiet until we reached the next block. "Derek, Sr., is clearly in charge. Derek, Jr., likes to add irrelevant things to the discussion, mostly to muck it up. Nobody else in the meeting will matter," he said without looking my way.

"What's their motivation?" I asked.

"Senior is tired of the business, I guess."

The *I guess* part was not encouraging. "He could step back and leave his son in charge, couldn't he?"

"That doesn't seem to be in the cards." Charlie still looked straight ahead as he spoke.

I was quiet for a bit, having gotten the hang of this don't-talk-when-others-approach situation. "Do you think the son is trying to torpedo the sale?"

"He doesn't have the clout to do that. Senior is keeping things moving."

That roundabout answer meant the son could still be an obstacle.

"Why the sudden change in timing?" I asked. "I mean, why last and best offers today all of the sudden?"

"No idea. Junior did say his father's minimum had been met."

"Isn't that an odd thing for them to admit?"

"I guess."

Charlie's continuing refusal to even look my direction when he spoke was unnerving. And I still had yet to see a genuine smile from the man.

I asked the next question as if I was inquiring about a blueberry muffin. "Are you angry with me for some reason?"

He lost a half step. His face contorted in clear confusion. "No. Why?"

"It just seems so, when you always look away."

He offered his hand. "We can hold hands while we walk, if that will make you feel better." The sarcasm in his voice was cold.

"That's just insulting," I shot back.

He stopped.

I did as well, preparing for the next insult.

"What is it with you? If I look at you, you complain. If I don't, you complain. Make up your bloody mind, woman."

His accusation stung because it hit home. I couldn't resist the urge to strike back. "Robot," I said walking away.

He caught up. "Ice queen."

"If you're done being juvenile, can we get back to business?"

"Me? You started this."

This was infuriating, and I stopped again. "Truce then," I huffed out.

"Truce." He offered his hand.

When I took it, his shake was firm, and warmer than I expected given his cold demeanor. "Let's do some business."

Before we made it to our destination, the text arrived.

JOHN: Don't forget you promised to talk to me about the wanker.

Of course he was still on his high horse about Gerald. And in John's terminology, *wanker* was right up there with *fuckhead*. I typed back to him as we walked.

ME: Later

*Later* was the operative word. It was completely up to me, and I still had no idea why there had been a box.

"Everything all right?" Charlie asked.

"Of course. Why wouldn't it be?"

"You don't need to be defensive."

He was right, but I didn't give him the satisfaction of agreeing.

∾

CHARLIE AND I ARRIVED AT THE HAWKER BUILDING, AND HE HELD OPEN THE door for me. "All the previous meetings have been at the hotel, so this probably means they're serious about finishing today. Things could get a little tense, so let me do the talking."

I gave him a little salute rather than let my tongue loose to say something inappropriate.

We stopped at the reception desk. After we announced who we were here to see, Charlie tapped a name on the sign-in log while the receptionist, Marjorie, wasn't looking.

Knightley.

They'd arrived an hour ahead of us.

Daddy may have had his issues with the Wentworth family, but his disdain for the Knightleys was on another level entirely.

A few minutes later, Abby came down to check us in. She was a cute, late-twentysomething brunette with a cheery smile and an even friendlier tone. "Charlie, you're looking better than ever."

He shifted from one foot to the other. His cold, "You too," didn't adequately acknowledge her nice greeting.

She turned to me. "Ms. Wentworth, so nice to put a face to the name."

"Thank you, Abby, and please call me Dani. I love that dress," I added.

She held the yellow skirt out for a second. "I got it at Bloomingdale's." She led us to the elevator. "Eighty-percent off. Can you believe it?"

"I'll have to check that store out," I answered.

"Oh, but you have Harrod's," she said. "And I loved shopping there. Weren't you scheduled for noon?"

"Yes. I'm early."

The elevator opened, and Charlie slid in, ignoring our banter. We followed.

Abby selected the top floor, and the elevator doors closed.

Turning to Charlie she asked, "What do you think of Beantown?"

"Pardon?" Charlie deadpanned.

I elbowed him. "It's a nickname for Boston. From the baked beans."

"Got it," he said. "Better weather than London."

The doors opened, and I held Charlie's elbow to let Abby go first.

"I can point you to the best place in town to get real Boston baked beans," she told Charlie in her singsong voice.

"That would be wonderful," he said with words nicer than his expression. "We'd like that."

Then it hit me. He'd said *we* as if Abby would assume he and I were together. I moved a touch closer to him. "Yes, we'd love to try your recommendation."

"I'll write down three for you," she said. "That way you have a choice, and you can never have too many baked beans."

"That's so nice of you," I said with a gentle touch to her arm.

"New England hospitality," she said with her broadest smile yet. "Just like you showed me in London. Well, not *you*, but your countrymen. New England, get it?" She giggled, and I joined her.

We stopped in front of a conference room. "Dani, you can wait in here." She pointed at the open door.

"Actually," Charlie said, "we'll be making a joint proposal on this rather than competing."

A flash of consternation crossed her face, but it disappeared as quickly as it had arrived. "Ah, well then." She continued and stopped at the room next to the corner office. "We'll put you both in the boardroom. Better view anyway."

I made eye contact with her. "Thank you." It did have a nice view.

"I'll round them up for you. Coffee, tea, and soda are on the cart," Abby told us as she left. She didn't close the door.

"She's nice," I said as I poured a Diet Pepsi into a glass.

"Yup," was Charlie's reply as he helped himself to coffee. At least he didn't ask me to fix it for him.

"And you know her from before?" I asked.

"Abby," a man outside the room said. "Ask the other group to stick around in case any questions come up."

"Okey dokey," she replied.

Charlie leaned close. "That means this could go more than one round. They may want us to bid against each other," he whispered. He didn't address my question about Abby.

When the four from Hawker arrived, Derek, Sr., was easy to spot even before he introduced himself. With a loosened tie, no jacket, and close-cropped hair, he looked the epitome of a company founder. He didn't need to impress anyone. He exuded casual and powerful at the same time.

Junior, on the other hand, was dressed to impress, and he seemed to be working a little too hard at it, all the way down to the expensive shoes. He shared his father's blue eyes, but wore his hair slightly longer, and he waited until his father had shaken both of our hands before coming forward himself. "You can call me Edwin," he said. "Having two Dereks in the office can be confusing."

His voice had been the one asking Abby to have the other group stay. "Thank you, Edwin." I nodded. "I go by Dani myself."

Their CFO, Stanfield Whitaker, and the lawyer, Maury Roth, were the last to arrive. Whitaker seemed to be the worker bee among them with two pens in his shirt pocket, a rumpled suit, and extra pounds around his midsection from long hours behind a desk. Roth wore a suit, but removed his jacket and rolled up his sleeves, the typical I'm-hard-at-work look they taught at all the law schools.

"I'm told your two companies wish to make a joint offer," Derek, Sr., said as he poured himself coffee.

"Isn't that odd?" Edwin asked, waiting his turn at the cart.

"It's a little uncommon," Charlie replied. "But both our families are interested in your company, and this way neither of us is a loser."

Edwin turned. "That assumes your offer is superior to our other bidder's."

From the sign-in log downstairs, we knew the Knightley-run hedge fund was the other bidder, and most likely the group behind the surveillance. Derek, Sr., didn't seem the type to condone methods like that, but nothing would be beneath Knightley.

The possibility that they might have another way to know our bidding strategy and outmaneuver us gave me a chill.

# CHAPTER 8

*Charles*

"Edwin, let's hear them out before making any judgments," Derek, Sr., said.

We took seats around the table. Senior at the end, and the two of us opposite Junior, Whitaker, and Maury Roth.

That strawberry scent of Danielle's was doing a number on my concentration. I closed my eyes. A beautiful girl was supposed to distract *them*, not me.

"Is that okay, Charlie?" Junior asked.

I opened my eyes and nodded at whatever I'd missed. This early it couldn't have been anything important.

They started by providing the updated financials they owed us from the last meeting. Whitaker had several dozen sheets distributed, and he stood to explain them on the screen in nauseating detail.

Roth sat back and silently took notes, shooting glances at Dani when he thought she wouldn't catch him.

Senior didn't pay much attention to Whitaker or Dani. He was probably old enough that he didn't have much lead left in his pencil.

Junior ignored both of us. Gay maybe? Or just a proponent of going with the Knightleys. He'd asked a few days ago if I planned to keep him on after the acquisition. He hadn't liked my lack of enthusiasm.

I asked a few questions as it went along. The important part would come later.

Dani watched attentively.

Junior added a number of comments, all inconsequential.

When we got to the jet-engine division, Junior got rude about it, implying that as a woman, Danielle wouldn't understand.

Senior stepped out of the meeting to take a call.

A minute later, Dani had a question again. "I've heard that the next generation will require a different protective coating on the turbine blades. How are you situated equipment-wise to handle that?"

Junior was an arsehole again. "The specifics of how the machines work is too complicated to explain."

His response was all insult and zero answer.

"That doesn't address your equipment situation," she said more calmly than I would have.

"Do you have an engineering degree?" he asked.

Dani shook her head. "No."

I didn't step in, not wanting to inflame the situation. We could get a specific answer later.

"Then you wouldn't understand," Junior said. "Think of them like spray-tanning booths, and we're in good shape. We have plenty."

Senior walked back in. "What did I miss?"

Dani smiled. "Edwin was telling me you have the equipment necessary for the next-generation turbine-blade-coating process."

"Yes," Senior said. "Expensive stuff, those chemical-vapor-deposition machines. We have enough to get started—about half the capacity we'll eventually need."

An hour later, Whitaker finished.

Roth still hadn't said a word, which was good, because lawyers tended to specialize in telling you all the ways something couldn't happen. But he'd perfected his timing on glancing at Dani when she wasn't looking.

I addressed Derek, Sr. "Perhaps we could take a short break."

"Good call," he replied, lifting his coffee mug. "This was my third this morning."

Dani walked out with Derek, Sr. "I realize I wasn't here for the earlier sessions, so I may have missed something," she said. "Do you think we could have another day, if we need it?"

I couldn't believe I'd just heard her ask that. It was a rookie move.

"That won't do," Senior said as he walked away.

I stood in the doorway and motioned her back into the conference room. She cocked her head as she came back in with a knitted brow.

I closed the door. "You can't ask that at this point."

A hand went to her hip. "And why not?"

"You were supposed to let me do the talking, and that question shows weakness."

"You didn't ask, so I had to. Or do you know why they insisted on the sudden speed-up in the process?"

"No, and it doesn't matter. It's what they want, and they get to set the rules. End of discussion."

"It's exactly because it's what they want that makes it matter." She pulled open the door. "I'm going to use the restroom, if it's okay with you, *sir*." She gave me an infuriating little mock salute.

Why did girls have to be so difficult?

∼

## Danielle

Derek, Sr., was in his office when I walked back from the restroom.

I knocked on the doorjamb.

"Come on in," he said, waving me inside.

His office had floor-to-ceiling windows and expansive views in two directions. But that wasn't what drew my attention. Instead, it was the multiple pictures of his wife on the credenza—and most likely in the two frames facing away from me on his desk as well.

"Daddy wanted me to ask how your arm is doing," I said. It seemed a more appropriate question separated from the group.

He rubbed his left forearm. "A lot better now, thank you. I tell you, fishing is more dangerous than it looks. How is your father?"

I caught a glimpse of travel brochures on his desk. "Well—very well. But I suspect busier than he'd like to be."

"Well, running businesses like these does take constant attention," he noted. "But in the end, it's a labor of love. It's the life we choose. Good people around us and hard work make for success. Sometimes we complain about the hours, but we don't really mean it."

"Yes," I agreed. "We all seem to feel that way about the family business. Daddy's never looked back and regretted it, I'm sure."

"Like I said, surrounded by good people."

That gave me one clue and left another question. He loved his company and loved running it. The sale wasn't driven by burnout. Something else was at play. The financials indicated it wasn't anything like a liquidity crisis either.

I pointed to the woman's picture on the wall. "She's lovely. Your wife?"

He nodded, and his eyes glistened. "Yes. Leslie and I have been married thirty-five wonderful years now." There was a quiver in his voice as he blinked back tears. "That's something I don't think your father can say."

The attack on Dad set me back. "True. Marriage isn't something he's an expert at. I hope to do better one day."

He sniffed once. "I apologize. That came out mean, and I didn't intend that."

All I saw in his face was sincerity. The question about his wife had triggered him in some way.

"You're not married?" he asked.

I held up my bare ring finger. "Still in the kissing-frogs stage, looking for my prince."

That pulled a chuckle out of him. "You'll know when you find the prince."

I nodded. "I hope so."

"We should get back in with the others." He lifted an arm toward the doorway.

I nodded. I had our clues.

"And the prince will make the frog phase worthwhile," he added as I passed through his doorway.

∼

CHARLES

I WAITED OUTSIDE THE CONFERENCE ROOM WITH WHITAKER, WHO WAS TALKING my ear off about inventory valuations.

Junior and Maury were in the room discussing Junior's latest car purchase, which was, as far as I could make out, a Ferrari. I'd missed the model number but heard it was new this year—red, of course, and he'd paid cash. *What a braggart.*

Derek, Sr., emerged from his office, accompanied by Dani.

I didn't get a chance to ask her what they'd discussed before Senior ushered us all back into the conference room.

"Edwin," Senior said. "I think your marketing update is the one thing we owe these people."

Junior seemed delighted to get up and point at the pretty graphics he'd created on the screen.

It hadn't changed. Marketing fluff was still fluff.

Dani spent a good portion of his presentation glued to her mobile, and although this was her area of expertise, she didn't ask anything.

All I could make out was that she was scrolling through images. How amateur could she be? Dad was an idiot for thinking pairing me with a rookie like her would lead anywhere but disaster.

So disaster it would be, and Dad would learn his lesson once and for all about the worthless Wentworths.

"That about wraps it up for the marketing update," Junior said. "Any questions?"

"No." I looked over at Dani. "What about you?"

She shook her head. "No."

Junior moved to take his seat, and the real business could begin.

"If that is all satisfactory," Senior said, "do you have a revised term sheet to propose?"

I'd brought three different sets with me. One each at two-point-seven, -eight, and -nine. "Yes, but first could we have a minute to confer?"

"Of course," Senior said as he rose.

The others followed his cue, and a moment later the door closed, giving Dani and me the room.

"This is not the time to be playing on your damned social media," I hissed at her, careful to be quiet so it didn't carry to the hallway.

"I wasn't playing." Instead of turning sheepish after I called her out, she broke into a smile. "I've got the keys."

Her self-satisfaction infuriated me. "What are you talking about?"

"I know how to cinch the deal with Derek, Sr."

"Yeah, beat the other guy's bid."

"That's totally not the point. Check these pictures out." She held her mobile out and scrolled up. "This is his wife three years ago. This is about a year and a half ago, this is six months ago, and this last one is last month. Tell me what you see."

"No. We're not messing around with pictures. We're on the clock here."

"Her hair." Dani pointed. "Six months ago she didn't have any to speak of, and now she does. That's a wig. She's had chemo. His wife is sick. He had travel brochures on his desk."

It started to sink in. "Because she's had chemo?"

"You're as dumb as a doorknob, Blakewell. He's spent his entire life building this company, and now his wife is sick. He needs to get out of here and go spend time with her. She could be terminal, for all we know, or it could just be a scary wake-up call. It doesn't matter."

It definitely seemed like she'd uncovered something. "Okay, let's say I agree with you, and that's why he's in a rush now. It doesn't change anything."

"Didn't you hear what I said? He spent his entire life building this place. He doesn't want to see it cut up and sold off."

I stopped her right there. "We're not going to do that, and you know it."

"Can the same be said for Knightley's hedge-fund group?"

We both knew the answer there was a solid no.

"I need the term sheet you brought," she said.

I laid all three on the table. "What are you thinking?"

"Here's what we do."

∼

AFTER WE'D MARKED UP THE TERM SHEET, WE ASKED THEM BACK IN TO PRESENT our new offer.

Dani started. "We understand how family control works in a business like the one you've built here. We both come from families that have the same focus—building sustainable businesses that provide solid and meaningful employment with more continuity than is found in firms run by boards of directors that are responding to Wall Street's pressures."

As I looked around the table, I rated Senior as attentive, Junior as dismissive, and the other two in-between.

She continued. "A primary strength we bring to the table is that we understand the management style a family-run business like this requires, the style the employees have become accustomed to."

"Are we going to ever get to the numbers?" Junior asked.

His question got an immediate stare from his father, but not a verbal rebuke.

"We are offering two-point-seven—"

"I've heard enough," Junior said, cutting her off.

Dani sighed, but didn't erupt at him the way he deserved. "And—"

He cut her off again. "This is below our other offer."

Senior sat forward in his chair. "Edwin, let them finish." His tone was clear: *shut the fuck up.*

"And an immediate close with no due-diligence phase slowing us down."

"So we could finalize this today?" Senior asked with obvious interest.

Dani had been right about him.

"Yes, sir," I said. "Although it's too late to wire money until tomorrow."

The corners of Senior's mouth turned up.

"In addition," Dani added. "We are willing to commit to an eighteen-month period of no layoffs or business-unit divestitures. Hawker will stay as Hawker has been, and its employees can feel safe in their jobs and their futures."

"How can you promise that?" Junior asked, clearly against our team.

She had the answer ready. This was the most ingenious part of her suggestion. "We would put two hundred million in escrow for the eighteen-month period, payable to you if we violate that agreement."

"No layoffs at all?" Senior asked.

"None," I confirmed.

Senior nodded, taking in the implications. "And who would you bring in to run the company?"

This we hadn't discussed.

Dani spoke up. "A member of one of our families." It was a sensible answer. "All we ask—"

"So there's a catch," Junior said.

"All we ask is that one hundred million of the two-point-seven be held in escrow for four weeks while we complete due-diligence checks after the transaction. If there are any discrepancies, they will be handled out of that sum at the end of the time period."

Junior sneered. "We'll never see a penny of that."

He really was an arse.

"We're happy to have any disputes handled by neutral arbitration," Dani added.

Senior's head bobbed in a slow nod.

Dani was clearly winning, in spite of Junior's complaints.

"Maury," Senior addressed the lawyer. "How quickly can we have the documents redrafted to incorporate these suggestions?"

Junior's face dropped.

"Half an hour, maybe a little more," the lawyer responded.

"But we should give the other party a chance to respond," Junior objected.

Senior ignored his son and stood, offering a hand to Dani. "I like what I've heard. Let's review the paperwork when Maury finishes."

Junior's jaw clenched, but he held his tongue for once.

I got a shake from the old man as well. "If you two could wait here while Maury does his thing, I'll be back. And, do tell your father that I said hello when you see him next."

Dani nodded. "I will."

The four of them filed out of the room and closed the door.

I was tempted to hug Dani, but I settled for a verbal pat on the back. "You did great."

"Be sure to tell my daddy," she said.

It was a line I wanted to repeat, but I didn't. We both had that issue.

Then, Junior's muffled words came through the door. "Why aren't we going for the Knightley deal? They're willing to go to three, which is a lot better than two-point-seven."

Hearing that the Knightley people were willing to go to three sent a shiver down my back. I hadn't anticipated that.

"I think going with someone willing to put a member of their family in charge makes more sense. We owe it to everyone who works here." Derek, Sr., was the other member of the conversation.

"But I'm family," Junior said. "And the Knightley Group would put me in charge, which is even better than these out-of-towners coming in. They're not even Americans."

"And how long would they commit to not replacing you or starting layoffs?" Senior asked. "You know their type. They'll be planning staff cutbacks before the ink is even dry."

"I'm sure I can get a commitment from them to hold off on layoffs," Junior said.

His father wasn't having it. "And how about putting money in escrow to back that up?"

"I can ask," Junior said hesitantly.

Dani smirked. The likelihood of that happening was dead zero.

"I'd say we structured that perfectly," I whispered.

An hour later, we had an inked deal and handshakes all around. Money would move tomorrow, and the Blakewells and Wentworths would each have half ownership of Hawker by the end of the day.

# CHAPTER 9

*DANIELLE*

WE HAD JUST COMPLETED SIGNING THE DOCUMENTS, AND MY STOMACH WAS IN knots from the excitement of it all.

I'd gone from zero experience last week to completing my family's biggest deal today.

Derek, Sr., put a hand on Charlie's shoulder. "Very nice meeting you two. And, Danielle, tell your father I said hello."

"Should I tell him you'd like to go fishing again?" I asked as they shook hands.

"Not in this lifetime. I'll leave that to the more adventurous ones like him." He turned to me with a card in his hand. "My cell phone is on the back. Call if you have a question I can help with."

I accepted it. "Thank you. I will." I hoped I'd never need to call and interrupt his time with his wife.

He leaned closer as we shook hands. "And thank you for accelerating this for me."

I smiled. "Enjoy your trip."

"We will." His eyes glistened with moisture again. "Feel free to use my office to contact your families," he added. "I'm headed home now."

Junior's sneer was hard to miss as we strode into his father's office. He was such a turd.

I closed the door. *Take that, jerkface.*

"Do you want to call first?" Charlie asked.

"Thank you." I pulled out my phone and held it up. "It's okay to use this one, right?"

"Not if you intend to say anything about Knightley."

I didn't feel like being restricted, so I chose the bat-phone he'd given me instead and dialed Daddy.

"Precious, how are things?"

I gritted my teeth. "Daddy, can you please not call me that?"

Charlie's grin at my expense was a mile wide.

Daddy sighed. "Okay, Danielle, what's the news? Just remember, you will always be precious to me," he added.

I turned away. "We have a deal."

He was silent for a moment "Very funny. Did John put you up to this?"

"This is not a joke. We signed the contract."

"Really? I'm here with Charles's father, Carter, right now. I'm going to put you on speaker." In the background he said, "Carter, they say they're done."

"Bullshit," Carter's response came across the line.

I put the phone on the desk and set it in speaker mode. "Your dad is with mine."

"Charlie, are you there?" Carter asked.

"Yes, Dad. We just signed," Charlie said. "And we need to have the money wired tomorrow."

"Other than paying up front, I assume it's exactly what we talked about earlier?" Daddy asked.

"Not exactly," I answered.

"How much did you work them down?"

"Let me explain," Charlie said. "Mr. Wentworth, this is Charlie Blakewell."

"I'm listening," was all Daddy said.

"The deal we negotiated is a little bit nonstandard, but I think it will work to everybody's benefit."

"I still want to know why we're paying up front," Carter said, and not in the nicest voice.

"Let me start at the beginning," Charlie said, ignoring the question. "The price will be between two-point-six and two-point-seven, depending on a few factors."

"I'm perfectly familiar with due-diligence adjustments," his father said with annoyance.

Charlie kept going. "We have one hundred million reserved for things we might find in due diligence within the next month."

Daddy's impatience showed in his voice. "You gave us a range of three hundred million. What is that about?"

"My question exactly," Carter added.

"The transaction closes tomorrow," Charlie said. "And the company is ours. The other two hundred goes into escrow, but we get it back at the end of eighteen months if we keep our commitment."

"What commitment?" Daddy asked.

Charlie answered. "That we won't lay anyone off in the first eighteen months."

"It doesn't make any sense to have our hands tied like that," Carter said.

Charlie didn't back down. "I thought it did, when the competition was the Knightley Group."

"I hate that guy," Daddy hissed.

"Me too," Carter added. "He should have his passport revoked and have to stay in America."

"They wouldn't have him," Daddy said, his speech slightly slurred.

"Then the Aussies," Carter suggested. "We used to send all the criminals there anyway."

Charlie just shrugged as we waited for them to finish.

"You're the duke," Daddy said. "You should be able to pull some strings and get him banished."

"Very funny," Carter shot back.

I couldn't believe they were bantering like school kids. I hit the mute button. "What's going on?" I asked Charlie.

"Dad said they were getting together for drinks and to make up."

"Sounds like it worked." Both our fathers were slurring a bit. And my daddy was more talkative than normal.

"Let's get this back on track." Charlie touched the mute button. "According to Hawker, the Knightley Group was willing to go to three. I think that makes the two-point-six to -seven I've negotiated a very attractive deal."

I hit the mute button quickly. "We, not just you."

He was making it sound like he'd done everything when I'd been the one with the no-layoff strategy that had cinched it.

"I agree," Charlie's dad said.

"Right," Charlie told me before un-muting us. "We need the money tomorrow or this goes to Knightley, so what do you want to do?"

"I say we go forward," Charlie's father said.

"I agree," Daddy chimed in. "We also need to call Jansen and get him on a plane, if this is closing tomorrow."

"Who is Jansen?" Charlie asked.

"A bloke we both trust to not play favorites between the families," his father answered. "We'll be putting him in charge."

Charlie's mouth dropped, but no words came out. We both knew that wasn't a wise plan.

I spoke up. "That won't work. Another stipulation we made is that the company will be run by a member of one of our families."

Charlie's father raised his voice. "You what?"

"Calm down, Carter. My son, John, is ready to step in, so we can deal with this."

"Your son?" Carter asked. "Why not someone from my family?"

Charlie listened intently. His father probably had him in mind.

"We'll close the deal and then bring Jansen in," Daddy suggested.

"You can do that," I told them. "But it will cost you the two hundred million in escrow."

"Dammit," Daddy said. "We'll work it out and call you back."

"Pistols at twenty paces?" Carter asked before the line went dead.

"Maybe we shouldn't have pushed the family-member-in-charge part of it," Charlie noted.

"You're a piece of work, you know that?"

He stepped back. "Why are you so pissy all of a sudden?"

"Pissy? A man is angry and a woman is pissy?"

"Sorry. Why are you so angry?"

"Let me count the ways. Coming in here, when I asked you what their motivation was for moving up the schedule, you couldn't be bothered to even think about it. When asshole Junior talked down to me in there, you didn't support me. And on this call, you took credit for the whole negotiation. There were two of us in the room."

"Uh—"

I cut him off with a finger. "Would it kill you to say *we* instead of I? We know Senior takes pride in Hawker being a family-run enterprise, that he feels responsible for his employees, and that he needed to get out of here and to his wife immediately. All those elements were required to clinch the deal. You can't sell a man half a horse. So grow a set. None of this…" I twirled my finger. "Maybe-we-shouldn't-have crap."

He opened his mouth to say something, but my bat-phone rang, cutting him off.

I answered it and put it on speaker. "Yes? We're both here."

"Charlie, you really should have called," his father started.

I huffed out a breath and moved around the desk toward the seat.

"We shouldn't have agreed to this family-member stipulation," his father continued.

I sat down to watch Charlie squirm.

"Hold it, Dad," he said. "We needed to."

At least he used we instead of I.

"I wouldn't have," his father responded.

So far Daddy had been quiet.

Charlie raised his voice. "Well, you two weren't here. Dani and I were, and it was clear as day that it was the only way to cinch the deal. It saved us three hundred million over what Knightley was willing to pay."

"I told you," Daddy said.

"And you're both sure of this?" Charlie's father asked.

"Yes," Charlie and I answered in unison.

"Then there's only one equitable solution," his father said.

I waited for the answer.

"The two of you will co-manage the company," Daddy said.

Charlie's expression, when his eyes darted to mine, wasn't enthusiastic.

I couldn't tell if it was working at this company that bothered him, or the idea of working with me.

Charlie spoke up, "But that—"

"Charlie," his father said, cutting him off. "That's the way it will be."

"You'd better be right, Carter, about him having grown up since—"

His father cut Daddy off. "Stop it, Jarrod. Of course he has."

Charlie stiffened at the implied slight.

We got off the phone after listening to a bit more of our fathers putting their differences aside and expressing confidence that this was the best way.

I set the phone down.

"I'm in. Are you?" Charlie asked.

This was one more of his last-chance-to-change-your-mind-and-get-off-the-train moments.

"All in," I assured him. I wasn't missing my chance at an operating position. More importantly, I wasn't backing down from any challenge.

"Okay, then." He went to the door and pulled it open. "I suppose that's all for today."

I agreed with a nod and followed him out.

Abby greeted him with a piece of paper. "Here's that list of places to get real Boston baked beans. If you want, I could take you to one tonight."

"Maybe another time," he said with a sigh. He turned to me. "I'll call you tomorrow."

"Sure." I nodded. "I'm going to wait for that printout Whitaker promised me."

"I have another call to make." After a curt wave, Charlie went back into the office.

Abby looked to me. "I'll tell Stanfield you're waiting on him."

"Thanks." I wandered into the conference room and took a minute to look out the window at the city that would apparently be my home for the foreseeable future.

*How did this happen?*

This deal was supposed to help me get to Paris, not move it out of reach.

I returned to Abby's desk. "Which way to Stanfield's office?" I wasn't big on waiting.

She pointed. "Turn left at the corridor."

Before I could escape, Junior intercepted me. "Can I have a moment?"

I moved us away from Abby's desk. "Sure."

"I'd like to offer my services…"

## CHAPTER 10

*CHARLES*

AFTER FINISHING THE QUICK CALL TO TELL MY BROTHER, ETHAN, I WAS STUCK here for a while because of the deal, I left Senior's office again.

Abby intercepted me with her usual smile. "Charlie, I guess you're my new boss." Before I knew it, she'd wrapped me in a light embrace.

I had no choice but to bring my arm around and pat her back. "One of them," I said. We'd been out to dinner a few times since I'd arrived in town, but that was over now that the deal was done.

She pulled back and cocked her head.

I nodded toward Dani, who was talking with Junior. "Dani and I are going to share the job."

Her brow creased. "Oh."

Dani was looking our way when I checked again.

Abby shifted back a step. "How does that work?"

I didn't give her the simple answer: that it likely wouldn't. Instead I fed her the company line. "We'll have to figure out the details." That was certainly true.

Co-chairmen, co-presidents, co-CEOs—there was a reason nobody did it. It didn't ever fucking work, unless maybe in a family business where the partners were siblings. But even that was difficult.

# THE RIVALS

My dad had to be crazy to have agreed to this, but there hadn't been any way to broach it with Dani and her father on the line.

Stuck here for the next eighteen months and saddled with that minx of a Wentworth girl? The universe had it in for me. It couldn't be anything else. What had I done to deserve this fate? Spending every day with Dani would be pure torture, and there was only one way to mitigate that—a clear rule between us that would keep me from doing anything stupid.

Junior turned to walk toward his office, and Dani strode my way.

Junior's door slammed shut. The man was understandably frustrated. His father had intentionally chosen not to give him control of the company for reasons I didn't know or care to know. Still, a temper tantrum was unprofessional.

"I hear I'm gonna be working for the three of you," Abby said to Dani when she arrived. "I can't wait."

"Neither can we," Dani replied. She didn't seem to have caught that Abby had said *"the three of you."*

"Three?" I asked.

"Yes," Abby said. "You two and Eddie."

Dani shook her head. "Edwin won't be staying."

Abby's face fell. "Oh." She seemed to be an Edwin fan.. "I better talk to him." She made her way to his office door, let herself in without a knock, and closed it behind her.

Dani canted her head toward Senior's nearby office. "We should talk."

I followed and closed the door behind us. "What did Junior have to say?"

"It started with him offering to stay on, and the normal wishing us well bullshit—he'd be happy to help, call him for any questions, maybe we'd like to hire him back as an advisor or consultant, that kind of stuff."

"And?"

"And what?"

"And what did you tell him?"

"You think I'm an idiot?"

I couldn't tell where this sudden anger was coming from. "I just asked what you told him."

"And in your exalted opinion, oh wise one, what should I have told him?"

I put my hands up in surrender. "Don't get all defensive. Just tell me you didn't commit us to anything."

"You really think I'm that much of an amateur?"

"Of course not," I lied. I had no clue how careful she'd be. Even verbal commitments at this stage could be dangerous. But even more dangerous would be feeding her anger at this moment. If she was going to be this emotional all the time, this arrangement didn't stand a chance of working.

"You want to tell me what that was about with Abby?" Dani asked.

"I guess she must like him," I told her. Abby had seemed quite concerned by Junior's tantrum.

Dani shifted. "You know that's not what I'm talking about."

"So maybe she likes him a lot."

Dani's jaw jutted out. "I meant between you two. What history is there that I should be aware of?"

"Nothing."

The corners of her eyes crinkled in disbelief.

It had only been to gather intelligence on Hawker, and the few times I'd dined with Abby wasn't something Dani needed to be concerned about. It would only rile her more, but it gave me the opening I needed to set down my rule. "We need to be clear about something."

She shifted her weight with annoyance still written in her expression. "You want Abby working under you?" she asked, with intonation that clearly underlined the double meaning.

"No." I pointed between the two of us. "If we're going to do this job properly, there can't be anything going on between the two of us."

Her jaw dropped, and her eyes widened. "There was never a fucking chance in hell of that, *your lordship*."

She turned, yanked open the door, and stomped off.

"Dani," I called after her.

She didn't stop. She didn't even look back.

She should have been more analytical about things.

With Abby still in Junior's office behind closed doors, I decided it was time to end my day here.

Why did women have to be so emotional? This was only business.

∼

## Danielle

The elevator doors closed, and I was safe from having the arrogant ass follow me.

I gave two middle-finger salutes to the office beyond the elevator before punching the button for downstairs.

Charlie couldn't see me, but with my telepathy he'd feel my anger through the steel. I'd almost barfed at the arrogance of the man. Assuming I was interested in him? Again?

My God. *And* he thought I didn't know enough to refuse all the stupid stuff Junior had offered. It angered me to no end—the pure gall of it.

By the time the elevator doors opened downstairs, I'd at least cooled off enough to not spit fire at the first person I saw. I let the click of my heels on the marble floor ground me as I crossed the lobby. *One, two, one, two, one, two.*

By the time I reached the sidewalk, I'd mentally replaced the numbers with *fuck, you, fuck, you, fuck, you.*

Retrieving the phone from my purse, I pulled up the app and asked for an Uber back to my hotel. I could've used the exercise, but I wasn't masochistic enough to try the walk in these shoes.

The tiny green car pulled up a minute later.

I noticed the stain on my skirt after I climbed in. How long had that been there? Pretty much first thing on my list was that I needed more clothes. My tiny suitcase held enough for a couple of days, and I was just about out of those. Eighteen months here was going to mean more than one serious shopping trip.

When we arrived at the hotel, I added a tip for my driver in the app. He'd been quiet and not asked any questions, which in my current state of mind was good for both of us.

Was it just me? Or did Charlie assume all women were dumb enough to fall for him? I was stuck with him for a year and a half. As I walked inside, I decided that could be a question for another day, another week, another month. That man got under my skin. Why was that? I wasn't sixteen anymore.

I knew I'd provided the keys to closing the deal. Wasn't that enough? I knew the truth. When the time was right, I'd explain it to Daddy.

As I entered the hotel, the restaurant caught my eye and became my first destination. Putting up with overbearing men was both tiring and draining to my sanity reserve. A stop for food would let me unwind.

Asking to be seated, I watched the petite hostess narrow her eyes after focusing them on my stain for a brief second. Everybody was judging me today, but fuck 'em. I wasn't putting off eating to go change.

Stupid Junior, Charlie, his father—even *my* father had been judgmental about everything from my knowledge to my suggestions today. Out of all of them, Hawker, Sr., had been the only one to treat me with respect.

And now this chick? Her only job was to walk me to a table and hand me my menu. Why did I care? She didn't know me, and I didn't know her. Did appearances really matter in front of a complete stranger? She could judge me after she'd completed a multibillion-dollar deal.

I straightened my back as I followed her. I didn't need her approval or anyone else's. After ordering a sparkling water to start, I laid down the menu and closed my eyes to relax.

*Breathe slowly. Full deep breaths, in and out, in and out.*

It took a minute to suppress the feeling that I was being watched and once again judged a weirdo. Continuing my breathing, I heard my water being set down on my table—without a word, but probably with a stare.

I ignored that as well. *Concentrate on the breathing.*

A half-minute later, I opened my eyes and blinked. A waitress stood a few tables away, eyeing me.

She marched over. "Have you decided on something?" This girl was in a hurry. Her nametag read *Lisa*.

I opened the menu. "Just a sec."

She tapped her pen against the pad.

I perused the menu quickly. "Cobb salad with the grilled chicken on top. Vinaigrette for the dressing."

"Anything else?"

Giving the sparkling water glass a tap, I asked, "Did you bring me this."

Her smile faltered. "Uh, yes. Is there a problem?"

I offered a sincere smile. "Not at all. Thank you for being quiet, Lisa."

"Hard day?" she asked, shifting out of efficiency mode.

"You could say that."

"The drug store down the street sells a dart set. When he drives me up a wall, I throw darts at his picture."

"Thanks. I'll consider that." I wondered how she knew a man was my problem.

Lisa left, and I added a trip to that drug store to my list, along with a stop at the business center to print off a picture of Charlie from the web.

I typed out a message to my girls on our group text.

ME: Awful day and I might be staying in the States for a while

I got my first reply just after Lisa dropped off my salad.

MENA: Cool
    MENA: I mean, is this good or bad?

That one required thought. Was it bad because it put Paris out of reach, or good because it gave me operating experience that would make Paris attainable later?

ME: Good I guess

ANDRINA: What's going on?

MENA: She's having a breakdown

ME: Am not

That wasn't exactly true.
I kept forking bites of salad into my mouth while reading and typing.

ANDRINA: What could be wrong with staying to visit us?

MENA: I want to know about the I guess part

ANDRINA: Me tooooo

MENA: How long?

I didn't answer them right away. Was it the timing, or was it having to work with Charlie? The choice was difficult.

ANDRINA: She's taking too long to answer

MENA: Is it the hottie from last night?

ANDRINA: It must be

ME: Sort of

MENA: Did he ignore you today?

ANDRINA: Or did he take you in the closet?

I laughed at that. They were truly good friends if they could make me laugh on a day like today.

ME: Neither. And stop that. I have a boyfriend.

ANDRINA: So????? More O-SEAM is always better and it makes you healthier. It scientific

I decided not to have this conversation with Andrina for the hundredth time. O-SEAM was her abbreviation for oxytocin, serotonin, endorphins, and more, which came from an orgasm. Orgasms were her solution to everything.

ME: I have to stay to manage the company for 18 months

MENA: You can come down here then

ANDRINA: She wants to go to Paris not DC

MENA: Sorry honey what does this mean about Paris?

ME: It's off for now

MENA: We should still get together

ME: When things settle down

ANDRINA: How big is this company you get to run?

ME: Very

ANDRINA: Then you get to boss a lot of men around?

MENA: And women, Andi

ME: Both but boss around isn't the right way to put it

ANDRINA: Still sounds like a step up

ME: True

MENA: Still waiting for the other shoe

ANDRINA: ??

MENA: There has to be a catch

ANDRINA: Got it

ME: I have to work with Charlie

ANDRINA: The hottie??

MENA: Of course

ANDRINA: Bossing him around should be fun

ME: We are going to run it together

They were quiet for a bit.

MENA: How does that work?

ME: I don't know yet

ANDRINA: I vote for wrestling

The couple at the next table scowled when I laughed at that. Andrina had a one-track mind.

MENA: Mud or jello?

ANDRINA: Maybe naked

ME: Cut it out. This is a serious problem if we disagree

I didn't see how having yelling matches over decisions would end up working well.

MENA: Try coin flips

ANDRINA: I have a double-headed coin I could send you.

I kept my response down to a giggle while I ate more salad.

MENA: What about Gerald?

I stopped chewing. *What about Gerald?*

ME: He likes flying to the States

He'd told me that at least once.

ANDRINA: What does he think about this?

ME: I had no idea it would turn out like this

MENA: You haven't told him have you?

ME: We only just signed the papers

I tried to remember where he usually flew to. Mostly New York, I think, but that wasn't far from here.

ME: Gotta go. I have shopping to do. I didn't bring much to wear

ANDRINA: See ya

MENA: Later

I put the phone down and attacked my salad with a better mood than when I'd walked in. My girls had my back.

When I finished eating, I added a big tip for Lisa, signed the check, and closed the leather folder.

"Which way is that drug store?" I asked her when she came by to collect the folder.

"Out the front door and turn left, two blocks down," she said with a smirk.

I thanked her and departed for the business center.

It wasn't hard to find a head shot of Charlie online, and I sent two copies to the printer.

"He's cute," the woman collecting printer output noted. "Boyfriend?"

"Coworker," I said—without adding that I would soon be tossing darts at the pictures.

Her eyebrow rose. "Be careful."

"It's not like that."

She put her pile in the three-hole punch and pressed the lever with a satisfying *chunk*. "It never starts that way." A minute later she was gone.

*She doesn't know what she's talking about.*

~

WHEN THE BAT-PHONE RANG IN MY PURSE, I SHIFTED THE BAG WITH MY NEW dart board to my other hand. "Hello?"

"Charlie here." The voice was unmistakably that of my soon-to-be dart target.

"Hi. Why are you calling on this phone?"

"It's a good idea to keep using them until we know Knightley isn't an issue."

"They're not," I pointed out.

"They could be—until we clear the due-diligence phase."

"You think they'd meddle after they've already lost?"

"It's happened before."

That thought chilled me. "Okay. You called me?"

"I expect the money to be wired by noon. It's probably best not to go to their building until then—less chance of some last-minute demand that way."

That would be convenient. "Okay. I have some shopping to do anyway."

"Shopping? Right." His tone was dismissive. "I'll call you when I know it's done, and we can go over and introduce ourselves to the staff. I can also help with your shopping."

I angled right to avoid a group of girls taking up most of the sidewalk.

"Don't bother. I'm also moving to my brother's apartment," I said in a tone to match his. I couldn't see straight, he made me so mad. He wasn't the one who'd been called across the ocean on no notice because his brother had been in an accident. "I need to visit my brother in the hospital." That ought to rub it in.

"How is he?"

He hadn't asked until now. Cold bastard.

I should have said John was peachy because he didn't have to deal with *you*, but I settled for, "It'll take a while, but he'll be okay."

"Glad to hear it. Give him my regards."

*Would those be the all-Wentworths-are-idiots regards? Or the why-did-you-have-to-get-in-an-accident-and-saddle-me-with-working-with-your-sister regards? Or maybe the I-don't-really-give-a-shit regards?* His tone made that last one the most likely.

I held my tongue. "Anything else?"

"How about dinner tonight?"

He had the audacity to ask me to dinner after the way he'd treated me today? "No. I have things to do." *Things like toss darts at your head—lots of darts.*

"But I thought—"

I cut him off. "No means no." It didn't matter what he thought. Dinner with him was not happening. "Have a nice evening, your lordship." I clicked the call off.

*Cheeky bugger.*

∿

CHARLES

SITTING AT THE DESK IN MY HOTEL ROOM, I LOOKED AT THE NOW-BLANK SCREEN of my mobile. Dani had abruptly rung off like a petulant child.

There was no way this could work if she continued to behave this way, and in my experience, issues like this with women only got worse.

We had things to discuss so we could get a running start on the very short due-diligence phase.

Even with the five-hour time difference, it wasn't yet too late to call London, so I dialed Dad, hoping he wasn't still drinking with her father.

"Charlie? Why are you calling from this number again?"

"I don't want the Knightley folks to overhear us. Where are you now?"

"Back at the house with your mother." He didn't sound drunk.

"Are you sober?"

"What kind of question is that? Sober enough. What's on your mind?"

"This co-management thing with the Wentworth girl isn't going to work." There, I'd laid it out in black and white. He wouldn't be able to accuse me of being insufficiently clear.

"I know. We'll have to ease her out down the road."

I huffed out an exasperated breath. "Then why are we going down this road?"

"Jarrod and I both know Knightley is the real enemy, but it takes time to build trust. He will have to see that you're not trying to screw him. And to be clear, I mean that. We are not trying to gain any advantage over the Wentworths in this."

"But she wouldn't even meet me tonight to prepare."

He laughed. "Finally, a woman who won't meet you after dark. What is the world coming to? I want you to make a list of her failings."

"Dad," I shot back. "This is serious. We have a lot to get through and very little time."

"Keep the list of her failings for now. Later, I'll make it clear to her father that this isn't working, and we can discuss it. But it can't be because you haven't been trying. He and I will have a frank discussion about simplifying the organizational structure."

I nodded to myself. "Okay. I'll keep your list."

After we got off the line, I pulled out a pad and started.

> Danielle Wentworth Failings.
> (General) Several emotional outbursts showed a lack of the necessary composure to captain a large enterprise.
> (1) Action: The day of the contract signing, she refused to meet to discuss next steps. Result: We failed to get a running start on any due-diligence items.

## CHAPTER 11

*Danielle*

First thing in the morning Thursday, I strode down the hallway of the hospital. I crossed my fingers on the way up the elevator, hoping John's prognosis would be good. His voice stopped me before I turned the corner in to his room.

"Of course I'd be happy to give you a private tour of London when you come out," John said.

I proceeded through the doorway.

Nurse Wendy pulled her hand back from his.

"How's he doing this morning?" I asked her.

"Much better. As a matter of fact, I expect him to be transferred downstairs today."

My brother scrunched up his face. "That's terrible. I really want to stay here with you."

She patted his arm and walked to the door. "We need to make room for more critical patients." Then she left.

I gave my brother a scowl. "I can't believe you."

"What?"

"I leave you alone for a single day and you're already hitting on the closest thing in a skirt."

"She's a very nice girl. I can tell."

"Of course she is, which is exactly why she deserves somebody better than you."

He moved a hand over his heart. "Oh, you wound me. And here I thought you were on my side."

I sighed and thought better of beating up on my brother. "You're obviously feeling better. What did the doctor say about your back?"

"Looks good for now. What can I say? Can't keep a good man down. Enough about me. We have to talk about the wanker."

He meant Gerald, though it was Charlie I was upset with today.

"We do not."

"What did he do? The other day you said *almost*..."

I sighed, unable to avoid the embarrassing admission. "We were at dinner. He'd just brought out plane tickets for a trip, and also a jewelry box."

"And?"

"And I got the call about you, so I had to leave."

"Was he going to give you a ring?" My brother's mind had gone to the same place as mine.

"Of course not." After not having heard much from Gerald, I still had no idea what had been about to happen at dinner.

"Whew. Good thing you promised me you'd hold off then."

"Yeah, and now that you're better, that's over."

He clutched at his chest. "It's happening again." The beeping of his monitor sped up. "I don't think I can take it."

"Stop it. That's not funny."

"Promise me I get to talk with him first." He winced in pain.

"Okay, I promise."

He sat up and smiled. "I'll be ready to interview him as soon as I get these casts off."

"You faker. That's not fair."

"You promised, and what's not fair is a wanker like that taking my baby sister and ruining her life."

"Who said anything about ruining? What if this is what I want?"

"You owe me."

"It's my life."

"I got you this Hawker opportunity with Dad. All I'm asking is that I get a chance to talk with the wanker first."

I sucked in an angry breath. "Stop calling him that. His name is Gerald."

"I will after I get a chance to talk with him and determine he isn't a wanker."

This wasn't one I was going to win. "I don't know what was in the box—probably earrings or a necklace—but I'll make sure you get a chance to talk to him."

"Good. Now tell me about the success you had yesterday."

I took the chair next to him. "You talked to Daddy?"

"Only briefly. He was sloshed."

"We signed yesterday, and it closes today."

He shifted up in his bed with obvious difficulty, given the two casts. "You're putting me to shame. After this he'll have us swapping jobs."

"Not at all. You got this one close to the goal line; it only needed a nudge."

"Dad said there's a catch. So what are you not telling me?"

I sucked in air to fortify myself.

"When you do that, it has to be bad."

He knew my tells.

I blurted it out. "I have to stay at the company and work with Charlie for a year and a half minimum."

"Charlie, huh?" He chuckled, though it ended on a wheeze. "Don't make me laugh, it hurts."

Hearing the laugh and seeing the tortured look on his face was priceless. "I'm serious," I told him. "It's going to be torture. We have to run Hawker together."

A broad smile replaced his grimace. "You finally found a way to rope him in?"

"Yes... No... What are you talking about?"

"I remember that crush you had on him."

"That was ages ago," I complained. "And this has nothing to do with that."

"Doesn't it?"

"This was Daddy's idea, not mine." That was the complete truth, and besides, now my Paris plan was ruined, or at least delayed.

"What did you used to say you wanted to be?"

No way was I going there.

"His cookie, right?"

I glared at him, pissed that he'd remembered that.

"I think I should stick around to see how this plays out between you two."

"No way. I'll tell Daddy you want to take my place and work with…" I almost said Charlie. "Blakewell, and then I can go off to Paris like I planned."

"Not happening. He hates me. This should be fun to watch. You and the Cookie Monster."

I stood and moved to the door. "It's not funny. You have no idea how infuriating he can be."

"So you still like him?"

"No way," I said. "I can barely tolerate him in small doses."

"And what does Gerald think of this arrangement?"

I paused, unsure how to phrase this. "We haven't had a chance to talk about it yet."

He smiled. "Very fun to watch, I think." He waggled his eyebrows. "A word of advice. Remember when I was running Orchard for two months until Ellis got freed up?"

"Yeah." I remembered well, wishing I'd had the opportunity.

"Dad roped me into daily calls with him to discuss things. Don't make that mistake. Tell him up front you'll give him bi-weekly updates and no more, or you're not taking the job."

"But I want this." I couldn't walk away now.

"You have the most leverage on day one. He'll give in."

I pulled in a breath, visualizing the conversation with Daddy and the ways it could go wrong.

"Trust me. He'll go along. He doesn't have a choice."

I nodded. I did trust John's judgment on this.

"Now, we should talk about ways you can handle the Cookie Monster."

I checked my watch. "Later. I have to go." I wasn't subjecting myself to more of that discussion with my brother.

"Later then. On your way out, could you tell Wendy I'd like a sponge bath?"

Skirt chasing never stopped with him.

"No. But I will tell her you feel constipated and need an enema." I opened the door. "I'll tell her cold water." I shook my head as I headed down the hall. Already working an angle with a girl. My brother was feeling a lot better.

Outside on the street, I tried Gerald again.

"Hey, Sugarplum. How are you?"

"Tired. John's going to be okay, so that's good."

"So when are you coming back? We have a lot to talk about."

"It could be a while. Daddy has me staying to run things here for a while. And it might be—"

He cut me off. "Sugarplum, I've got to run. Why don't you text me your contact info there? Where you're staying, your office, and the like. I'll be in touch soon. Ta-ta for now."

Just like that, the call was over, which was probably a good thing. Trying to explain the situation while I was walking on the street might not be best. I texted him the company address, Abby's number—because she would most likely be able to track me down—and John's apartment address.

How was I going to explain eighteen months separated by an ocean?

∼

### CHARLES

THE NEXT MORNING, I PACED THE SUITE AND NIBBLED AT THE REMAINS OF MY room-service breakfast. The bowl of strawberries had reminded me of Dani. Something about that scent of hers drove me batty.

I'd already been downstairs to tell the desk I'd be keeping the suite for a while. And after calling for a dry-cleaning pickup, I was out of things to keep me busy.

Waiting for notification that a deal had been completed was always the most stressful time.

It wasn't quite eleven when I got the call from Whitaker. "The money's all arrived, boss."

His use of *boss* actually excited me. I'd gotten that kind of response before, but they always meant *owner* instead of *boss*. Today I was the real boss, with thousands of people under my control.

"Great," I said. "I'll see you in a bit. Is Derek, Sr., around? I'd like to talk to him." It was always good to touch base with the seller after the fact.

"I haven't seen either him or Edwin this morning. Would you like me to check with Abby?"

"No thanks. I'll be by shortly." No sense chasing them.

I cinched up my tie and checked it in the mirror. The look wasn't right. I changed it out for a solid red one—a power color. First impressions made a difference.

I picked up the mobile again, and my finger hovered over the screen for a few seconds. I pocketed it after remembering Dani's curt responses, and her telling me to not bother calling her. There was no upside to getting her riled up again. She was a big girl, and she could organize her own schedule. She'd said she needed to shop, and who was I to consider the job more important than that?

The walk to my new building was a short one. Overnight rain had rinsed the city clean, and the late-morning air invigorated me. Finally in charge of a business of my own—this was truly a new day.

After passing through doors that needed a cleaning, I walked toward the lift.

"Good morning, Mr. Blakewell," the receptionist said.

Word had traveled fast.

I changed direction for her desk. Her badge read *Marjorie*.

"How are you this morning, Marjorie?"

She beamed. "Fine, thank you."

Needing something else to say, I asked, "Have you seen either of the Hawkers this morning?"

"Mr. Hawker, no, but Edwin is here somewhere. Shall I find him for you?"

"No, I'll be fine." I departed her desk for the bank of lifts. Remembering all the names was going to be a task. *Marjorie*, I said to myself.

Upstairs, Abby was at her desk with that perpetual smile. "Good morning."

I returned her greeting and asked, "Have you seen Edwin?"

"He was here earlier. I'll find him for you."

I nodded. "Thank you." I slid the nameplate for Derek, Sr., out of its holder on the wall and brought it to her. "Could you get me a new one?"

"Of course. I've already boxed all of his things. The office is ready for you. If you'll give me a list of things you need, I'll round them up."

"Paper and pens, to start with." I walked into the now-empty office and took a seat behind the desk. A set of cardboard boxes with Senior's name on them filled the small conference table. The walls were bare, but the view out the windows onto the city was magnificent.

I'd arrived.

Abby popped in a few minutes later. "I found Edwin. He'll be up in a minute."

"Thank you. Let's set a staff meeting for one thirty."

"How big?" she asked.

"What are my choices?"

"Just the direct reports, or I can fill the boardroom to standing capacity with people that work for your direct reports."

"Big, I think."

She left with a nod, and I turned to the windows.

Dani was out there somewhere, but I'd said I'd wait until noon to call her.

Why had that thought popped into my head? Dani could and should handle her own schedule.

I opened the door on the right-hand wall. Instead of a closet, I found a private loo, complete with a urinal for quick breaks. The small shower stall would come in handy if I wanted a midday run. Or if the right lady was in here.

I quickly put that image out of my head. A job like this was my future. I'd need to concentrate if I was going to keep this opportunity and get out of the cubbyhole Dad had put me in.

Junior's former office lay on the other side, but Senior hadn't put in a door to give him access. Hierarchy was everything.

I returned to the windows and the view of the city. As expected, Edwin arrived quickly. "You were looking for me?"

I turned. "I wondered if I could get a contact number in case I have any questions later."

He looked around the office before pulling a card from his wallet. Clearly, he'd had it in his mind that this office would one day be his. "I've left a few things in my office to make it easier to consult."

"Appreciate it." I accepted the card, and he left. The implication that he expected to be paid was one I hadn't foreseen.

Abby was back a moment later. "Raymond is on his way up to take your picture…for your badge," she explained. She offered me a key ring with three keys. "Your office, desk, and file cabinets. Raymond will get you the cardkey for the rest of this building, and all the other offices."

I took the keys. "Thank you. You're very efficient."

She giggled. "Remember that when it's time for my performance review."

She stopped at the door and ushered in the security guy, Raymond. He was a big, burly fellow, straight out of Central Casting as a bodyguard type. He already had the cardkey, and the photo for the badge took only a few seconds against a blank space on the wall.

Abby returned after he'd finished. "Should I put Ms. Wentworth next door?"

"Makes sense. Is Edwin out of there?"

"I'll see."

That sounded like a *no* to me. "Use a flamethrower if you have to, but clean it out now." Dani needed space.

∼

*Danielle*

My morning shopping after visiting John had netted me a few outfits, so I bought some time before I'd run out of clothes. I checked out of the hotel and dropped everything by the apartment. A look at my phone yielded nothing.

Charlie had said he'd call by noon, I thought. It was twelve thirty, but rather than be pushy with him, I dialed Abby's desk.

"This is Abigail," she answered.

"Abby, this is me. I mean Dani."

"Hi. Are you coming in this afternoon?"

"Charlie said he was going to call when things were complete, but I haven't heard from him."

"Stanfield said everything is done. Maybe he forgot to call."

*Forgot my ass.* "I'll be in shortly."

I changed into one of my new purchases, a gray suit, and the Uber ride took only a few minutes. *How could he forget? Is this his way of making me feel irrelevant?*

Once inside the tall, glass-and-steel building that was now mine—or half mine—I marched past Marjorie, the receptionist. Inside the elevator, I practiced my breathing on the way up.

I found Charlie chatting with Abby. "You promised you'd call," I said at perhaps too high a volume level based on Abby's reaction.

Charlie nodded toward Senior's office. "Let's talk."

I marched into the office. Boxes of Senior's things sat on the small conference table.

He followed and closed the door. "You can't go doing that."

"Doing what?" I demanded.

He pointed to the door. "We have to show a united front, and if we have disagreements, it needs to be behind closed doors instead of out in the open like that."

"But you said you were going to call."

"There are no buts to this, Dani. Out there, we have one voice, and one viewpoint. It's like parenting. We don't argue in front of the kids."

What would he know about parenting?

He walked to the window. "What do you see out there?"

We were two dozen floors up, and a whole city was laid out in front of us. I kept back from the glass. "Boston, Cambridge, I don't know all the names."

He waved me closer and leaned against the window. "Look down at the street, and tell me if you see one person who matters to us."

I shivered as I got only a little closer to the window and shook my head, not knowing where he was going with this.

"That's a city full of people who don't give a shit about us, and we don't care what they think." He turned and pointed at the door. "But behind that door are hundreds of people looking at us, judging us, and deciding if they want to stay or leave. We need them to trust us, and that means we don't argue in public."

I nodded and shifted away from the glass.

His brows creased. "You're afraid of heights."

I stepped back again. "You never know if the glass is strong enough." I'd heard of windows in buildings like this breaking, and I had no desire to test this particular one.

I got us back to the issue. "That doesn't change the fact that you didn't call."

He stiffened. "You said, and I quote, *'Don't bother'*, so I didn't."

I felt my face heat with anger. "I meant you didn't have to help me shop."

"Nice of you to make that clear now. I made the mistake of thinking you were old enough to manage your own schedule."

I huffed. "You are impossible." I stomped my foot and regretted it as soon as I did. He'd goaded me into taking the low road.

"And you're being childish. Grow up."

I gritted my teeth and didn't shout back because there was more than a grain of truth in his words. "I take it the closing went off without a hitch," I said calmly, remembering to breathe slowly and deeply.

"That's right. While you were busy shopping, everything was completed."

Now he was back to insulting me, and I was done controlling my anger. "I'm sorry if I didn't have enough time to bring a full set of clothes with me. I got a phone call at dinner and had two hours to be on a plane to come see my brother in the hospital who was possibly dying. So pardon me for—"

"Sorry, I didn't know." He actually looked a little sheepish.

I pressed my advantage. "He'll live, by the way."

"That's good." He stepped around behind the desk. "Are you done yelling at me now?"

I didn't see the trap in the question. "For the moment."

"Turn around, then."

"No. You turn around." I wasn't a doll to be commanded by him.

He let out an exasperated breath and pulled scissors from the desk drawer. "You have a tag on the back of your skirt." He walked my way. "Or…" He offered the scissors. "You could slip out of it and cut it off yourself."

I looked behind me and was mortified to see he was right—a price tag showed back there. The last time I'd ripped one of those off a skirt this nice, the little plastic thingy had made a hole in the fabric.

For a second I considered having Abby help me, but decided that would make me look even more childish. I turned toward the door. "Okay." When he knelt down behind me, I looked away.

He pulled at the hem.

The heat of his hand brushing against my leg sent an unexpected jolt through me. Then the sound of a snip and a pull on the skirt.

"All done," he said.

When I turned back, he held out the tag.

*How stupid could I look?* "Thank you." I took it and crumpled it in my fist.

"I wouldn't want you to be embarrassed in front of the troops."

I nodded and dropped the tag in the trash before leaving the office.

Abby was in the next office, boxing Junior's things. "This will be ready for you in a minute."

Then I looked at the wall and noticed it.

Junior's nameplate had been replaced by one with my name. But more importantly, Senior's larger office now had Charlie's name next to the door.

Ducking back into the corner office, I asked, "And why exactly are you in this office and I'm next door?"

He looked up. "I think adjoining offices shows the right optics, don't you?"

I crossed my arms. "That's not what I mean, and you know it."

His eyes went back to the desk, refusing to meet mine. "You've heard the saying, the early bird gets the worm?"

I stood my ground, ready for the stare down.

Instead, he asked, "Would you like to get lunch? We could—"

"No," I said quickly.

"But we—"

"No means no." There was no way sharing a meal would help me calm down. Refusing to throw a tantrum, I left without another word and asked Abby to get me a few things to set up my office.

Charlie was trying to get me to quit. That had to be it.

I wouldn't give him the pleasure. There was nothing he could do that I couldn't do better, and time would show that to be true.

# CHAPTER 12

*Charles*

Walking up behind Dani to cut that tag off, the whiff of strawberry had nearly done me in. I absolutely had to keep my distance from her. It was as if she had a force field around her—no, make that a gravity well—that drew me in.

As I'd knelt down, I'd been faced with a close-up look at those legs. Oh my God those legs, and that arse. My mind had gone instantly to her legs wrapped around me as I took her against the wall. It had taken all my concentration to clip the tag away and behave myself.

After she left in a huff and once again refused to meet, I adjusted my trousers. If episodes like this repeated, it was going to be a very long year and a half with her next door. At least her closing the door had limited my distraction.

I pulled out the sheet of paper I'd started and added another entry to my list for Dad. It was my version of a mental cold shower to calm myself.

>   (2)Action: The day money arrived and we closed the transaction, she refused meeting with me to discuss our upcoming presentation to the staff. Result: We are about to

introduce ourselves to the company, and we do not have a coordinated message.

With my dick calmed, and naked thoughts of her banished, I put the paper back in my drawer. I turned my chair to the window view of the city I'd be calling home for a while. Boston didn't have the grandeur of New York, or the history of London, but it would do quite nicely. This side of the pond was better than a posting in the UK. I'd gotten the distance I wanted from Dad's meddling, but it didn't come without its cost. For eighteen months, I'd have to endure working with Dani.

A bit later, as I was familiarizing myself with the financial report Whitaker had dropped off, my secure mobile mobile rang.

"How are things?" Dad asked. "Money should have arrived."

"It did, and I'm getting settled in."

"You'll want to meet with the senior staff right away and calm nerves."

I didn't point out that it was insulting for him to think I didn't know that myself. "Dad, we already have a meeting scheduled for this afternoon."

"Good job."

I decide the best way to deal with the Dani situation was to keep him abreast of it. "I've started keeping your list and already have two items on it."

"You mean the girl?" Dad asked.

"Yes. Basically she's refusing to meet and talk with me about things ahead of time."

"I see. That may sort itself out over time, but if not…"

I waited for the other shoe to drop.

"I've already got a call from Derek Hawker's son. He's offered his services to run the company, which would free you up to keep working on other things, as well as fix our issue with the girl."

His emphasis on freeing me up to do other things didn't sit well. Sounded a lot like sending me back to do more acquisitions and putting off my transition to operations in Berlin.

"I thought we agreed I'd be getting Berlin."

"Yes, of course. As soon as the time is right."

Putting in time here at Hawker, even if it meant working with Dani, would burnish my credentials in operations and make it hard for him to deny me.

I didn't have to embellish the facts to put a stop to this for now. "I wouldn't trust him just yet—at least not until after we've had time to review what the staff here thinks of him."

"What do you suspect?" Dad asked.

"A quick review of the financials shows they weren't in a liquidity crunch," I observed. "One has to ask, though, when Derek, Sr., decided to step back, why did he not put his son in charge?"

I let the question hang in the air.

"I could ask him," Dad suggested.

"I'd rather you didn't. Instead, let us poke around a bit and develop an opinion. If you ask his father and it gets back to the son, it would poison the well and destroy mutual trust. We wouldn't be able to call him in later to help, if that's what we decide."

"I agree," Dad said after only a moment. "Very astute of you."

It was the kind of compliment I didn't often get.

"Thanks, Dad." I turned my chair toward the window and smiled.

"One other thing, Charles. Since I'm not able to pop in, given the distance involved, I expect regular written reports on Hawker's progress."

Maybe I'd overestimated how much protection the distance from London would provide. "Certainly." I would've preferred phone calls, but he clearly wasn't going to let those suffice.

"I'll let you get back to it then," he said.

After we rang off, I contemplated how I might have just dodged a bullet. Dad's suggestion that I could get back to work for him—living out of a suitcase and pursuing deals—bothered me. The *"right time"* wasn't very definitive.

He hadn't suggested that he'd move me directly into Berlin operations next, as we'd previously discussed. Had I misread that, or had he let his guard down and I was seeing how he really felt about my capabilities?

Either way, this was my opportunity to create an operations track record he couldn't argue with. Turning back to my desk, I pulled out a pen and started to jot down notes for the introductory meeting with the staff.

I moved my Dani problem list into the top desk drawer. Best to keep it handy to note things as they came up.

∼

*Danielle*

. . .

After spending some unproductive time locked away in my office, I scolded myself for letting Charlie get to me.

I opened my door. "I could use some help," I told Abby.

She followed me in and took the chair across from me with her pen at the ready. "Shoot."

I opened my wallet and slid my driver's license and credit card across the desk to her. "I need a rental car. If they could drop it here, that would be good. Make it a monthly rental, a midsize sedan. I don't care what make or particular model." Uber and taxis weren't going to suffice.

She nodded, making notes, and took my ID and credit card from the desk. "What else?"

I slid my phone across to her. "Please add all the top staff phone contacts."

She took it. "Certainly."

I liked her efficiency. "And yours too," I added.

"Of course."

I pulled the apartment key out and wrote down the address for her. "This is where I'm staying."

"That's a nice area."

She was a local, so she should know.

"Also, if Gerald Durban calls, I want to talk to him, so pull me out of any meeting."

She didn't ask, but her look implied the obvious question.

"He's my boyfriend," I explained.

"I'll be sure to find you."

"Who handles our HR?"

She looked up. "That would be Ron Wroblewski."

"Could you ask him to come see me, please?"

"I'll tell him. He was expecting to talk to you before the meeting."

"Meeting?" I asked.

She nodded her head toward the wall. "Charlie asked me to set up a meeting for you two with the senior staff at one thirty."

And again Charlie hadn't mentioned it to me. "Tell Ron before the meeting would be best."

Abby nodded and disappeared.

A few minutes later, a big bear of a man arrived at my door. "You want to see me, Ms. Wentworth?" He carried a binder under his arm.

Lucky for me, everybody wore badges with prominent first names. I stood and walked over to offer my hand. "Ron, it's nice to meet you, and please call me Dani. This has been kind of a tumultuous day for everybody, I would guess." My hand disappeared in his massive one.

He stepped inside the office to join me and nodded. "You could certainly say that."

"Could you please bring me an org chart we could go over?"

He pointed to the small, round table in the corner. "I thought you might be interested, so I have one with me."

We took seats at the table.

He opened his binder and pulled out a neatly printed organizational chart. "Should we invite Mr. Blakewell to join us?"

"No. I think it would be more productive without him."

His eyebrows rose, and I realized I should have thought more about those words before I'd spouted them. They did sound a bit catty.

"He's busy," I explained to get out of having to deal with another dose of Blakewell right now.

He pointed to the top of the chart, where my name and Charlie's already shared a box. "This arrangement where you share the job... It's a bit unusual."

"It is what it is. We'll make it work." I should have filtered those words better as well. The troops didn't need to know we'd been forced into this. I laughed to break the tension. "You know what they say about two heads being better than one. We're going to prove it."

He gave the slightest nod. "The employees are used to hearing a single set of directions. With two heads, a single voice may be challenging." He leaned forward in his chair. "Derek told me once, my primary job was to keep an ear to the ground, so to speak, and let the boss—that would be you now—know what the troops are feeling. So, I'll be keeping you abreast of things."

I nodded. "Thanks, Ron."

"If you need advice on working through the dynamics, I'm here to help." His eyes conveyed more empathy than I would have expected. The man was offering to help me with my Charlie problem.

I nodded. "I'll remember that, Ron." Showing weakness now would be bad. And why was the HR guy offering to help the poor woman navigate the situation instead of realizing the problem originated with the man next door?

"My office is on the third floor," he said before sliding the org chart closer.

Twenty minutes later, I had a basic understanding of the upper-level structure of the company and a fair number of the names I'd need to know.

Ron pointed to the diagram. "This group here, the jet-engine division, is located in Fallwood, in the western part of the state. And the cosmetics division here..." He pointed to a different spot. "...isn't in this building either. They're located out in Framingham."

"Are there any particular issues we should be aware of?"

His brow creased. "I'd say the big one is the machinists union contract extension."

"How so?" I asked.

"They're a prickly group to work with, I would say." That wasn't a unique viewpoint for somebody in his position. "Derek—I mean, Mr. Hawker—has always taken the lead in dealing with them. He's had a personal relationship with the union president, Tony Califano, for a long time, and has managed to keep the peace."

I sat back. "And you sense there may be a problem now?"

"We had a contract extension pretty much finalized, but when this discussion of selling the company got started..." He didn't finish the sentence.

"I don't understand."

"Everything came to a standstill. We were almost ready to sign, but things kept getting put off."

"So this is an open issue in your mind?"

"In my experience, contracts like this are only done when they're done. I would expect it's gonna take at least one visit from you and Mr. Blakewell. You should let me know when you want me to set that up. Time is not our friend on this."

"Right." I checked the time. "Looks like we have a meeting to get ready for. Thanks for the heads-up, Ron. Can I keep this?"

"Sure thing." He stood.

I got up as well. "One more thing. Do you think the union knew the negotiations for the sale were going on?"

He lifted a shoulder. "It's fishy is all I'm saying. Outside of me, Abby said the group who knew was limited to the Hawkers, Whitaker, Roth, and her, of course."

"Maybe Mr. Hawker told him," I guessed.

"It's possible, but it would be out of character. It's more likely that people just acted differently rather than saying anything in particular, and the union picked up on it. They know people. I wouldn't call them informants, but you can learn a lot by calling around and talking to people. It's common for them to stay plugged in to what is happening at headquarters."

I nodded slowly. "Thanks for your time, Ron."

"Let me know when you want to set a meeting with them. It's probably best if we take the initiative."

"Will do."

He reached for the door. "And I'm here if you want to talk."

I nodded as he left, and I only rolled my eyes after he was gone. I could handle Charlie Blakewell.

~

THE MEETING WITH THE UPPER-LEVEL EXTENDED STAFF WENT QUITE WELL.

Charlie turned out to be a skilled presenter. In front of the group, he was personable and quite animated, even surprisingly human. He smiled, a side of him I hadn't seen in private.

As I watched him, I wondered why that wasn't the Charlie who talked to me. The Charlie he showed me seemed distant and cold by comparison—all robot.

Was I doing something to cause that? Or was I reacting differently when I was close to him? Probably the Charlie in front of the group was the fake one. It was definitely something I was going to have to dissect if we were going to spend the next year and a half working together.

The relief of the group as we confirmed not doing any layoffs was obvious. Both Charlie and I made a point of the fact that we had committed to that promise, and we added that both our families ran companies opposed to that business practice. You could see the shoulders around the room loosen as people took in our words. The group that departed seemed much happier and more at ease than the one that had arrived for the meeting.

I ended up shaking more hands than I could count, and certainly taking in more introductions than I could remember. But I did get a chance to put some faces with the names on the chart.

Charlie found me as the meeting broke up. "If you have some time, I thought we would get together with Whitaker."

"Of course," I told him.

"My office then."

Whitaker was a finance guy, the CFO, and it made sense that we should get into that aspect of the business as quickly as possible.

I followed the two of them to Charlie's office, and I found my eyes drawn to Charlie's ass. I had to consciously work to pull my gaze away. Why was that?

Inside, we took spots around the large conference table in his office.

"I had a concerning visit today," Whitaker started.

Charlie shifted forward in his seat, clearly with the same interest I had.

"It was our banker, Woolsey," Whitaker continued.

Problems with bankers were par for the course, but never good.

"And?" Charlie asked.

Whitaker gulped. "It seems our credit line is under review."

"What exactly does that mean, under review?" I asked. "Is there some problem we're not familiar with?"

"Certainly not. And I told him there was no change in our debt structure having to do with the sale of the company."

"Maybe they just need written confirmation of that," Charlie suggested.

Whitaker nodded. "Could be, but I thought you should know. And it would probably be good if you talk to him. The last thing we need is for them to lose confidence in the company."

After Whitaker left, I stayed in Charlie's office for a second. "What do you make of that?"

"Something spooked them is my guess. Banks by their nature are cautious. The only upside for them is that we pay what we owe them plus interest. The downside is that we default and they lose not only the interest, but all the capital. The imbalance of the two makes some skittish."

Charlie's analysis didn't add anything to what Daddy had already taught me.

"Changing subjects," he said. "How do you think the meeting went?"

"Very well. The no-layoff commitment was a big plus for all of them, obviously."

"As it should be. I think your words about the meaning of family were also well received. They certainly hit home with me."

"That's because family is not the most important thing, it's the only thing."

"You did well. Thank you for your help." He added a smile—the first that he'd shown me. Cute dimples appeared that I hadn't known were there.

His compliment surprised me, and I returned it in kind. "I thought you did a good job. They like you." Yesterday I would have added *so far*, but I held it back today. Even I'd been taken in by the different Charlie who had spoken in that meeting.

"What's not to like?" he added.

It was a cocky line worthy of my brother.

"We should talk about the personnel situation," I told him.

"Later. I have to make a call." He walked over behind his desk, giving me my cue to leave.

I gave him the laugh he deserved. "I'll ask Abby to have this door widened to fit that ego of yours."

Pulling open the closest door, I realized it wasn't a door out of the office. "You have your own bathroom?"

"Don't blame me. I didn't install it."

The space wasn't large, but it was well appointed, and it had obviously been built by a man, because the corner contained a urinal. I exited and closed the door. "My office doesn't have one of these."

He cocked his head and gave me the second smile of the afternoon. "We could add a door on your side."

"And have you walk in on me? I think not." My tone didn't match the tingle I felt in my belly at that smile.

"That's what locks are for."

When I turned to leave, I felt the weight of his stare on my ass.

I chose the correct door on the second try, and a quick glance back made him look away. He had been checking me out.

*Or was it my imagination?*

I shut the door securely behind me, lest I be tempted to hear more from this new side of Charlie—the side that knew how to smile and make me tingle, the side that watched me.

*Shut that shit down, sister.*

I retrieved the org chart Wroblewski had given me from my office. I had people to talk to, more faces to match with names, and people to put at ease.

Abby quickly put her phone away when I came out.

I held up the list. "I'll be downstairs for a while."

∼

## Charles

Upstairs that evening, in the Covington Industries flat the security guy, Ben, had given me access to, I looked out over the city before settling down to go through the financials again.

I'd double-checked with Bill Covington before accepting the offer to use this place, as I'd felt a little uneasy about it. I was still getting used to the concept of a cousin in America who I couldn't acknowledge.

But he'd insisted, and I was glad he had. After one night here, I wasn't going back to even a *suite* at the hotel.

Still staring at the financial reports, I thought back over the day.

Things had gone well, exceedingly well. From signing papers yesterday to having all the money wired this morning and walking stupid Edwin Hawker out of the building this morning, it had been a whirlwind.

I opened my mobile and pulled up the photo I'd taken of Dani this afternoon as she walked out of my office. Sure, I needed one of her facing me, but this one was driving me nuts.

Big willy was instantly hard as I looked at the picture, just as he had been this afternoon as she left my office after discovering the private loo.

She'd seen the shower. Had she instantly thought of getting it on under the hot water the way I had?

How was I supposed to last a year and a half with her constantly in front of me?

The woman was smart and overflowing with empathy. When I told her how well she'd done this afternoon with the meeting, I hadn't expressed half of what I'd seen.

Her speech to the troops had been one I wished I could bottle and keep for whenever I needed to raise people up and make them feel good. Her words about family had been both powerful and heartfelt. Everybody in the room could see and feel that.

There had been more than a few wet eyes in the crowd as she spoke.

How she did that, I had no idea. If it was a class she'd taken, I needed to attend. Unfortunately, I doubted that was how she'd come upon the ability. In her realm, she was a force of nature, which is what probably made her damn near irresistible.

It likely had something to do with her brains, body, and beauty as well, but who knows? Questions like that didn't often have answers. She was a multifaceted package, and just thinking about that got me aroused all over again.

The only way I was getting any sleep tonight would have to involve whacking one off to her picture. Denying myself wouldn't work. I would only end up sleep deprived in the morning.

That wouldn't be fair to the people at the company, so in a way, I owed it to them to take care of business. I moved my hand down to do just that. My cock was rock hard and begging for release. I didn't try to stretch out the process, and I came quickly.

I leaned back in my chair a moment and breathed deeply. When I opened my eyes, the damn financials were still waiting for me, as well as a minor mess to clean up.

# CHAPTER 13

*DANIELLE*

I CHECKED MY PHONE THE NEXT MORNING AS I WAITED FOR MY BREAKFAST IN THE restaurant downstairs at the hotel. I'd decided on one more night here until I'd stocked the apartment with food.

The screen showed the bad news—still no call from Gerald.

I turned the phone over, not wanting to see the evidence of my failure. I couldn't even do the girlfriend thing right. Maybe I should have stayed just a few more minutes to find out what had been in the box and thank him.

Andrina would have stayed, I bet.

It was too early to expect a response, but I sent a text to my girls anyway.

ME: Gerald hasn't called. Should I be worried?

ANDRINA: I'll call when I get a chance

Gerald was probably traveling again. That had to be it. And, the time difference certainly didn't make connecting easy. It would have been so much simpler if Hawker had been in Britain.

Looking around at the guests in the restaurant, I decided they were almost all travelers, as I'd been two days ago.

To make up for my recent lack of exercise, I decided to walk half the distance to the Hawker building before calling an Uber.

Even after my extended journey, when I reached our floor of the office, Charlie's door was closed. I'd beaten him in.

Abby didn't notice me walk up as she talked on her phone. "I'll see you at noon... Me too." She made a kissing sound before hanging up. The phone moved hastily down when I came into her line of sight. "Good morning," she said in greeting. "I wish I had a brother as thoughtful as yours." She pointed inside my already open office.

I glanced in to see a vase with what must have been two dozen red roses. "For me?"

She nodded. "Just arrived."

"If Andrina or Mena call, please put them through."

"Sure thing."

I put down my purse inside the office and read the card. It was from John. *You promised*, it read.

Blackmail flowers.

I returned to Abby's desk and pointed at Charlie's door. "When he gets in, please ask him to come see me."

"He's in a meeting already," she said. "With Whitaker, and he said he expects it to last all morning. But I'll let him know when he comes up for air."

I shook my head. Was it impossible to get a step ahead of him? "Thanks."

Half the names on my org chart had been crossed off and introductions made. I'd get to some of the remaining ones this morning. I left the office with my chart after a minute of admiring my roses. John was the best.

"I'm going to wander around some more and get introduced this morning," I told Abby.

She nodded. "There's a meeting that had been scheduled for this afternoon, and I'm not sure how you want to handle it..."

"Go on," I said.

"New-product reviews for the personal-products division are due. You see, Edwin..." She hesitated, obviously formulating appropriate words. "Well, he felt a little squeamish dealing with them, so he had me sit in in his place."

"Squeamish?" I asked.

"The products are feminine," she answered. That said it all.

"What time?" I asked.

"One thirty."

"I'll be there." I raised a finger. "One other thing."

She cocked her head.

I hesitated, unsure if this showed a lack of self-confidence. "How do you think the meeting went yesterday?"

A smile overcame her. "Very well is the word through the grapevine, if that's what you're asking."

That was exactly my question. "I know this is nerve-wracking for everybody, and it is for me too." I rephrased that. "For both of us." Charlie deserved my support.

After we finished, I checked my phone. It had been on silent.

ANDRINA: Depends

MENA: I say make him wait on you. Don't answer right away when he calls

ANDRINA: I agree with Mena

They'd decided on texts instead of a call, and they weren't much help. Still nothing from Gerald.

Charlie's door remained closed when I left.

My next stop was downstairs.

A little while later, between offices, I returned a missed call from my brother.

"Guess what?" he answered.

"I'm not into guessing games this morning," I told him.

"Dad sent a plane to pick me up, so I'm leaving you alone here."

I processed that for a moment. "I thought Daddy wanted you to stay for a while in case…" *In case I'm in over my head.*

"I told him he should have confidence in you."

His kindness gave me a lump in my throat. "When do you leave?"

"This morning. But I'll only be a phone call away."

I spent a minute giving him a hard time about leaving the pretty nurses behind before letting him go. I'd hoped we'd have time to hang out while he healed. With those casts, he wouldn't be able to run away, and he'd have to listen to me.

Now the success or failure of this Hawker acquisition rested entirely on me. This was my chance to show Daddy.

# THE RIVALS

*Charles*

The next morning, I'd just finished a marathon session with Whitaker when Abby poked her head in my office. "Ron Wroblewski would like a few minutes of your time." She probably noticed my confused expression. "He's the HR VP."

I stood to stretch. "Okay. I've got time now, if that works. Just give me a second to get something from the machines." I'd noticed the tempting yellow bags as I walked by yesterday.

"I'll have him up here in a few minutes for you."

I followed her out of the office and headed to the break room. There I exchanged money for two lovely bags of peanut M&M's and a can of Coke. I returned to my office with the perfect mixture of sugar, caffeine, and protein.

When Wroblewski arrived, I was surprised by the size of the man. We shook.

"It's nice to get a few minutes with you, sir," he said.

"We can drop the sir, Ron. It's Charlie." I held up one of my yellow bags. "Would you like some?"

He shook his head. "I shouldn't." He shifted in his chair. "I want to start by telling you how well I thought yesterday's meeting went."

"You think so?" I popped a few of the candies into my mouth.

"Absolutely. A very good start."

I noted that he'd called it only a start. "That's not why you wanted to talk, I assume." I had more things to get to with Whitaker and didn't want to spend a lot of time jawing. That could come later, after the diligence phase had been completed.

"I got a call from Califano today, and he wants to set up a meeting."

I didn't recognize the name. "And who is Califano?"

"As I told Dani yesterday, he's the machinists union president representing the workers at our jet-engine division. And I thought this was likely."

I had no idea why Dani hadn't mentioned it, but that wasn't right to bring up with Wroblewski.

"Is there a problem?" I asked.

"Things are going sideways, in my opinion. We seemed to be on track for a contract extension until a little while ago. When Derek, uh, Mr. Hawker, got serious about selling the company, the union went quiet, and the signing got put off."

"And you need us to get things back on track, I assume?"

"That's about the size of it," he said as he stood. "Have you two decided on a date to go down and meet with them?"

I didn't let on that this was news to me. "We'll get back with you, Ron."

He left, and I found Dani outside looking over Abby's shoulder at her screen.

Both of them turned to look at me. "Can I have a word with you?" I asked Dani before heading back into my office.

She followed.

I closed the door after her. "I just had a visit from Wroblewski. Why didn't you tell me we had a union boss who wanted to set up a meeting?"

"That just happened yesterday, and you've been holed up in your office all morning."

"A union problem could really fuck us right now. But maybe you wouldn't understand that," I shot back. "While you've been busy shopping, I've been doing real work."

She waved a piece of paper. "And I've been meeting the staff all morning. You're the one who had his door closed."

"We're supposed to be doing this together. You need to tell me about important things like this as soon as they come up."

Dani held her ground. Her gaze didn't stray. "I would have if you'd been around. Or would you prefer I kick the door down?"

I wasn't taking this abuse from her. "I was busy with Whitaker, going over the financials."

"Speaking of doing this together, why didn't you invite me to your meeting with him?"

I tried to ignore the way her tits lifted as she crossed her arms under them. "I didn't see you here when we started it."

"Nor did you leave a note for me to join you when I came in."

I gave in on that one to lower the tension. "Point taken. I was wrong about that, same as you were wrong not to tell me about the union issue. Now, we need to move on and do these things together."

"And you can work on being more polite, while you're at it."

"I'm direct. It saves time."

"You're rude, and that's different."

"I'll use nicer, fluffier words, if you'll keep me informed."

She went to the door and opened it. "Together. I agree. You shouldn't be leaving me out of things."

"Anything that's appropriate," I clarified.

She seethed. "Anything."

I let her have the last word, otherwise we would never finish this argument.

After the door closed, I let myself smile.

Dani had proved more impressive than I'd thought. Pushed into a corner, the woman had the guts to fight back. She'd need that tenacity when she finally got to run something like this company.

We'd still need to settle the issue of a meeting with Califano, but that could wait until she'd calmed down.

I pulled out my pad to add a note on another sheet.

> (3) Action: She met with HR and learned of an imminent union problem in the jet-engine division. Rather than alert me so that we could deal with it in a timely manner, she dismissed the issue as minor and kept it to herself. Result: We could be facing a dire situation with the machinists union, and time has been lost dealing with it.

At this rate I was going to need more than a few sheets of paper for this list. Our fathers would have no choice but to put me in sole charge of the company.

Next I called Whitaker and set a meeting for the three of us at four thirty so Dani could get up to speed. Then I ventured out of my office.

Dani's office was open and empty.

"Inform her," I told Abby, "that we have a four thirty with Whitaker, and it's important."

## *Danielle*

After the yelling match with His Highness Charles the Righteous, I marched into my office and closed the door—firmly, but without the slam I felt like giving it. I wouldn't give him the satisfaction of knowing he'd gotten to me.

*Anything I could handle?* The arrogance of the man knew no bounds.

He'd been the one hiding behind a closed door. Abby had known where I was the whole time, if he'd cared to ask. I'd had my phone with me, if he'd bothered to call. Clearly all the arguments lined up on my side, not his.

After what had to be ten circuits around my desk, I grabbed my purse and headed for the door. I'd calmed myself enough, and lunch awaited me out there somewhere.

When Abby looked up, her eyes shifted quickly to Charlie's door. It was still closed. She held out a folder. "I have that new-products information for your meeting Monday."

"What's good around here for lunch?" I asked. "Something quick, but not the normal fast food."

"If you go out to the left, there are usually two or three lunch trucks on the street. I like the one that serves gyros myself. And the Starbucks down the street has tables outside, which are pleasant."

I held up my phone. "Gyros sounds good." I held up my phone. "I'll be available if his highness is looking for me."

She rolled her eyes and added a smirk. "Do you really want me to tell him that?"

I thought better of it. "Maybe not, but you know how to reach me."

Downstairs, I easily located the truck she mentioned. The smells emanating from its window were heavenly, but I kept my food wrapped until I ordered my cappuccino at Starbucks. The wait to snag an outside table was only a few minutes.

Abby had been right. This was relaxing—delicious food and drink, just watching the people go by.

Opening the folder, I started through the material for the new-products meeting and had an idea.

Abby picked up on the second ring. "Everything okay?"

"Perfect," I answered. "The gyro is scrumptious."

"Your car is ready, and they're dropping it off for you here in a few minutes."

"Thanks. That's quick." Silence hung on the line for a second while I formulated my question. "You said you and Mrs. Hawker tried all the products before they were released?"

"Yeah, those are the launch rules."

"And they'll bring prototypes?"

"Of course."

The plan came together in my head. "Then please ask them to bring extras of the trial packages, and tell Charlie to join us for the new-product meeting on Monday."

"Sure. Also, Charlie set up a meeting for the two of you with Whitaker at four thirty."

"Of course he did."

~

I HAD ANOTHER MISSION WHEN I RETURNED TO THE OFFICE.

After closing the door between us, I dialed Abby's desk a minute later.

"Yes?" she answered.

I double-checked the facilities director's name on my org chart. "Please have Giorgio come see me."

"Is something in your office broken?"

"And have him bring the upstairs layout with him."

She gave up trying to get more information. "Sure thing."

~

GIORGIO HAD COME PREPARED, AND IT DIDN'T TAKE LONG TO EXPLAIN WHAT I wanted to accomplish.

"Should I discuss this with—?"

"Absolutely not," I said, cutting him off.

Concern crept across his face. "You sure about that? I don't want to get in trouble with this."

"It's my responsibility." I'd make sure there was no blowback for him. I walked to the door and opened it. "And it has to be complete for Monday."

He stood, shaking his head slightly. "That'll cost extra."

"Monday." There were some advantages to being in charge of the company, and I planned to exercise this one.

## CHAPTER 14

*Danielle*

Friday afternoon, Charlie, Stanfield Whitaker, and I were going over endless financials when Abby let herself in.

Charlie looked up, but didn't say anything.

"Dani, that man you mentioned is downstairs asking for you."

"What man?"

"Mr. Durban."

"Here?" My mouth must have dropped to the floor. *Gerald is here?* That couldn't be true.

She nodded. "Should I bring him up?"

It took me a few seconds to get my mouth working properly. "Yes, in a moment?"

Charlie eyed me. "I guess we're done for now." His voice sounded as if interrupting his precious meeting had been my plan.

*Well, screw you, Charlie Blakewell.* I stood and gave him my straight face. "It must be important, and I didn't ask him to come."

He slid his papers together without looking at me. "I didn't say you did. We'll continue this tomorrow morning at ten."

Not a question of *how about* meeting at ten, just an order to meet tomorrow.

Whitaker's eyes darted between us, and he stood. "On Saturday?"

Charlie's eyes held the big man's. "Is there a problem?"

"Of course not," Whitaker answered as he shuffled his papers together.

He beat me to the door, clearly not wanting to be in the line of fire if things got more heated between Charlie and me.

"Fine, ten," I said as I closed the door behind us, just hard enough to make my feelings clear.

"Shall I bring him up now?" Abby asked, pointing to my office.

"Yes, please." I released the door handle. The cold metal reflected the heart of the man in the office. A cathartic yell at Charlie fucking Blakewell would have to wait. It wasn't like he would deserve it any less tomorrow when fewer people were around. It would be easier to step out of lady mode and give him a good yelling without an audience.

I entered my office and closed the door. What was Gerald doing here unannounced? I checked my phone. I hadn't missed a message, a call from him, or a voicemail.

He'd meant this to be a surprise. Why wouldn't he have called first and set up dinner again or something instead of appearing at the office?

Checking myself in the pocket mirror from my purse, I decided on a quick trip to the bathroom to touch up my mascara and lipstick.

He stood just inside the door of my office when I returned. His smile was as broad as ever. "Hey, Sugarplum." He gave me a quick kiss on the cheek—no hug, which was just as well in front of curious eyes.

"I must have missed your call," I said as I closed the door and blocked out listening ears.

"That's because I just hopped on a plane."

"Well, that's nice." It was all I could think to say. I pointed to one of the chairs in front of the desk. "Let's sit." I didn't want to explain a year and a half apart just standing here.

He checked his watch—the Patek Philippe he was so proud of. "We don't have a lot of time." He didn't move toward the chair.

"I don't understand."

"You left so abruptly from our dinner."

"I explained that. John was in the hospital. I had to leave that instant to catch the plane."

"You said he's going to heal up."

"Yes, thank you. It'll take some time, but he'll make a full recovery, they tell me."

"Good. Then your job here is done, and you can come with me to Las Vegas. We can get our plans back on track."

"I can't just pick up and leave."

He moved toward me and took my hand. "Sure you can. You're going to be my wife, and everything will be fine."

My eyes widened. *Excuse me?* This was all wrong. He hadn't asked me to move in with him first. And he hadn't asked if I would marry him; he'd just told me. This scenario was all backward. Where was the ring? Screw that—where was the damned question? There was an etiquette to this, or at least a tradition, even if I wasn't ready for it.

I pulled my hand back. "You intended to propose at dinner?"

He glanced down. "Yes. I've been wanting to for the longest time, and I finally got up the courage."

A ring had been in the box after all. But that didn't make me happy.

"We need to get to the airport. Security these days is a nightmare."

I straightened my shoulders. "No." I said everything in that one, simple word.

"You said we were good together. You said that more than once."

I had, sort of. After taking a deep breath, I started. "I told you I can't leave. Not today, and not soon." There was also my promise to John, but I didn't need to spell that out to Gerald.

"Sure you can. You have to."

The words out of his mouth were all wrong. Everything about this conversation was upsetting. How had this become mandatory? How had emotion been left out?

"You're not listening." I moved behind the desk.

His eyes followed me and landed on the vase of flowers for the first time. His face twisted in anger. "A few days apart and there's already another man?"

"Of course not," I shot back. "Those are—"

"Forget whoever this is," he yelled. "You have to come with me now. Our flight to Las Vegas leaves tonight. Then it's back to London to plan our honeymoon."

I shook my head. He'd mapped it all out, without any input from me. And I was done with this. He wasn't the Gerald I'd known—or thought I'd known. This lunatic Gerald was a man I'd never seen, and didn't ever want to see again.

I matched his volume. "No means no."

"Oh."

I pointed at the door. "Get out."

"What?"

"Now. You can't just show up here and demand we get married."

Complete disbelief came over his face. "But I thought you wanted to."

"You didn't even ask me."

"I'm sorry. You're right." He didn't sound sorry, or contrite, or anything approaching that. He sounded angry, or cornered. Before I knew it, he was on one knee. "Sugarplum, will you marry me?" He held out his hand. It didn't contain a ring. Everything about this was fake—the emotion, the question, the motivation, everything.

I breathed slowly and gave him the only answer that wasn't fake today. "No."

"Why not?"

A better question was why? Why now? Why like this? Why me? Why him?

He got back on his feet. "Let's go to dinner and talk about this."

"No," I yelled. "What has gotten into you?"

Maybe I'd almost gotten up the courage to say yes to a suggestion that we live together. But not marriage, and certainly not like this.

"Sugarplum?"

"I said no. Get out now," I yelled even louder.

He marched to the door. "You're going to regret this."

Then the door slammed, and I was alone.

I was no longer his Sugarplum. I'd never even liked that name. It was over. It had to be. He'd shown his true colors. He cared even less about what I wanted than the idiot in the office next door.

Slumping into the chair, I put my head in my hands. A week ago I'd been looking forward to him coming back to London. And now, I couldn't stand another minute in the room with the arrogant ass he'd shown himself to be.

My stomach rioted. I closed my eyes and willed myself to calm down. It was no use. I got up and left my office. I avoided looking in Abby's direction and headed down the hall.

I made it to the restroom. Luckily it was empty. As I leaned against the counter, my stomach settled somewhat. The visage that looked back at me in the mirror was one of a loser. I really was terrible at the whole girlfriend thing if the man I'd spent a year with was a psycho.

Things were beyond having Paris pushed out now, way beyond. Everything about my world was crashing in on me. How had I missed how controlling Gerald could be? How demanding?

I grabbed a tissue to clean up around my eyes. *Be strong*, I told myself. *You're a Wentworth.* We were strong stock. Little problems didn't make us fall apart. We were the kind of family that had created the English empire. This was just a hiccup in my life's journey.

The door opened, but I dared not look over.

Abby walked up beside me.

I couldn't avoid glancing at her in the mirror. Another tear ran down my cheek, and I swiped it away. Strong women didn't need to cry. They could handle anything. I was that strong woman.

"What happened?" she asked.

I couldn't hold back the sniffle. "Nothing."

"It didn't sound like nothing. And don't give me any of the British stiff-upper-lip crap."

With nobody in the entire town to talk to, I opened up. "He wanted to marry me, and I told him to leave."

"He proposed?"

I nodded and wiped my eyes again. "I guess, but it was more like he *told* me I was marrying him—like it was ordained. You know, like an arranged marriage or something."

"Your father did that to you?"

I shook my head. "No. Of course not. It was just... I don't know how to put it. Gerald thought we'd already agreed. But we hadn't. He hadn't even asked. I mean, I thought he was going to...ask me to move in with him before I left. But somehow he skipped that step. He said I had to go with him to Las Vegas and get married."

"Tonight?"

I sucked in air through my teeth. "Crazy, right? He just demanded it."

"What kind of turdball does that? And then says you'll regret it. That's pretty low."

"You heard that?"

"Yup."

"Turdball?"

She smiled that infectious smile of hers. "It's my work-appropriate substitute for douchebag fuckhead asshole." A moment later she pushed at my shoulder to turn me and wrapped me in a hug.

A woman I didn't recognize pushed open the door.

"Use the one downstairs," Abby told her.

Without a word, the woman left, a testament to Abby's clout in the organization.

"Anyway, this isn't exactly the best place to talk," Abby said after a moment, backing toward the door.

I nodded and followed. Reaching my office, I made a decision. "I think I'm going to leave for the day."

Abby's bark was immediate. "To a depressing hotel room? No way."

"I moved to the apartment."

"Alone? Still depressing." She shut down her computer and pulled her purse from its drawer. "Grab your purse. It's happy hour at the Saddle Rack, and you need some eighty-proof liquid mood corrector."

"I don't know…"

"I do." She ushered me back into my office.

I didn't bother with anything other than my purse.

After locking my door, I went with her to the elevators.

The doors were closing when she said, "Repeat after me: Gerald, you fuckhead. You don't deserve me."

I did.

"Louder," she said. "You need to yell it."

So, I yelled, "Gerald, you fuckhead. You don't deserve me."

The doors opened at street level just as I finished.

"Feel better?" she asked.

I nodded. Screaming at Gerald, even though he wasn't here, had been cathartic. But what did it mean?

We reached the street, and the first woman I saw had a large diamond on her finger. Tears welled up again when I realized that wasn't in my future, and I stopped.

Abby turned. "It's this way."

"I think I'll just go back to the apartment." I raised an arm to flag an approaching taxi.

Abby pulled me away from the curb. "No, you don't. It doesn't matter if you cry or scream or laugh, you're not doing it alone tonight. That's not healthy."

I was probably going to do two of those. I was both hurt and mad. "But I don't want—"

"And we're both getting good and sloshed while we do it. Not alone, and definitely not sober."

She pulled me along.

I didn't resist.

# CHAPTER 15

*Danielle*

When my alarm sounded on Saturday morning, it took two tries to silence the monster. Why did they have to make them so loud on hangover mornings?

Hiding under the pillow for a minute didn't help the throbbing in my skull. But an urgent need to pee forced me out of bed and to the bathroom anyway. A minute later, I'd downed the suggested number of Excedrin with a glass of water. Then another glass. Water was good for a hangover, wasn't it?

I almost didn't recognize the bleary-eyed woman in the mirror. I definitely had to avoid tequila next time.

*"Don't worry. It'll erase all your problems,"* Abby had said. What she hadn't mentioned was the pendulum swinging from numbness last night to excruciating pain this morning.

My memory of the night at the Saddle Rack was spotty. A few details came back to me as I tried to brush away the crap in my mouth that felt like I'd chewed on a cat's tail.

There had been the shots, of course. Lots of shots. Who wouldn't want to lean back in a dentist's chair and have someone pour tequila down your throat? Fun at the time, but I was paying the price this morning.

And cowboys, or at least guys dressed like cowboys, and lots of them. Dancing. I remember dancing with… I don't know how many.

The faces were blurry, and the names were a jumble. No, wait… There had been a Jett something, or was it Bret—not that it mattered.

I'd ridden the mechanical bull. And my back told me I wouldn't be doing that again anytime soon.

I remembered lots of jokes about riding a cowboy, or being ridden by one. I was pretty sure Abby had kept me safe, though. At least I couldn't remember taking one of them up on the suggestion.

I put the toothbrush down and went to open the curtains.

Bad idea.

I pulled them closed again. The sunlight was too bright for me. Maybe more Excedrin? Definitely another. They built a safety margin into the recommended dosage for sure. The bottle didn't say anything about the dose being weight dependent, and I wasn't the skinniest girl on the block, so I'd be safe with another.

The bedside clock said I had to get moving to make it in time for the meeting with Charlie. If the Excedrin didn't kick in soon, I would be useless, but at least I should be there. I started coffee in the little machine. Tea was too weak to deal with the way I felt.

The full weight of the meeting with Gerald yesterday came back to me. *"You have to,"* he'd said like the spoiled brat he was—as if all that mattered was how something affected him. What about me? What about how I felt?

That was the whole problem, wrapped in a neat box. How much could he care about me if his only reaction to my needing to stay here a while was related to how it affected him. Like a spoiled brat, he'd kept repeating that we needed to get to the airport.

In London, we'd have a four-week waiting period between getting the paperwork and the wedding. In Vegas, that became instantaneous. What was the rush? What about having my family there? That hadn't even factored into his thinking.

I'd cried last night while explaining the whole shitty situation to Abby. But this morning, I was all cried out. Instead, I felt like a weight had been lifted from me. Better to learn how self-centered he was now than after I lived with him or worse—had a gold band on my finger tying me to him.

*"Every crappy experience is an opportunity to learn,"* Daddy liked to say. I hoped he was right, because I didn't ever want a repeat of Gerald.

Last night's clothes lay strewn on the floor. I picked up my bra and instantly regretted it. Leaning over with a throbbing headache? Not a good idea.

"Fuck you, Gerald. I'm too good for you," I said loudly to the empty room. It helped a little, but it didn't resolve the emptiness I felt.

I'd failed at the one thing a woman should be good at—attracting a man to share time with, share things with, perhaps share a life with.

Everybody I knew had been able to find someone to pair up with, someone to get serious enough with to at least live together—everybody but me. Even Andrina had been in a relationship once. Gerald had been the closest I'd come, and in retrospect, it hadn't really been a relationship worthy of the name.

Work and the family business were important to me. But was I working hard at that to make up for my personal failings?

I pulled fresh panties from the shopping bag on the bureau and only realized I hadn't taken the tag off after I'd slipped them on. Of course, I could go into work and have Charlie snip it off for me.

Why had that just popped into my brain?

I was a basket case this morning, but I couldn't skip the meeting and prove Charlie right about me. Giving him that satisfaction was not an option. "Screw you too, Charlie Blakewell," I said to the empty room. Somehow the words didn't give me the same satisfaction as yelling at Gerald had.

The coffeemaker finished.

After adding a packet of sweetener, I poured the concoction into the Starbucks mug I'd picked up. The way I felt, the mug would be empty almost as soon as I left the apartment.

After locking up, I headed downstairs and out to the parking lot. I stopped beside my rental car with a gasp.

It had a flat tire.

*My fucking luck. What else can go wrong?*

Crossing to the other side, I realized it wasn't one, but all four tires were flat. I quickly turned to check the nearby bushes.

I was alone.

*Who the fuck?* I didn't have enough swear words to describe how I felt right now. If this was what Abby called a safe neighborhood, then what the hell was a bad one like?

∼

CHARLES

. . .

Saturday morning, I arrived at work early. Partly it was because I hadn't slept well. I'd heard the yelling that came from Dani's office yesterday. It had been impossible to ignore.

She'd looked terrible when she came out after jerkwad Gerald left—like a wounded animal.

Abby had quickly followed Dani to the bathroom, and it was probably best that I didn't intervene. Comforting a woman after a boyfriend problem was best left to another woman.

I'd lain awake last night and told myself it was normal. Dani and I had to work efficiently together as a team. That's why I was concerned about her and her state of mind. It made perfect sense for me to be invested in her emotional well-being, didn't it?

As I paced the office and looked out the long windows at the city, all I could do was wonder where she was, and hope she was safe.

I'd been at my desk for an hour before I heard Abby unlocking her desk outside my door. I grabbed a coffee cup and headed out, acting surprised to see her at her desk. I lifted my cup. "I'm getting a refill. Would you like any?"

She looked up at me with bloodshot eyes. "I'll join you." She retrieved her coffee cup from a drawer and followed me to the break room.

"Rough night?" I asked as I stood aside so she could make the first cup of coffee.

"Why don't you ask me what you really want to know," she said as she pressed the buttons to make hers with a double shot.

Her directness surprised me. "I heard some of the arguing, but I don't know the specifics. Is Dani all right?" That last part was my real question.

"She's hurting because she realized the guy she's been going out with is a total turdball. I think now she might realize she's better off without him." She pulled her cup out from underneath the spout.

I placed mine in the machine. "Is there anything I can do to help?" I pressed the buttons to duplicate the coffee she'd selected.

"Cut her some slack, for a change."

The *for a change* comment cut deep. Her tone indicated she thought I hadn't been fair.

"I feel like crap," she said. "And I only drank half of what she did. She's going to feel even worse."

"Should I call off our meeting?" I asked.

"I wouldn't. Calling it off would be saying you don't think she can handle it."

"I was just—"

She cut me off. "She needs your support, not your sympathy."

My cup finished, and I pulled it from the machine. "You're a wise lady."

She half laughed, half snorted. "Just remember that when it comes time for my performance review." Stopping at the door, she turned. "Do you want to do dinner tonight?"

I let out a breath. "I don't think that's a good idea, given the situation."

Her mouth fell slightly open. "Oh…right." She left a second later.

The conversation hadn't been as awkward as I'd expected.

## Danielle

When I climbed out of the back of the Uber I'd summoned to get to work, there he was.

Gerald stood on the sidewalk outside the Hawker building, *my* building. The sight of him didn't do anything to calm my throbbing head.

"I'll give you one last chance to say yes," he said.

Was it a threat or an ultimatum? I couldn't tell. One thing it for sure was not? An appealing proposition. I'd declined to marry him, and this is how he reacted? This made it crystal clear that yesterday hadn't been an aberration, but a view into his true character, one he'd kept hidden until now.

I went past him to the building's door. "My answer hasn't changed. No, as in no way. It's over between us. Now get out of here before I call the police." I passed inside, shivering.

He didn't follow.

A guard I didn't recognize sat at the reception desk.

I pointed back. "If that man tries to come into the building, call the police."

His eyes widened, and he looked past me to the street. "Yes, ma'am."

Gerald had said I'd regret it, and if this is what he meant, it only made me more sure I'd made the right decision. I might regret how many shots I'd had last night, but I most certainly didn't regret kicking him out of my office. Now he was officially out of my life. Stalking me at work was miles past unacceptable.

*How could he? How could I have not seen this coming? What's wrong with me that I attracted a man like him and hadn't figured it out?*

I made it upstairs with time to spare. Charlie's door was open. Of course he'd beaten me in today.

I passed his door on the way to the break room for another cup of coffee, and I didn't see him at his desk.

The Excedrin had kicked in and helped, but it didn't eliminate how crappy I felt.

He wasn't in the break room either when I added Kona roast to my cup. I brought the mug to my nose and inhaled. The aroma, along with the warmth of the mug in my hands, soothed me for a moment.

Today was a new day, a better day. It had to be. It could hardly equal yesterday.

Wandering back to my desk, I realized there were people I would have to tell about Gerald. I couldn't keep this from Andrina or Mena—and then there were Daddy and Alicia.

John needed to be on the list as well. He would be back in the UK by now. I could already hear the *I told you so*.

Sitting down behind the desk in my office, I sipped my coffee. An interoffice envelope sat on the corner of my desk. The *From* column had Giorgio's name in it. Opening it, I unfolded the plans to find a note.

> Call me if you want to make any changes to this. Otherwise we are a go for Sunday. I even found a guy to do the carpet. - Giorgio

The layout was exactly what I wanted. With a smile, I folded it back up and returned it to the envelope.

Fishing my phone out of my purse, I selected John's number.

Before I could start the call, Charlie was at my door. "Good morning, Dani."

I should have closed it, and there was nothing good about this morning.

He walked in carrying his coffee mug and a paper bag. He kicked the door closed behind him. "I thought we could talk."

I set the phone down. "This isn't a good time."

He ignored me, put the bag down on my desk, and took a seat.

I was about to tell him to leave, but then he opened the bag and the aroma reached me.

"I only wanted to pass on what I learned the hard way about recovering from a hard night." He pulled out paper plates, plastic utensils, and then the food. "Breakfast burritos," he announced.

My mouth watered.

"It's a scientific fact," he said. "I've found that food in your stomach the next morning helps. Well, maybe it's unscientific and just my experience." He chuckled. "It may be anecdotal, but it's still evidence."

This was the most friendly and talkative he'd been with me yet.

I started to unwrap the warm bundle. "Really?"

He started on his as well and handed me a plastic knife and fork. "They may be a bit messy, but trust me, this is exactly what you need."

"Based on your vast personal experience?"

He pulled napkins out of the bag and handed me a few. "More times than I would like to admit, I'm afraid."

For some reason he was sharing personal details this morning.

After I unwrapped it, the burrito was a mouthwatering monster. The first forkful was like heaven, and it was all I could do to keep from humming to myself.

"Bon appétit," he said, cutting a piece of his. "This is the best bloody hangover medicine. Well, this plus pain reliever and coffee. But I'm guessing you have those other two covered already."

I nodded

We ate together in silence, and I had my food almost finished before I got up the courage to ask, "Why this?"

He shrugged. "A little birdie told me you might have had a rough night."

That could only have been Abby, although I hadn't seen her yet this morning.

"Thank you," I said.

"I'm also available to talk."

Another uncharacteristic utterance from him.

I forked more food into my mouth without answering.

"Only when you want." He lifted a bite to his mouth. "And if you want."

I didn't look up to catch his eyes. My feelings were too raw. A nod was all the response I gave him.

This was a side of Charlie Blakewell I hadn't seen since arriving, and I decided I liked it.

The meeting with Whitaker was short, and we went right into another with Wroblewski.

By the time the second meeting concluded, my headache had subsided, and my eyes didn't ache anymore from the glare streaming in the window.

Wroblewski gathered his papers together. "Anything we didn't cover? Or anything you want to go over again?"

We'd set up a meeting with the machinists union, and we'd addressed everything we needed to prepare in nauseating detail, it seemed to me. I shook my head.

Charlie leaned back in his chair. "This is fine for all the facts and issues, Ron. But what about the personality side of dealing with Califano? What's he like? What are his hot buttons?"

Wroblewski closed his folder. "I've only met him a few times."

That surprised the hell out of me, given Wroblewski's position.

"Mr. Hawker had most of the dealings with him," he explained."

Charlie pushed back his chair and stood. "Thanks, Ron. I guess we're all set for the meeting."

Wroblewski left, but I was still gathering my things when Charlie spoke again. "I have a car. If we drove together to the meeting, it would give us a chance to talk on the way."

"Sure," I agreed. "Sounds good." I didn't have a vehicle with working tires at the moment anyway. Who knew when I'd have a chance to sort that out. Either way, mentioning what had happened to my rental car this morning was not a place I was going to go. "See you Monday," I said on my way out.

"I hope you feel better," Charlie said as I left.

I turned at the door. "I do already. Thank you for the burrito." Thanking a coworker was normal, wasn't it?

Why did I even have that thought?

"Just looking out for my most valuable employee." He turned away.

I didn't work for him, but unable to see his face and judge whether he'd meant it as a joke or not, I didn't respond.

## CHAPTER 16

*Charles*

Monday morning, I rode the lift up to our offices. I now considered this *our* building. It said Hawker on the door, but between Dani's family and mine, this was now ours. Joint ownership would just take a lot of getting used to.

"Good morning, Mr. Blakewell," Abby said as I strode up.

I'd been able to get her to call me Charlie during the day, but somehow her morning greeting was always more formal.

Her smile was different in a way I couldn't place. She quickly averted her gaze to look down at her desk.

"Very nice necklace." Maybe a personal comment would loosen her up. She wore a sapphire pendant on a gold chain.

"Thank you." She fingered the pendant.

It wasn't something I'd seen her wear before. I took a wild guess that could be construed as a compliment, even if I was wrong. "He has good taste."

She nodded.

My door was open, and since this conversation wasn't going anywhere, I walked in.

The sight inside stopped me in my tracks. "What the bloody hell?"

"Morning, Charlie," Dani said from behind a desk where my conference table used to be.

I was speechless.

Everything had changed. A red stripe ran diagonally from the door to the corner, dividing the space in half. My desk had been moved to the left. Dani sat behind a desk to the right, and a small round table with four chairs, instead of my bigger table with eight, straddled the line near the window.

"Like it?" Dani asked in a cheery voice.

I was rooted in place, not wanting to accept this invasion of my space. "What the hell did you do?"

She stood. "You insisted, excuse me, *suggested*, that we work together on everything, and this..." She swept her arm around the space. "...is to make that easier. And since we're equal partners in this, I thought it best we share this office. It has much better light than the one I was in. And it still has room for the small conference table."

I sighed and walked to my desk. Things were arranged as they had been, and the wood was the same color, but it seemed different somehow. It was smaller—that was it.

"We swapped the one you had for that one—to make the two identical, since we wouldn't want anyone coming in to think less of me because my desk was smaller."

"I liked that desk." In desks and offices, I definitely preferred larger to smaller.

"You'll be fine. Abby was very careful moving everything for you," she said. "And, it's not like anyone will think your dick shrank just because the desk did."

Her vocabulary surprised me, not because I was above it, but I hadn't expected it from her. The woman was more resourceful than I'd given her credit for. Or would *cunning* be a better description?

I'd have to watch my back with this one.

She stood. "I'm going to get some coffee." She held up her cup. "What about you?"

"That's a lovely idea." I grabbed my cup and followed her. The alluring hint of strawberry trailed behind her.

"Thanks for the heads-up," I told Abby as we passed her desk.

She raised her hands. "Sorry."

Dani looked back. "Don't blame her. I swore her to secrecy."

As soon as Dani turned away, my eyes were drawn back to her arse. I wasn't above watching delectable scenery when presented with the opportunity. Cunning vixen, this one.

She approached the machine and punched up her coffee.

"You should have talked with me first," I said.

"Like you did when you claimed that office for yourself last week?"

She had me there.

"And you think sharing an office is going to work?" I asked.

"Why wouldn't it?"

I put my cup in place after she withdrew hers. "No reason. Just it's unusual."

What could I say? *Because I'll spend too much of the day stealing glances at you?* I couldn't say that. *Because your beauty is distracting? Because you smell incredible? Because I'm having trouble keeping my thoughts of you strictly in the coworker category?* That last one summed it all up.

But none of those was appropriate in an office environment. Especially because they were all truer than what I'd said. Silence was the true discretion in this situation.

I lifted my cup. "Abby said you put a new-product meeting on my schedule for this morning before we head out to meet with Califano."

The smile that curled her mouth was mischievous, if I read it right. "Meetings together, as you suggested." She checked a paper from her purse. "I have an issue with my rental car I need to take care of. But I'll be back in time."

I shrugged. Having her out of sight would make my morning easier.

Not long after finishing my coffee, I needed to relieve myself of the extra liquid.

On autopilot, I pulled open the private bathroom.

Abby giggled from beyond my door.

I ignored her, closed the door behind me, unzipped, and turned right for the urinal.

I saw it as I whipped my dick out.

A fucking plant.

Not only had Dani rearranged my office, she'd planted a fucking fern in the urinal—my urinal.

I was absolutely going to find a way to get back at her.

When I finished up over the toilet, I left the seat up on purpose.

∼

## Danielle

The look on Charlie's face when he came in to see our divided, joint office had been priceless.

Giorgio and his crew had done a superb job. Everything was symmetrical, with the one exception of having the door to the private bathroom on his side. But that couldn't be helped. We had to share it.

When I came back from dealing with the car rental company, I handed Abby the new paperwork.

"What was wrong with the first one?" she asked.

"Leaky tire."

"And they changed out the whole car? Impressive."

"Yeah." I nodded absently. "Are they here yet?" The personal-products-division people were due for the new-products meeting.

"They went to get water in the break room. Vanessa is the division VP, and Willow is her new-products manager. I have the boardroom cleared for you."

I pointed to the empty office I now shared with Charlie. "We'll do it in here. The table is more intimate than the boardroom."

The corners of Abby's eyes crinkled. "Are you sure? In the past—"

"Absolutely," I assured her. "Charlie and I both want to be involved in this. His rules."

The two women appeared, and I introduced myself. "Welcome," I told them. "I've been looking forward to this."

Willow carried the bag of sample items, and they moved into place around the table just as Charlie arrived.

"You're right on time," I told him.

"Aren't I always?"

I didn't have a comeback to that.

Vanessa and Willow introduced themselves.

"The VW girls—I think I can remember that," he quipped.

That got a giggle from Willow. Vanessa seemed less impressed.

*Note to self: Vanessa prefers a professional approach.*

"And which division again?" Charlie asked.

"Personal products," Vanessa explained as we sat. "We have two items ready for launch approval today."

Charlie remained standing and checked his watch. "I have another meeting. Perhaps you should just go ahead without me."

I patted the table top next to me. "You told everyone that nothing was changing. This is the company's process, and you also insisted we both be involved in these types of meetings."

Vanessa fidgeted.

I had Charlie trapped with his own words.

The wrinkle that formed across his forehead gave him away. He knew it, and after a moment, he pulled out the chair next to me.

"Are you sure?" Vanessa asked, directing her question at me. "These are primarily targeted at women."

I smiled in Charlie's direction. "He's an expert when it comes to understanding women, aren't you?"

He gritted his teeth briefly. "Not all women, it would seem."

"We have a couple of new items to show today," Vanessa began.

"Oh, before we start," I said. "There's another part of the process. Management tries out the new products before they're released, isn't that right?"

Both women nodded.

"We've always done it that way," Vanessa said. "You are the final arbiters of product quality." She pulled out the first item. "This is a personal waxing kit." She laid the box on the table.

Charlie's eyes widened. He'd spotted the key word: *intimate*.

Tormenting him was going to be fun if he reacted this way at just the sight of the box.

Willow opened the kit for us. "It contains everything a lady…" She looked at Charlie. "Or a man, would need to make it the easiest possible experience."

"It can certainly be difficult," I added.

Both women nodded.

Charlie was still and silent.

Willow pulled out a packet. "It comes with three pads saturated with our numbing cream."

"The same formulation we use for our PE product," Vanessa explained.

I asked the obvious. "PE?"

Willow's face reddened with a glance toward Charlie. "Premature ejaculation."

Vanessa was more businesslike. "Test subjects report a significantly less stressful time when waxing using the numbing wipes."

"Can they be used anywhere?" I asked.

"Yes, as long as you avoid the mucus membranes, which is not an issue for men."

"Men?" Charlie asked.

"Yes," Willow answered. "A unisex kit simplifies the logistics in the sales channels. Some men prefer waxing to shaving."

"Shaving their...?" he didn't finish the question.

Vanessa was unfazed. "The pubic area, including the scrotum."

Charlie looked ready to puke, but controlled himself. "Really?"

She nodded. "Men account for about twenty percent of our sales."

I looked him square in the eyes. "I'm sure a lot of women like the velvety softness without hair."

He gulped.

Willow pulled out the next package. "The strips are extra long, with a loop on the end for pulling."

"Don't you just hate it when you can't get a good-enough grip to yank it off quickly?" I asked.

Willow nodded.

Charlie closed his eyes for a second and sucked in a loud breath.

"Here is the second real improvement," Willow said as she pulled out the jar.

"We're very proud of this," Vanessa added.

She pointed to the side. "The plastic strip on the side is thermosensitive. It starts blue when it's not warm enough, turns green when the temperature is right, and red if it's too hot."

"Avoids burns," Vanessa added. "Especially for the men. The scrotal tissue burns more easily, the doctors tell us." She looked at Charlie. "We're told that can be very painful. It has something to do with having no fat or muscle in the area to protect the testicles from heat transfer. The temperature is only a bit lower than a curling iron—"

"We get the idea," Charlie said, shifting in his chair, drawing his legs together.

Vanessa's smile in my direction indicated she understood what I was up to.

Willow pulled out another package. "Soothing wipes are also provided for the last step." She started placing things back in the box.

"We have a second item," Vanessa said as she produced another small box from the bag. "A redesigned shaver." She removed it from the box and handed it to Charlie.

"It's light," he said as he held it under his chin. He pulled it away. "The head is a little on the small side.

"That's intentional," Willow said, holding her hand out.

Charlie relinquished it.

Willow ran her finger over the small, rounded head. "This is intended for intimate use. It's designed to be maneuverable in the area between the labia and the thigh, which is tight."

"Razors are also difficult," Vanessa added, "because the area is not as flat as your cheek or neck."

Charlie gulped again. This was getting to him.

"The shape also works well at the base of the scrotum," Vanessa said with a smile, getting into the Charlie torture. "The feedback we'll need from you is whether the oscillation of the head is a bother."

Charlie's eyes went a notch wider. "Me?"

"You said yesterday you didn't want to change anything, isn't that right?"

I nodded. "That's what we said."

"Well, you two are our final test subjects then," she said triumphantly.

Charlie turned the shaver on and off, again bringing it under his chin. "It vibrates a lot."

Willow's face lit up. "Why didn't we think of that?" she looked at her boss. "If we add a silicon cap, it could do double duty as a toy. That would be a first in the marketplace."

Vanessa typed a note into her phone. "Removable silicone cap for the shaver. Very good, Mr. Blakewell. We'll look into that and get back to you," she said.

Willow unloaded two fresh boxes of each product onto the table.

"What time next week should we get back together for your reports?" Vanessa asked.

I turned to Charlie. "How about next Monday?"

He sucked in air but didn't answer right away. "Uhhh... I think we'll need more time for this. At least I will."

"Okay. We'll give you a call," I told the women.

They made their way out, and I gathered up my two test boxes.

Charlie shut the door. "What was that all about?"

"What?"

"You know damned well what. Curling-iron-hot wax to the balls? No fucking way am I waxing anywhere, much less down..." He cast his eyes downward and huffed, without finishing the sentence.

I put the boxes down and crossed my arms. "You said you wanted to follow the procedures they had in place, same as last week. Those were your exact words." I caught the glance he stole at my chest, but I didn't call him on it. Instead, I pulled back my shoulders and lifted my boobs a bit.

"I'm not doing it."

I narrowed my eyes at him. "And I thought you were trustworthy."

"I am, but I'm not waxing."

"And shaving," I said. "Fine. Don't then. The way the company grapevine works, it will probably take about two days for everyone who works here to know your word means diddly-squat."

"But that—" He pointed at the radioactive boxes. "Is not what I meant."

I picked up my samples. "Fine. You try splitting hairs like that with the employees and see how it goes." I made a show of checking my watch. "Took you less than seventy-two hours to break your word. Is that a record for you?"

"That's not what I meant," he argued again.

I stopped at the door, with my free hand on the handle. "If you don't have the balls for the job, have your daddy send someone who does." I pulled open the door. "Man up, Blakewell, or go home." I closed the door before he could respond.

Abby's eyes were wide, apparently having heard at least part of my pronouncement.

Stopping at her desk, I summoned my calm voice. "We have things to try this week."

She glanced at Charlie's door. "Is there a problem?"

"A waxing kit and a shaver." I nodded toward the office. "I don't care what he offers you. Do not let him rope you into doing the testing for him." I failed to restrain the giggle that got out.

"Understood." She offered a knowing smile as she let out a relieved breath. "And, Mr. Califano's office called. They have to reschedule the meeting."

That smelled like a crock of shit. "Let Charlie know." I retreated to the conference room and closed the door. My phone had vibrated while in Charlie's office. When I checked it, I found another missed call from Gerald.

It deserved the attention I gave it: none.

When I opened the door again, Abby was telling Charlie, "I can't this time. Sorry."

He stiffened, and for a moment I thought he might yell at her, but he didn't. He turned and saw me. "We have a meeting at five thirty today with Wroblewski, and we need to set another time with Califano."

"I'm flexible."

The corner of his mouth turned up. "I'll bet you are."

My cheeks flushed with the inflection in his voice. "I meant, I'll make time for it." I turned back to our office before I said something more foolish.

∼

At the end of the day, I reread the messages that had arrived this afternoon.

> Gerald: I'll be back for you!
>
> Gerald: We need each other!
>
> Gerald: You need to reconsider!!
>
> Gerald: You are making a mistake!!!
>
> Gerald: We are good together, I know you know that!

The man had a serious issue with exclamation points. They didn't help his messages.

Everything about them annoyed me. I started to type back.

> ME: Leave me alone. We're done

My finger hovered over the key to send the message for a moment. Instead, I moved to *delete* and erased everything I'd written.

No response back was my message to him. Giving him the courtesy of a reply wasn't what I felt like after what had happened between us.

*And what had happened?*

I didn't need him. I hadn't made a mistake. I didn't need to reconsider. I didn't know that we were good together. Just the opposite. I'd woken up to the reality of our lack of a relationship. Even at the dinner before I'd left London, I'd missed another in the series of obvious signs. It should have been clear that night that Gerald would never move with me to Paris.

*I'm such an imbecile.*

He knew how important the Paris job was to me—how much it meant to me, how much I wanted it. Or if he'd been listening, he would have known. Maybe he'd been listening, but hadn't cared.

What did it say that I didn't know the answer to that question for sure? Why didn't I know if he'd heard me or not, or if he simply didn't care enough to want what I wanted?

At least his text message that he'd be *back* hinted that I wouldn't find my tires flattened again this morning—not if he wasn't in town.

For a moment I toyed with the idea of asking Charlie if his father could get a hold put on Gerald's passport. Just as quickly, I realized how awful that would make me appear. Vengeful wasn't a good look.

I hadn't suspected Gerald of being capable of anything so low as vandalizing my car, but everything about his visit to my office had screamed desperation. And desperation drove men to extremes. *But why is he suddenly so desperate? Did I really know him at all?*

## CHAPTER 17

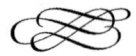

*DANIELLE*
 *(one week later)*

MONDAY MORNING A WEEK LATER, I ARRIVED AT THE PARK AHEAD OF CHARLIE for our morning run.

Last week, he'd suggested running both as a way to get exercise and a time to talk before the day began. *"We could get ourselves on the same wavelength,"* he'd said. Working as a coordinated pair was harder than it had sounded at first, and the early-morning conversations had helped. Our truce had lasted, and every day with him had become easier.

He'd also been right that the exercise invigorated me for the day.

I opened my phone and reread the text again.

DADDY: I think it's time for an update call

John had been right that Daddy's first suggestion had been daily updates.

I'd said every two weeks, but I'd already fended off two requests for earlier status updates.

*Be strong.*

I typed the message and hit send.

ME: Status update this Saturday at 9am my time. Love you.

Then I deleted another text message from Gerald. A little over a week of being officially single, and I was over him. And, my girls Andrina and Mena had cured me of feeling sorry for myself with their suggestions of sticking pins in a Gerald doll. The stick figure lay on the counter back at the apartment. It had gotten two fresh pins this morning. Every stick made me feel better.

I put my phone in my running armband. It was safer than dropping the fool thing. I'd made that mistake before. I squinted into the early sun and started jogging in place to stay warm.

"You beat me here," Charlie called from behind me.

I turned to see him jogging up. "Somebody once said something about the early bird getting the worm."

The sight warmed me, as it had each day since we'd started this ritual—not just the muscular legs, but the chest, shoulders, and arms that were either exposed or hugged by tight fabric. Andrina's advice was rubbing off on me.

"Wise man." His long strides ate up the distance between us. He checked his watch. "Ready?"

I nodded. "Just go easy on me."

"Okay. Let's do this." He started off.

I ran alongside him.

He glanced my way several times before he sped up significantly.

I kept my pace steady.

He could tire himself out all he wanted. This wasn't a competition.

A guy running the other way was a bit obvious as he checked me out as he passed. A few paces later, Charlie reversed course and ran back to me. He circled behind before joining me at my moderate jog. "Sorry. I needed a little burst to warm up."

"Fine by me."

What he'd really needed was to show off by speeding ahead—such a typical guy move.

I smiled, realizing his showing off had worked on me—just a little. Seeing his backside, along with the power and speed he possessed, was admittedly appealing. I mean, what girl wouldn't want to run behind a guy like him and watch that ass and those legs?

I liked legs almost as much as broad, powerful shoulders. What was wrong with that? Nothing, of course. Guy-watching was as much a thing as girl-watching, or it should be. We were just more discreet about it than the guys. I hadn't let my mouth hang open or done any drooling.

Gerald hadn't been the least bit athletic.

I coughed, realizing I'd just compared Charlie to Gerald. *Why had I done that?*

"You all right?" Charlie asked between breaths.

I nodded. "I think a fly just flew in my mouth." It was a stupid excuse, but the first thing I could think of.

He pulled me to a stop. "Open up."

"What?" I panted.

"Your mouth." His hands moved to my forehead and jaw, pulling my mouth open. "Open your mouth."

I did, losing the ability to argue with his strong, warm hands on me. His elbow brushed my breast, and my heart sped up even more.

He moved close, tilting my head side to side. "Good," he said, releasing his firm grip on me. "I had to be sure it wasn't a bee."

Another pair of runners passed us.

He tilted his head in the direction we'd been going. "You good?"

The buzz of excitement from his touch hadn't passed enough to allow coherent speech. I nodded.

He started off, and I followed him along the path a few seconds later when my legs finally responded to my commands. *Left foot, right foot, left foot, right foot.*

Charlie slowed to let me run alongside. "You can't be too careful about bees. I got one in the mouth once."

I jogged and listened, unable to form a question that wouldn't sound moronic. Processing the fact that I'd just compared Charlie to Gerald took all my concentration—that and being afraid my mouth wouldn't work with the tingling I still felt from his touch, or that I'd trip if I tried to run and talk at the same time as the question swirling in my head used all my mental energy.

Why had I gone weak in the knees from a medical check? Making sure I wasn't about to swallow a bee sounded necessary.

"Damned thing didn't sting me at first, but when it did..." He moved right to let a guy pass us going the other way.

The thoughts tumbled through me at light speed. He hadn't taken my face in his hands to kiss me or anything like that. He was just responding to the excuse I'd made up, of course. It wasn't that he'd wanted to touch me, or that I'd wanted him to. What did it all mean?

"But when it did," he continued, "my tongue swelled up so much they had to take me to the hospital."

A few seconds later, my brain function returned enough to allow a simple response. "That's terrible," I panted.

"I couldn't have you dying on me out here," he said between breaths. "I mean, what would your father think?"

"Or my brother," I added in jest.

He looked back for a second. "That would be bad." He laughed. "I was starting to like him. It would be a shame to have to kick his arse."

I laughed at that. "I wouldn't be so sure of yourself. He was trained by a Royal Marine."

"It won't help him."

We dodged another pair as the path turned to the left.

"I was trained by the SAS."

I didn't believe that line for a second. Everybody knew the SAS didn't train civilians like him.

After the turn he looked back.

"You're full of it. The SAS doesn't—"

"Listen to me," he said cutting me off. His words weren't loud, but they were harsh.

"That bee story wasn't real either, was it?" I laughed.

"This is no joking matter." His voice shifted to insistent, almost angry. "Look straight ahead and listen carefully."

"But—"

"Bloody stop arguing for once, and do exactly as I say. We're being followed."

*Followed?* As I jogged, I looked over, slack-jawed at his arrogance.

"Straight ahead, I said." His words had turned angry. "And for God's sake, shut up."

Reluctantly I turned my head to look forward again. If we hadn't been running, I would have stomped my foot to tell him how I felt about it.

"Don't look back."

Of course that meant I desperately wanted to turn around and look.

"Keep running. Unlock your mobile and hand it to me."

We moved over for another bicyclist, and I did as he asked.

He took the phone. "We're going to halt up by this tree and take a selfie. And remember to smile—you're having fun."

I hadn't smiled since he'd started talking to me like a child, but surely I could manage to fake it.

By the tree, he pulled me to a stop just off the path. His arm came around and pulled me to his side.

Sparks jolted my skin.

He held the camera up in front of us. "You're happy to be here with me. Act like it."

I snaked an arm around him. It only intensified the shock of being in his grasp.

He clicked off several pictures. "Better… Don't forget to smile and giggle. We're a happy couple."

I melted into his side as his body heat made the giggling easy—almost natural. For a second I forgot we were staging this for someone else's benefit and pulled myself closer, very aware of my breast against his heaving chest.

"Very good. Just like you're my girl." He clicked a few more pictures.

I could see on the screen that he'd aimed the camera high enough to pick up people behind us. Then it hit me.

He'd called me his girl—not actually *his* girl, just a fake girlfriend.

"We're going to kiss." That was all the warning I got. He turned toward me and pulled me fully against him. His lips claimed mine.

The instinct to fight it evaporated as our mouths melded together, and I closed my eyes. My free hand twined in his hair as I pulled myself up to meet him. It may have only lasted a few seconds, but time slowed. I felt warmth over every square inch where our bodies touched. I heard every heartbeat like the slow tick of a clock while his lips held mine. My mind buzzed with the excitement.

Charlie released my mouth and pulled back a few inches.

Our eyes locked, and for a moment, all I heard was the rushing of my blood. All I felt was the warmth of my chest against his—that and the schoolgirl butterflies in my stomach. Then the pressure of his arousal against my belly got my attention.

Gerald hadn't reacted that way to a kiss—not ever. *My God. I'm doing it again.*

It was Charlie's eyes that kept me still, not his arms. The more I looked into them, the more at ease I felt. *Happy couple.* I liked the sound of that.

He released his hold on me, the instant lack of body warmth hit me like a cold shower. "Look at the mobile and giggle." He held the phone up for us.

I couldn't stop thinking about how his lips had felt against mine, and how the warmth of his body had flowed into mine. The tingles he'd caused had been real.

The bulge in his pants hadn't been fake either. He'd felt the same attraction, and his gruff exterior couldn't mask it.

*Now, what am I supposed to do with that realization?*

"Watch the mobile," he said pulling me out of my trance. He scrolled back a few frames and pointed at a man in a gray tracksuit. "This guy here. I've seen him following me before."

"Are you sure? He looks like he's just stretching."

"Positive." He turned toward me. "I wouldn't lie to you."

In his eyes I saw the truth. He meant it. His eyes contained a warmth I suddenly realized had been missing in Gerald's. They had a depth I hadn't noticed before, too.

*Damn. I'm doing it again.*

He took my hand, and our fingers twined together. "Are you ready?"

My reactions told me I hadn't been ready for any of this. What should have been a relaxing run in the park had become a whirlwind of emotions I didn't understand. But if he'd asked, I would've been ready for another kiss, and the way my belly buzzed, a whole lot more.

"Let's go." He pulled my hand to get us running again before letting loose.

I knew we couldn't hold hands while running, but that didn't stop me from wishing. Concentrating on holding hands would have kept my mind from going back to how the kiss had felt, and what those feelings meant.

Nothing about this morning made sense. It took a few hundred yards of concentrating on not tripping to get back in the groove and my strides to feel natural. Finally, my mind was coherent enough to ask the question. "What happened back there?"

"I'm going to find out who he is and what he's up to." He hadn't answered the question I'd asked—or hadn't he understood?

I didn't repeat it. The more I thought about it, the more I realized I could be reading into what had happened. How foolish would it be for me to ask him how he'd felt about the kiss when all he'd meant was to position us so we could take a picture of the guy following us? Talk about awkward.

A quarter mile later, we reached our starting point at the parking lot.

"Are you good for another lap?" he asked.

"Sure." I didn't ask if we were going to stop by that tree again and make out in our less-than-pretend way, but I'd be ready if he wanted to. Just the thought made my feet lighter.

"Have you put any more thought into the issues of the union contract extension?" he asked.

And we were back to work. Had the kiss truly been no more than an act, to get a picture of the man following us?

We discussed a few more work items as we ran before getting back to the looming union issue.

"When do you expect we'll finally meet the elusive Mr. Califano?" I asked between breaths.

"Soon. He's flexed enough muscle by jerking us around to make it clear who's in charge."

We approached the parking lot at the end of our second lap and slowed to a walk.

He stopped. "Mobile." He extended his hand. "And don't look back."

I handed him the phone without giving in to the temptation.

His arm came around me again.

I molded myself to his side as he held up the phone and snapped pictures. "Are we kissing again?" The question escaped my damned lips before I realized how much it sounded like a request.

He pulled down the phone and turned toward me.

I closed my eyes and raised up on my toes.

"No."

His rejection pulled the breath out of me. "But..." I didn't finish the sentence. What could I say?

Had he found kissing me so disgusting that he couldn't fake it again?

I settled back on my heels and lowered my head. I didn't need his acceptance. "Good. Because I didn't like it either." I pulled back.

He didn't let me. Instead, he lifted my chin and his forehead came down to meet mine. In spite of the rejection, my body reacted as it had before.

"Liar," he said softly. "And I don't do things halfway. If you kiss me again, rule or no rule, I'm not stopping. I promise you that." A scant second later he'd released me and backed away. "See you in the office."

*Was that a warning, an invitation, or maybe a promise if I accept the invitation?* I couldn't figure it out.

"See ya," I responded. I'd been tempted to say more, but wisely didn't. Letting my hormones control my words right now would be a very bad idea.

At my car, I turned away to towel off. I couldn't stop rolling those words around in my head, *"I'm not stopping."* I'd been right about it after all. The kiss had gotten to him too. *"I don't do things halfway."* That was a lie. He hadn't French kissed me.

If a French kiss included tongue, did that make what we'd done an English kiss? He was English, after all. Gerald was English, and he'd French kissed me. Oh well. Andrina would know the answer. She knew everything when it came to men.

The sound of a car horn and the screech of tires drew my attention to the parking lot exit.

Charlie swerved and barely avoided the collision.

I looked away and shook my head. If he couldn't learn to drive on the right side of the road, maybe he should stick to taking an Uber.

After I unlocked my car, I decided not to rib him about his driving when I got to the office. Telling a man he couldn't drive safely wouldn't go well. I'd save it for the next time I got mad at him.

Anyway, my brain was plenty full. There was so much I couldn't understand about this morning. Why had I compared Charlie to Gerald? Why hadn't I been able to control my reaction to him? Why had the kiss felt both exhilarating and natural? He was a Blakewell. It didn't make sense.

After starting the engine, I pulled down the visor to check my lips in the mirror. They looked normal. But they still tingled. I had to get control of myself. Melting into a puddle after a simple kiss wouldn't do. I was a Wentworth with a job to do.

Nonetheless… *Threat or invitation?* Either way, his words hinted at danger in my future.

### Charles

All the way back to the condo for a shower, my thoughts had danced back and forth between Thin Man and Dani.

He represented an unknown danger. Why was he back, or still around?

She represented a different kind of danger, one I understood all too well. Getting involved with her was the one thing I'd said I wouldn't do. The one rule I'd put in place for both of us. Nevertheless, I couldn't get her out of my mind. The feel of her lingered with me—the warmth of her tits up against me, the softness of her lips, the feel of her bum under my hand, and that damned strawberry scent.

I had to cut this shit out. We Blakewells were strong stock, and I had a job to do that couldn't be jeopardized. *Stay in control.* I could do that. I had to.

Sure, the embrace had been an expedient way to get a picture of Thin Man, but had the kiss been necessary? Of course not. Yet in the moment, it had felt like the right thing. I hadn't realized how dangerous it would be until too late.

At least I'd avoided a second kiss, and I hoped I'd warned her strongly enough to keep her away. The comment that I wouldn't stop had clearly scared her, and I hoped it would solve the problem going forward. Fear worked with her, and I'd remember that.

Once I reached the condo, I knew I needed help on the first danger, so I dialed Ben, the security guy.

"What can I do for you, Mr. Blakewell?"

"Charlie," I reminded him. "I saw that tail again this morning. The same guy as before. But this time I have a picture of him."

"Send it over, and let me know when you want me to try to tail the tail and figure out who he is."

I thanked him and sent the picture we'd taken. "I'm going to get you," I said to Thin Man on my phone.

After my shower, my mobile rang with Dad's name on the screen.

"Are you somewhere you can talk?" he asked.

"Yes."

"There's a chance we'll be making a change soon," Dad said.

"What kind of change?" I hated when he sprang things like this on me.

"We've been approached again by Hawker's son."

"Edwin?" I asked, just to be clear.

"Yes, and…" He cleared his throat. "I know it's been hard for you and Danielle to work together jointly, sharing the title, and I'm inclined to hire him to run Hawker."

"And Dani's father?"

He ignored the question. "I want you to come back and run our operations on the continent."

My heart sped up. "You mean Berlin?" That had been what I'd hoped for all along, my own division, and not in the same office as Dad—a double win. I fist-pumped the air of the empty room.

"That's right. Gerhardt has told me he's thinking of leaving, and in my estimation, you're ready."

I paced around the table, thinking through the scenario. "That still leaves Mr. Wentworth."

"It does. How is that list of the girl's failings coming along?"

My list was now up to nine items, but mostly minor issues. "I'm working on it."

"Keep at it. Just add your recommendation that she's not qualified based on your observations, and send the whole thing to me when I call you. I'll soften him up to the idea in the meantime."

We rang off, and I went downstairs for a walk to get something at Starbucks and calm down.

My goal was within reach.

*Berlin, here I come.*

## CHAPTER 18

*DANIELLE*
   *(eight days later)*

IT WAS TUESDAY, EIGHT DAYS SINCE OUR KISS IN THE PARK. YES, I'D KEPT COUNT. Even worse, I hadn't told Mena and Andrina about that episode. That would have meant endless critiques I didn't need, not to mention another O-SEAM lecture from Andrina on the health benefits of sex.

Both Charlie and I were getting more familiar with the people and operations at Hawker. And despite our complication that morning in the park, each day working with him had been easier than the last.

My phone dinged with a reminder of the lunch Charlie and I had scheduled up the street with our HR guy, Wroblewski, to discuss our continuing union problem. Califano had once again called off the meeting we'd had scheduled with him last week, and we'd yet to agree on a new time to get together.

"Time to go?" Charlie asked from behind his desk.

I grabbed up my planner and stood. He knew the answer to his question.

"Put that down. We're just talking with Ron."

He'd hassled me about my planner numerous times.

I put it down and followed him to the elevator.

The sun was bright in my eyes when we exited to the street. I heard him before I saw him.

"Sugarplum, we need to talk." Gerald's voice grated on me as much as his name for me did now. I halted.

He came into focus as my eyes adjusted to the light, and Charlie started forward to intercept him.

With one quick step, I grabbed for Charlie's hand and pulled him back. "No, we don't," I told Gerald. "We absolutely don't."

I could feel the tension in Charlie's grip, but I held his hand tighter to keep him from leaving my side. I made the introduction. "Charlie, this is my ex, Gerald Durban."

"Ex?" Gerald asked.

Charlie's face hardened. "Maybe you didn't understand the lady, turdball. She doesn't want to talk to you." His free hand clenched into a fist.

Gerald didn't get the hint. "And who might this chap be, Sugarplum?" There was that name again, and even more annoying this time.

"I work with Dani," Charlie answered. "Now bugger off."

Gerald stood his ground. "Not until I have a chat with my Sugarplum."

It was time for more drastic action. I turned my gaze on Charlie. "Don't be coy," I told him.

Charlie's befuddled look was about to get tested.

"He's also my new boyfriend," I told Gerald. A second later, I wrapped a hand behind Charlie's neck, stepped in front of him, and raised up on my toes. My lips met his. I held on tight, pressing myself to him to create the show that would get Gerald to leave.

Charlie wrapped his arms around me tightly, and his original startled reaction shifted to something more demanding. Quickly, his tongue ran across my lips, demanding access.

The feel of him quickly grew intense, and as if we'd done this a thousand times, I opened my mouth to him. But it hadn't been thousands of times, and the feel of his tongue stroking against mine nearly undid me.

One of his hands lowered to my ass and pulled me close with a determined squeeze. Melting into him, I closed my eyes and surrendered control. Tingles buzzed under my skin in all the places our bodies came together, as if he was electrified. Heat ran to my core as our tongues continued to dance.

As a teenager, I'd fantasized about kissing Charlie. In the park last week I'd gotten a simple kiss. And even that brief taste of him had lit a fire inside me I couldn't explain. This kiss was on a whole new level—one I hadn't experienced before, one I wasn't ready for.

The street noise faded away as the beat of my heart filled my ears. Gripping the nape of Charlie's neck, I stayed glued to him. As I breathed in the woodsy scent of his hair, it transported me miles from here, miles from the city, from Gerald, from everything. I was sixteen, hiding in the trees and watching Charlie swim in the lake, wishing I had the courage to join him.

I hadn't back then.

He moaned into my mouth, more of a growl than anything else—half human, half animal, and all sensual. He tasted of power and desire. And he wasn't playacting for Gerald's benefit. He wanted this. He wanted me.

The heat built in my core. I wanted this more than I'd understood, and I wanted him as well. I wasn't the shy girl any longer.

What I'd said to Gerald had been a lie, but in this moment, I wished it were true. I wished I was Charlie's girlfriend—the one he took home at night, the one he woke up next to in the morning, the one he rained kisses on each day, kisses like this. Kisses like I'd never gotten before.

He shifted against me, his growing erection obvious now.

He likely couldn't feel it the same way, but my nipples were equally hard, trying to poke their way past the fabric separating us to meet his skin. Every inch of me craved contact with him, but here on the street, the back of his neck was the only bare patch I could reach, and I wasn't letting go.

What felt like minutes went by as we traded breaths and moans and swipes of tongue. The passion of his kiss only intensified as it went on. I felt like I'd burst with pleasure now. I could feel it in his every movement, every squeeze, and the heat that flowed between us. This wasn't the same Charlie as before. I'd unleashed something primal in him, and my urges were equally primitive.

Finally he pulled back.

I pushed forward to make contact again, but only got a lip full of his stubble. My eyes fluttered open, like waking from a dream, a dream I didn't want to end—not now, not yet.

Mere inches away, his eyes held mine in a tractor beam that wouldn't let go. "You shouldn't have done that," he told me. "I warned you." The words rumbled out of him. Suddenly he was Mr. Grumpy.

"Huh?" I sighed. More complicated speech eluded me. My brain was still processing all the sensory input, and at the same time craving more, more Charlie Blakewell. In the moment, I'd thought he'd liked kissing me. Had I gotten that wrong?

"I told you if you kissed me again, I wouldn't stop." Evidently his no-dating rule meant no kissing as well, not even fake kissing.

I barely nodded, having forgotten that warning when I'd made my move to piss off Gerald. In this moment, I couldn't decipher his meaning. Had I gone too far?

At least Gerald had disappeared. Fake kiss number two had apparently worked like charm, as far as that went. And good riddance to him. If I never saw him again, it would be too soon.

"We'll continue this later." Charlie's baritone reverberated in my chest with a combination of danger and excitement. He pulled me along down the sidewalk. "We don't want to be late for our meeting."

Would that mean more kissing or a discussion of my mistakes? I didn't give a shit if we were late, so long as I got another minute with him like we'd just had.

But it appeared I didn't.

It was like falling through the ice of a frozen lake. One minute I was warm and cozy in his embrace, and the next he'd said it was a mistake and plunged me into the frigid water of reality. He'd thought it had been wrong, and wanted to berate me later.

He pulled on my hand. "We have to hurry, or we'll be late."

I pulled my hand free from Mr. Grumpy and followed behind.

A professional work meeting lay ahead. I could be a professional. Nobody had to know I'd just made a fool of myself. Nobody except Mr. Grumpy.

I'd make sure I sat where I could kick him in the shins, if required.

~

*Charles*

That kiss had come out of nowhere. One minute we were confronted by Turdball on the street, and the next she'd plastered herself to me and demanded the kiss I'd both threatened and promised earlier—the one that wouldn't be either short or sweet.

I gave it to her, or rather took it. I'd given her fair warning, so it was her fault if it was too much. I'd had to stop because the urge to move my hands to less-appropriate locations on her body wouldn't have gone well on the public street. Her tits called to me. Another few seconds and I would have palmed them, being the caveman I was.

The woman was a tigress beneath the understated business clothing, and once we got started, it was clear she wasn't in any mood to stop. She tasted like honey and smelled like strawberry. Oh, the strawberry. It was definitely from her hair.

If we hadn't already had this meeting scheduled, I'd have yanked her back into the office to extend our make-out session and take it further, take her further, wherever that would lead.

She followed a pace behind me the rest of the way to the restaurant.

I shortened my stride, but she still stayed back a bit, not walking alongside me. "Hurry up. We don't want to be late." I hated being late. I hated even more that she suddenly wanted space from me. Had I screwed up in kissing her so hard and long? It hadn't seemed so while she pawed me like a tigress in heat.

After that taste, I wanted to learn all of her.

If her unspoken reaction had been any indication, she didn't care to wait either. But my guess at her state of mind didn't matter. All that mattered was what came next. We needed to be clear about dropping the no-dating rule. The words needed to be said. The answer needed to be clear.

"I got us a table inside," Ron Wroblewski announced as we walked up.

He held the door for us, and once again my cock took notice as I caught a slight hint of Dani's strawberry scent.

∼

## DANIELLE

OUR AFTERNOON WAS PACKED WITH MEETINGS AND NO TIME TO TALK. THINGS went nonstop until the customer dinner we'd been scheduled to attend this evening.

It wasn't until that ended and Charlie and I were on the sidewalk outside the restaurant that we finally had a minute alone to talk.

"I was wondering…" What a pathetic way to start off. Was I a moron? I'd wanted to know how badly I'd screwed up by kissing him on the street before lunch. He'd pretty much ignored me since then. Naturally, that should have clued me in that when we got to it, I'd get a lecture about the rule.

"We'll talk after the drive," he said before I could formulate the right words for my question.

"Drive?"

"That's what I said, but you'll need to dress warmer than that."

"Why?"

"Because it'll be cold by the harbor."

That didn't explain why we were driving somewhere just to talk. "Then I'll need to stop off at home first. It's not far."

"I'll drive; you navigate," he said.

If I hadn't wanted to talk so badly, I probably wouldn't have agreed to put my life in his hands this way, but I did.

Twice he deflected my questions about why we were going to the harbor after my apartment, so I gave up.

As we made the turn onto my street, the blue and red reflections on the buildings indicated police presence.

"Slow down," I cautioned, but he already had. "It's the third building on the right."

As we approached, I could see that the police SUVs were not just on my street, but parked in front of my building.

Charlie exited the car after pulling to the curb. "I'm coming with you," he said.

I didn't argue. The blue and red flashes created an eerie, cop-movie vibe, the kind where the camera moved through the scene to land on a dead body.

That thought chilled me. Three cars seemed like a lot for the simple domestic disturbance I'd figured it was. Or maybe they were responding to a medical emergency, like somebody had a heart attack.

"Which unit is yours?" Charlie asked as we approached the door.

"Twenty-three. Second floor."

At the top of the stairs, we encountered a cop with his hand up to stop us. Another one was partway down the hall.

"I live here," I told him. I gestured behind me. "He's with me."

The cop keyed the radio on his shoulder. "A woman claiming to be a resident is here."

"Send her through," a voice from the other end of the radio said.

Moving down the hallway, my stomach roiled at the realization that the second cop was standing outside the doorway to my apartment.

It was open.

As I turned the corner, I gasped at the sight. I couldn't avoid recoiling as angry horse hooves flashed back to me.

Charlie urged me forward with a hand at the small of my back.

His touch, right on my strength tattoo, gave me the willpower to move forward. *I will not give in to fear.*

We walked in. The apartment had been trashed—my apartment.

Why would anyone do this?

## CHAPTER 19

*CHARLES*

HER DOOR HADN'T STOOD A CHANCE. THE DOORJAMB WAS SPLINTERED.

Dani's hands went to her face at the sight inside.

This was not a simple burglary. They would have grabbed the expensive items, if she'd had any, and hightailed it out of here. Instead the place had been demolished—the lamps, the furniture, holes in the walls, everything destroyed.

"Why?" Dani asked, sobbing.

I didn't have an answer for her.

She wandered toward the bedroom, and I joined her.

That scene was even worse. Clothes were everywhere. The room was an utter disaster.

A man in a suit with a badge hanging on his belt stood at the door to the bathroom.

"I'm sorry. You can't be in here," he said when he noticed us.

"But I live here," Dani responded.

The man consulted his notepad. "Danielle Wentworth?"

"Yes," she answered.

"Detective Bosco," he said, glancing between us. "You live here alone?"

"Yes. Only just moved in."

"You're not married, Ms. Wentworth?"

"No," Dani said.

He wrote a note. "And where were you earlier this evening?"

"She was with me all day," I offered. "At work."

"Do you have a boyfriend?" Bosco asked her.

I answered for Dani. "No." Turdball didn't fit that category anymore.

"And you would be?"

"Charles Blakewell. I work with Ms. Wentworth. We just got back from a day of business meetings."

He made another note.

"Do you have a card, detective?" I asked.

He produced one for me before turning back to Dani and waving a finger around the room. "Do you have surveillance inside?"

Dani looked stunned. "Pardon?"

"A camera system?"

"Uh… No."

"Divorced or separated?"

I stood back.

"No," she said.

"Enemies?" he asked.

"I only just arrived in town. I haven't had time to make any that I know of," she said.

"You're English?" he asked.

The question surprised me, because I'd heard her accent before, but today it was American not British.

"Yes and no," she said. "I'm American, born here, but my parents are British."

"And you recently arrived from there?"

"Yes, I told you that already."

I could see her frustration building.

The Inquisition continued. "That's a very nice necklace you're wearing."

Dani fingered the ruby-and-diamond necklace. "Thank you."

"Is it real?" he asked.

"Yes, it most certainly is."

"Did you have other expensive jewelry here in the apartment?"

She shook her head. "No. Not much."

"Would you check to see if any of it's missing?"

She went to the closet, and a moment later called from there, "It's all still here."

"What do you make of this, detective?" I asked him.

He ignored me.

"Do you have any other valuables you kept here? Cash, perhaps?" he asked when she returned.

"No."

The detective moved away from the door to the bathroom and motioned inside. "Does this message mean anything to you?"

Dani gasped.

My blood boiled with anger.

*You need to go back to England* was scrawled on the mirror in red.

∼

## DANIELLE

AT THE SIGHT OF THE AWFUL MESSAGE, MY KNEES BUCKLED. MY VISION narrowed and the room darkened. I shoved back the image of the rearing horse.

Instantly Charlie propped me up with a firm arm around me.

"Well, Ms. Wentworth," the detective said, "whoever did this really didn't like the idea of you being here… And you know who did this, don't you?"

"Not for sure," I said with a shaky breath. It wasn't exactly a lie. I was pretty sure, but not one-hundred percent. You were supposed to be certain when you accused someone, weren't you? The small room had turned distinctly cold.

"I can't help you if you don't help me," Detective Bosco said. "Who do you have in mind?"

The look on Charlie's face said he knew exactly who I was thinking had done this. Maybe I was more certain than I'd thought…

This hadn't been random kids destroying things for the hell of it. This wasn't a determined thief looking for my nonexistent stash of jewelry. Only a handful of people knew I lived here. Only one person wanted me to go back to London, and only one had threatened me.

I hated that fucking Gerald wasn't out of my life yet.

Charlie's lips opened to speak.

I cut him off with a raised hand. "It's okay."

"You sure?" he asked.

His eyes and his smile gave me the strength to speak. "His name is Gerald, Gerald Durban."

Bosco wrote the name down. "And why does he want you to go back to England?"

"He lives there." Just the thought of what I was about to say made me shake. "He wants me to marry him."

Bosco kept writing. "Where do I find Mr. Durban to talk to him?"

"I don't know." I sniffled.

The detective sighed and wrote another note. "It looks to me like the door to this place won't lock, not until it's been repaired. Do you have a safe place you can stay tonight?"

Charlie's arm around me tightened. "She can stay with me."

I looked up to catch his smile—a smile I desperately needed right now.

"Can we take some of her clothes?" Charlie asked.

"Of course." The detective moved to the door. "You can pick up the report at the station in a day or two."

I managed a nod as tears formed. I blinked them back, determined not to show either of these men how vulnerable I felt at the moment. "Report?"

"For your insurance," the detective said.

"Aren't you going to take fingerprints?" Charlie asked.

Detective Bosco tried to hide his smirk. "It's not like on TV. We can only afford to do fingerprinting if there was an assault or a lot of valuables are involved. That's why I asked about cameras. These days that's mostly how we catch them."

Charlie nodded.

"Break-ins are not like lightning. They can strike twice."

I winced at the thought.

"I'd consider adding surveillance," the detective said.

Charlie looked my direction. "We'll think about it."

"Sounds like a good idea," I said. "Thank you, detective."

After Detective Bosco left, Charlie moved me to the bed and sat me down. "Rest here while I pack up a few things."

Once again, a nod was all I could manage.

He found a suitcase in the closet and started with a pair of jeans from the floor. Then he stopped and started taking pictures with his phone. "As a record," he said.

Feeling raw, I couldn't stop the shakes that swept over me. My anger at Gerald shifted to fear as well. What would have happened if I'd been home?

Gerald had yelled at me in the office with other people just outside the door. He'd completely destroyed my apartment in an obvious rage.

What would come next? How bad would it be if he caught me alone? That thought only increased my trembling.

Charlie came back from taking pictures in all the rooms and resumed packing. A half hour later, he had my suitcase and several garbage bags full of my clothes and toiletries.

We left the destruction behind as he led me to the street.

"I'll go back to the hotel," I said.

"No, you won't," he said as he guided me toward his car.

I felt like arguing, but all I could focus on was my anger at Gerald. I'd only been renting this place, taking over for my brother. I hadn't owned it, but still, the destruction had been aimed at me, and it made me feel violated, scared, and vulnerable.

He opened the backseat door and loaded my things in. "You're coming to my place." He closed the door.

"But—"

Before I could say another word, a finger was in my face. "Walk or be carried." The finger lowered, and he grasped my shoulders. "Those are your only choices," he added firmly.

The warmth I felt from his touch made me even weaker. "You wouldn't dare." The words embarrassed me as soon as I said them. He'd been nothing but helpful and supportive, and here I was being combative.

In an instant, he'd leaned down to sweep my legs up and take me in his arms. "Carry it is. I told the detective I'd take you to my place tonight, and I will not have you make a liar of me."

Wrapping my arms around his neck to hold on, I gave in to his caveman move and melted into him rather than fight. At least he hadn't slung me over his shoulder. As he carried me around the car, my fear subsided.

He brought me to the passenger door. "Are you going to behave now?"

"Do I have a choice?" For some reason he brought out my argumentative side.

He set me down next to the car. "That's what Turdball got wrong. You always have a choice."

"Thank you." I closed the inches between us and wrapped my arms around him, hugging the man who'd just said the one thing that mattered to me. He understood.

He hugged me back and kissed the top of my head. "Does this mean you'll behave?"

I nodded into his chest. "Yeah." The feel of his arms around me was like a shield keeping me safe. My mind went back to the kisses we'd shared.

Pulling out of my grasp, he opened the door for me. "Then get in."

John's admonition that I shouldn't trust Charlie as far as I could toss him rang hollow now. If only that moment earlier today hadn't been for show.

∼

## Charles

I closed the vehicle's door after Dani slipped into the seat. It still felt odd to have to walk to the left side of the car to drive.

Her offer to go back to her hotel had been my first out, but I hadn't taken it. It had been her suggestion, so accepting it wouldn't have been forcing anything on her. And it would have put the distance between us I needed to make walking away comfortable.

By this time tomorrow, I could be on a plane to Berlin and the future I'd wanted for years. It had been my sole goal in life, the next logical step, the step I wanted.

I belted in and looked over. "I'll drive slowly."

She nodded with a faint smile.

All I had to do was send my memo to Dad tomorrow, relocate Dani to her hotel, and get on a plane to Berlin. It would be mission accomplished here, and goal reached.

*Simple as pie*, as they said. Get on the plane and leave this mess behind. My future was ahead of me, not here. With the union situation buggered up, this place was going to get worse before it got better.

Yet here I was. I gritted my teeth as I made the left turn onto the main road and went to the right of the center divider. It was all wrong. The driving, the scene at her flat, and my plan for tomorrow. It didn't fit.

"You all right?" she asked.

"Of course," I lied. Nothing about tonight was right.

I should have been asking her that. It was her flat that had been destroyed, and she who'd been attacked. It was an attack, but to what purpose?

"Do you think he'll try again?" Dani asked.

The turdball couldn't possibly be deranged enough to think tearing everything up and scrawling a warning on her mirror would win her back. He wasn't that stupid, was he?

I didn't have an answer for her. "Probably not." But this clarified the choice for me. If I left, she would still be in danger. Glancing over for a second, I added, "Regardless, I'll keep you safe."

"Thank you."

The way her face softened from fear to gratitude sealed the decision for me. As a gentleman, the right thing to do was stay. She had to be protected. It was the only option.

It was what I'd promised Detective Bosco, and now her.

Dad could find someone else to handle Berlin when Gerhardt left. There would be other opportunities for me, and the threat to Dani was clear and immediate.

She needed me, and despite her protests, I'd be here for her.

## CHAPTER 20

*Danielle*

The tall building bordered the Common, Boston's small version of Central Park. The doorman held the glass entrance open for us as soon as he saw Charlie.

"Carl, this is Ms. Wentworth," Charlie said. "She is to have full access to the building and any assistance she desires."

"Certainly, sir." Carl tipped his hat to me. "Very nice to make your acquaintance, Ms. Wentworth."

I nodded. "Thank you, Carl, and it's Dani."

"Understood, Ms. Wentworth."

Charlie ushered me through the quiet opulence of the building's lobby. Inside the elevator, he pressed the button for the twenty-fifth floor, one below the top.

My ears popped on the way up, and my legs were still shaky from what I'd seen. Leaving the elevator, I stumbled.

He dropped one of the bags of clothes to catch me. "You need to lie down."

That wasn't the answer. Lying down wouldn't erase the images running through my head. "I need a drink." Without some alcohol, I'd never be able to get over the shock. "And more than one."

He picked up the extra bag with his other hand and kept a steadying arm around me. "A drink I can handle." He let go of me momentarily to unlock the door and disarm the security system. "But I'm not letting you overdo it."

I wasn't prepared for the sight of the place. *Big* wasn't enough of a word. It was immense and decorated tastefully with manly, black-leather furniture, as well as the requisite monster flat-screen television on the wall.

He guided me around the corner. "First one on the right." He opened the door to a bedroom that defined the word *gargantuan*. "This will be your room."

After setting the things inside, we returned to the large front room.

"This place is yours?" I asked.

"No. It's one of the Covington Industries flats. I'm just borrowing it for the time being." He walked to the far wall after sitting me down.

"How'd you manage that?" I asked, thinking of my dinky apartment. Slipping off my shoes, I leaned back into the soft leather and watched him.

Once again I found myself seeing Charlie as the anti-Gerald. It calmed me to think he'd keep me safe from the terror Gerald had unleashed. He'd had a fury I hadn't foreseen—not one bit.

"I know a guy." He opened a cabinet and turned back. "What's your pleasure?"

"Scotch, bourbon, anything but tequila." Now that I knew where the liquor was, I could help myself and *overdo it* later, if I wanted to. The way I felt at the moment, that was likely how it would play out. I needed to calm my nerves and forget.

He retrieved a bottle and started to pour. "Scotch it is, then." He poured a second as well.

"You know a guy?" I asked. That was a lame explanation. If it was a corporate apartment, I'd expect a family business relationship or something.

He walked over and offered me one of the two tumblers.

I sat up to guzzle the first of what I expected to be many. The amber liquid burned lightly as it went down. Another glass or two would fix that unpleasantness.

He'd only managed a single sip before I held out my empty glass. He took it and walked back to the liquor cabinet. "Just one more."

"Then make it a triple."

He returned and handed me what looked more like a double. "This is all."

I stood and knocked back the amber liquid. I needed all the help I could get if I was going to sleep tonight. The image of that awful message on the mirror reappeared again and again—not to mention the old, familiar pounding horse hooves that appeared anytime I was rattled.

The scotch soon soothed my jitters enough to allow a normal walk from the couch to the full-length windows on the far wall. "You have quite the view here."

"Just borrowing the flat, as I said." He joined me in looking out. "But it is quite nice, I suppose."

*Nice* didn't begin to describe the uninterrupted view over the Common and the rest of the city to the north and west. The people strolling on the lighted paths of the park were mere ants from up here. "More like spectacular."

"If you'll excuse me, nature calls." Charlie walked off and turned in to the bedroom across from the one he'd told me to use. The door closed behind him.

It was my chance. Scooting across the floor, I grabbed the scotch bottle and added to my glass. I quickly found another bottle in the cabinet and deposited it in the bedroom he'd shown me before returning to the window just in time.

He rejoined me as I drained the last of my glass. "You should take it easy on that."

"It's not tequila, so I'll be okay." I held the glass out—almost, but not quite steady. "I'll take another."

With a sigh he took it. "Okay, but this is your last."

"Don't be mean."

"It's for your own good."

No doubt he meant that, but we had different opinions of what was best for me tonight. My opinion started with lots more alcohol. Gerald was such a…*shit*. I couldn't come up with a bad-enough word to describe him. I didn't use a lot of swear words, and none of them I could think of was right for Gerald. Maybe if I tried stringing several together…

Charlie brought back the tumbler, but with less liquor than last time.

We stood together, me a little ways from the glass, watching the scene outside the window.

"What's going on in that head of yours?"

I took a gulp of the amber liquid before replying. "Trying to come up with a bad-enough name for fucking Gerald."

He sipped from his glass. "And what do you have so far?"

"Fucking dickhead jerkwad," I sighed. "But somehow it doesn't seem enough."

"I agree."

"Abby told me *turdball* really means douchebag fuckhead asshole."

"That's closer. Let's add yours and make *turdball* mean fucking dickhead jerkwad douchebag fuckhead asshole."

I laughed. "That's closer." Swaying slightly from the alcohol, my shoulder touched his.

His arm came around behind to steady me. "You've definitely had enough."

I leaned into his strength. "Nope. Not yet." If more liquor meant more of him holding me up, I surely hadn't had enough. "You make me feel safe," I admitted. It was the truth, and truth was always good, right? For the moment I was protected—behind a doorman, secure locks, and most importantly, beside Charlie.

"I promise I'll keep you safe."

His words flowed over me like warm water. I switched hands with my drink and snaked an arm around him, pulling myself tight against my anchor, my rock, my armor, my protector.

The solid feel of his body dissipated the Gerald-dread that had filled me.

Although I wasn't sure I wanted to talk about my mistake kissing him today, the liquor loosened my tongue. "You wanted to talk?" I asked him.

"Tomorrow."

I tried again. "We should talk."

"Tomorrow."

***

CHARLES

SHE TURNED MY WAY A LITTLE AND PULLED HERSELF IN MORE SNUGLY. HER TIT squished against me in a way I was acutely aware of.

"Why would Gerald do something like that?" she asked.

I reveled in the feel of her. "There's no accounting for crazy, it seems."

"I think I like you," she said before settling her head against me.

That came out of nowhere. "What's not to like?" I joked.

"Yeah. I can see that now."

We needed to talk about the rule and today's kiss, but it couldn't be tonight—not after what had happened to her, and not with her drinking. This conversation was already getting into dangerous territory, so I shifted to my other foot and changed the subject. "How did Turdball know where you lived?"

"I don't know."

"Did you tell him?"

"Not that I..." Her head came away from my chest. "I don't think I did." She loosened her grip.

"Don't beat yourself up over it."

She leaned more heavily into me. "I think I should sit down."

We'd found her drink limit.

"Give me that." I held my free hand out for her glass.

She swallowed the last of it. "Only if you give me a refill."

I guided her toward the spare bedroom—the only safe place for her tonight.

She veered toward the couch.

"Time for you to head to bed." I pulled her back on course and set the glass down as we passed the end table.

She leaned into me. "Are you going to tuck me in?"

My eyes widened. Tucking her in sounded tempting, but it was a bad idea. It would involve her getting out of some of her clothes, and that would be dangerous given her inebriated state and my current libido.

Inside the room, I sat her on the bed and returned to the door. "I'll see you in the morning. Yell if you need anything."

I returned to the large front room overlooking the city. It seemed much emptier without Dani. After refilling my glass, I settled into the sofa. The wanker turdball had to be dealt with, but first I had to locate him. Pulling out my wallet, I fingered the card the security guy, Ben Murdoch, had given me.

The hour was too late now, so tomorrow I'd give him a call. He seemed like a capable chap, most likely with the kind of connections that would help him find this Gerald wanker. What to do after I located him? I wasn't sure of that yet.

Once we got him out of this country and back to the UK, I'd be able to relax. Dad knew the sort of blokes who'd be able to persuade him not to come back to visit Dani again.

Swallowing the last of the smooth scotch, I refilled the glass for my nightstand and padded off to bed.

I thought back over the day once settled under the covers, and I ended up with a raging hard-on that couldn't be ignored. Dani had been that alluring.

I'd never get to sleep like this. If sex was the best insomnia medication, whacking one off came in second. I started to stroke to the memory of Dani against me today, and a week ago at the park. A vision of her up against a tree in the park at night filled my imagination—just the two of us, lost in the passion of the moment…grunts and groans, followed by ecstasy.

Panting raggedly after finishing, I cleaned up with a few tissues from the side of the bed. Looking at the dim glow that emanated from under the door only made me wish I'd had the courage to tuck my girl in. I rolled onto my side, facing away from the door.

Maybe I would have offered a gentle backrub. Naturally that would have meant pulling up her shirt to massage the skin directly. And maybe she would have *ooh*ed and *aah*ed, requesting more. And maybe that would have led to more touching, and more nakedness.

Then again, maybe not. She was only here because her flat had been trashed—no other reason. She'd even suggested the hotel. That had to mean something.

Still, only two doors separated us. A gentleman would handle the situation with restraint and proper manners, just as I had. The odd part was I'd never regretted being a gentleman before tonight.

I sat up and grabbed the glass on the nightstand, gulping it down. Normally I didn't use liquor as a crutch, but this was not a normal night.

Eventually, sleep overtook me.

∽

## Danielle

After Charlie closed the door behind him, I went to the bathroom for the scotch I'd hidden. He'd confiscated my glass, so I was reduced to drinking directly from the bottle.

After what had to be more than a few drinks' worth, I stumbled my way to the bed, shed my clothes, and slipped in between the sheets.

Whoever owned this apartment certainly knew a thing or two about sheets. These were an eleven on the ten-point softness scale. If I remembered in the morning, I'd have to ask where someone got sheets like this. It was as if they were spun from fairy hair.

But as soon as I closed my eyes, the scene at my apartment came back to me, and the shakes began. How had I not seen this about Gerald? Wrapping my arms around myself, I tried to quell the fear.

Gerald had found the apartment I'd only been in for a few days, which meant he had the resources to find me almost anywhere. The rage driving him had been evident in the destruction, and there was no telling what he would do next.

I heard Charlie out in the great room. It took all my willpower to keep from putting on a bathrobe and going out to snuggle against him some more. Being clamped up against his side this evening had been the only time I truly felt safe since seeing what Gerald had done.

The room swayed as I got up to take another gulp of scotch. Staying awake and cowering in fear wasn't a good option.

~

THE SOUND WOKE ME.

I froze, not even daring to breathe. *What is happening? Where am I?*

A thud? A clank?

I could barely hear over the pounding of my heart. Sitting up too fast, I concentrated on making my head not spin and listened.

No sounds, but the room was unfamiliar and cold.

My breath came in pants as the fog cleared somewhat.

*Charlie brought me here.*

Charlie, the one I could count on.

But what if Gerald had found me again? Alone in this bedroom, I felt vulnerable.

I slid out of bed and shivered against the chill. The blue numbers on the clock said ten after three. After listening at the door, I opened it. My heart still raced. Had he gotten into the condo? Was he waiting for me out there?

No sounds came from the hallway. And only the light from the city at night and the stars came through the great room's windows down the hall.

I paused. How did I know Gerald wasn't already in the condo? The door across the hall beckoned—the one room in the entire city where I knew I'd be safe. Charlie had promised.

Pulling the comforter off the bed, I wrapped it around me and slid across the hall, quietly twisting the door handle.

I closed the door behind me. Charlie's bedroom was even darker than the one I'd been in. Not even the digits of a clock lit the space. The sound of his breathing was all that indicated he was here. The rhythmic pattern calmed me.

*Good going, silly girl. You escaped that scary bedroom. Now what's your plan?*

## CHAPTER 21

*CHARLES*

THE NEED TO PEE WOKE ME UP. I SLID OUT FROM UNDERNEATH THE COVERS AND sat on the edge of the bed with a raging hard-on. My mind was a bit blurry, and this place was still new to me. The monstrously effective blackout curtains in this room made it pitch black.

Toilet? The toilet was to the left, I knew. I rose and felt my way around the bottom of the bed and turned left. Putting my hand out to keep from banging into the wall, I tripped over something.

Instinctively, I twisted as I went down. "Fuck," I yelled. I hit the floor of this dark hellhole hard.

"Shit," she yelled.

She? I'd tripped over a girl?

She yelled again, "You kicked me."

"Dani?" I struggled to my knees and felt for the doorway ahead of me somewhere. "What the fuck? I almost broke…" At least I didn't land on my hard-on and fracture my bloody dick.

"You kicked me," she repeated.

I located the doorway to the bathroom and stood, bracing myself against the doorjamb. "Don't move. I can't see a blasted thing."

"I'm sorry. I was scared."

She wasn't making sense. What the hell was she doing on the floor of my bedroom right where I would trip over her?

"Give me a minute," I mumbled.

I closed the bathroom door behind me and flicked on the light, which immediately blinded me. The bad news was my bladder was about to burst, and having a rock-hard erection made emptying it impossible. The good news—no bruising. I hadn't injured it in the fall.

That had happened to poor Allister Flood. The bugger tripped over his fucking dog first thing in the morning, with a complete boner, and broke his dick hitting the floor. He was never the same again. He told me it healed crooked.

I don't recall him having a girlfriend after that. Come to think of it, I never saw his dog again either.

Just realizing I'd barely escaped poor Allister's fate deflated my problem appendage enough to be able to piss. And how would I explain a broken dick to the nurse on duty at the hospital? I shuddered at the thought.

I washed up and forced my mind to the problem at hand. Dani had snuck into my room to lie on the floor. What was up with that?

Grabbing a towel to cover up, I opened the door. "What is going on?"

Dani blinked at me, wrapped in a comforter on the floor beside the bed. She'd shifted out of my path. "Can I use the bathroom?"

"Sure." I walked around to the other side of the bed and slid in.

She went into the toilet with the blanket wrapped around her.

The door closed, and the room went dark, save the sliver of light from under the doorway.

She turned off the light before returning, and we were in total darkness again.

I heard a rustling as she settled onto the floor again.

"Wentworth, what are you doing?"

She sniffled. "I heard something, and I was scared. I don't know. I just thought I'd be safe in here with you. But I didn't want to wake you, so I... I guess I sound silly, but I don't know how he found out where I was living... And maybe he could find me here... And the noise... And we hadn't talked about this morning yet... And—"

"That's enough." I couldn't blame her, I guess. Coming back to a flat that had been as thoroughly trashed as hers would give a lot of people nightmares. "I locked the door myself. You're safe in this flat."

"I'll be quiet," she said. "And you can go back to sleep." She meant she was staying here, and on the floor of all things. Not only was she babbling, but her words were still slurred from the whiskey.

"Not acceptable." A gentleman wouldn't make her stay on the floor. "I'll take the other room, and you can use this bed."

"No. Don't leave me… Please, I don't want to be alone."

"Then get in the bed, and I'll take the floor."

"No. It's your room. I can't make you sleep on the floor." She wasn't making any sense.

"I'm bloody well not letting you sleep on the floor either."

She sighed. "The bed is yours."

There was obviously only one alternative left.

"Then, hop up and get in. It's plenty big enough—unless you think you can't behave yourself with me." I shifted farther to this side of the bed and turned away.

She giggled.

It felt good to hear a little mirth from her.

"You have an overinflated view of your appeal."

She slurred the words, but they still hurt.

"Ouch. You don't have to be mean about it," I told her. "Just keep to your half of the bed. It's my flat, and a lady is not allowed to sleep on the floor. Full stop, end of story. Now make up your mind, woman."

After a minute, the sheets rustled and the mattress shifted as she climbed into bed. "Thank you."

"Mmm-hmmm," I said curtly. I didn't do drunks. Anyway, she'd just said she didn't find me appealing, hadn't she?

I lay awake for what felt like the longest time, focused on not rolling toward her and not slipping a hand or foot closer. It was torture.

I wasn't supposed to give in to her. It didn't matter how attractive she was, how nice she smelled, or how warm her tits felt pushed up against me. No, none of that mattered.

"Can we talk?" she asked softly.

I turned my head in her direction, and the hint of her strawberry fragrance went straight to my dick. God, I loved the smell of her.

"Please?" she added.

"In the morning." I turned away. *I don't do drunks*, I repeated in my head.

# CHAPTER 22

*DANIELLE*

I PRIED MY EYES OPEN. ONLY ONE COOPERATED. I RUBBED THE OTHER UNTIL THE glue holding it shut let go. It was darker than shit in this room. After a few blinks, I could make out the outlines of two pictures on the wall next to me. A faint sliver of light came from underneath the bathroom door.

I stretched my legs. The sheets were still soft as angel hair against my bare skin.

What?

It came back to me like a snowball hitting my head. I was in Charlie's bed.

No. It was worse than that. I was stark naked in Charlie's bed.

I ran a hand down my stomach and gave a gentle sigh of relief when my fingers found the waistband of panties. So, topless, but not completely naked.

The sound of the shower started in the bathroom, so I didn't have to risk sliding a hand over to find out whether Charlie lay next to me.

Last night came back in a rush—coming to this building with Charlie, being unable to sleep, and then being so scared from the night sounds that I'd sought safety on the floor here in Charlie's room. Great idea that had been.

He'd coaxed me into the bed. I'd wondered for a few minutes where it would lead. But he'd remained turned away, and probably for good reason.

I must've fallen asleep quickly, because I couldn't remember anything after that. Without a watch or clock that I could see in this room, I had no idea what time it was. But if he was in the shower, evidently it was time to get up.

Slipping out of bed, I fumbled my way to the door, across the hall, and into the bathroom of the scary bedroom I'd escaped last night. The lights blinded me for a second, and looking around, I realized all over again how plush this place was. I hadn't noticed much about the bathroom in my inebriated state last night. The counter was stocked with toothpaste, a toothbrush, a hairbrush, and even deodorant. The shower had shampoo and body wash on a ledge.

The shower stall was more like a shower *room*, big enough for a small party, which instantly sent my brain in the wrong direction.

*How much fun could a couple have in here?*

With warm water running in the sink, I splashed my face and finished with a washcloth. Two rounds of brushing and rinsing got what felt like road gravel off my tongue.

While I braced against the cold marble counter, last night's events ran through my head on repeat. I should've grabbed ibuprofen or something. It wasn't as bad as the morning after my tequila misadventure with Abby, but it wasn't good.

I ran the hairbrush through a dozen times, and at least I was no longer a horror-movie character. The thought that Gerald was out there somewhere tried to push its way to the fore, but I refused to let it.

I turned to view my tattoo in the mirror. It was still there—a daily reminder that fear was behind me. I was a survivor.

Letting Gerald control my life would be letting him win. I would survive this, survive him. I had to. If I came face to face with the evil he now represented, I'd kick him in the balls so hard he'd never have children. Just the thought made me smile.

"Fuck you, Gerald," I yelled at the mirror. After repeating it a few times I mentally thanked Abby for teaching me the exercise.

∽

CHARLES

. . .

She was gone from the bedroom when I finished my shower, which was a good thing. It kept me from having to decide whether or not to wake her and whether or not to do more than that.

Lying mere inches from her under the sheets and not reaching for what I knew would be soft skin had been agonizing.

I'd resisted whacking one off in the shower to thoughts of her, and after wrestling my partial stiffy into my pants, I made my way to the kitchen. Perusing the refrigerator, I decided something simple, something American, would be most appropriate for her. Bacon and fried eggs would fit the bill.

I was almost done when I heard her behind me. "Good morning," I said as I turned. "How do you feel about some breakfast?"

"I'd love some." She came closer, dressed for work in a button-down shirt and skirt. "Sorry about last night."

She held a liquor bottle that looked suspiciously like the scotch I'd served her. Putting the spatula down, I asked, "Where'd you get that?"

She smirked as she held up the bottle. "I might have helped myself to a little extra last night."

"How little?"

"Not as much as you think," she shot back.

Deciding against a verbal sparring match, I turned back to the pan. When the eggs were finished, I fetched orange juice from the refrigerator. Like we were a well-oiled machine, she'd retrieved glasses by the time I had the lid off the juice. I poured for us and offered her the first glass.

"Thank you." She gulped down half the juice.

"Thirsty?"

She nodded. "I want to apologize for—"

I raised a hand. "No," I said. "You have nothing to apologize for."

"But I—"

Setting my glass down, I grabbed her shoulders. I didn't trust myself to touch her anywhere else. "I said I will not listen to an apology. You had every right to be scared. That psycho ex-boyfriend of yours is the one with a problem. It's not your fault. Do you understand me?"

She nodded.

"One other thing..."

She bit her lower lip.

"Until I locate Turdball and deal with him, you're staying here in this flat with me." I squeezed her shoulders to make my point. "No arguments, and send me a few pictures of him."

She nodded again, but her lips firmed into a hard line, telling me she'd held back an objection.

*Screw that.* She'd have to deal with it.

A few seconds later, it came out. "Do you have to be so pushy?"

"Only when you're so bloody argumentative."

As far as I was concerned, the issue had been settled. I'd promised to keep her safe, and I damned well kept my promises. But we still had to get one thing straight. "The rule is, you have to trust me completely. I'll handle the turdball."

"Have to?"

"Think carefully. There's no going back on this. You either trust me or you don't. And if you can't, then I'll ship you off to your blasted brother and let him be responsible for you."

She gritted her teeth.

"I'll put you on damned plane myself." Just noticing how pretty she was sent blood rushing to parts of my body that didn't need any more encouragement.

"Okay, I trust you," she huffed.

I let her go and turned around. "It's settled then. Let's eat."

"But I'm not your slave," she said as I took my juice to the table and returned to gather up the plates.

"All I said is trust. I'll keep you safe. You can count on it." I didn't turn to let her see me smile. Winning an argument with this woman wasn't an easy task.

She followed me. "I want to talk about yesterday."

Taking in a calming breath, I turned to face her.

"On the sidewalk," she continued, "I kissed you again, and—"

This was not going the right way. She needed an easy out. "You had to get the wanker to piss off. I get it." I turned to pick up the plates.

She stepped behind and wrapped her arms around me. "Yes... No. Not exactly. I wanted to."

Her words froze me in place. "No, you didn't. I mean *don't*. Because there would be no turning back." I couldn't let this go further. "Believe me, I'm not right for you. I'm not a nice man."

That was the truth, but I didn't turn to let her see my face. She'd see right through my words to how much I wanted her as well. She was both what I wanted *and* what I had to deny myself, for both our sakes.

She hugged me tighter. "Yes, I did, and I still do."

Scaring her would be my only escape. It had worked before. I spun around and crashed my mouth to hers, kissing her hard to scare some sense into her.

Her hand circled my neck.

If the Turdball was any indication, she was used to the slow, gentle type. Going past her safe zone like this was sure to trigger her. I'd show her a taste of the dangerous side, and little Miss Prim and Proper would back away for sure. The problem would be solved.

## CHAPTER 23

*DANIELLE*

WHEN CHARLIE TURNED AND OUR MOUTHS MET, I PULLED MYSELF INTO HIS KISS. If he was going to be rough and demanding, I'd run with that. I speared my hand through his hair.

Everything slowed, and I saw my truth clearly. Danielle Wentworth had *settled* for meek Gerald as her boyfriend. *She* would have heeded Charlie's warning and taken his offer to back away. But I wasn't that girl today. I knew what I wanted, who I wanted, and I wasn't accepting less.

I'd read *Cosmo* articles about taking charge of your love life to get beyond mild and boring—both words that described Gerald. It was time for a change. I was done settling for meek and mediocre. It didn't matter that Charlie represented risk. I was ready for risky this morning, wherever that led.

The danger he presented scared me, but it also challenged me to have the courage to let my inner lioness loose.

Our tongues dueled as he kissed me with fervor. I mirrored it back to him as Andrina's voice echoed in my head: *"Go for it."*

He smelled of spice and manliness. We traded breath and desire like wild animals. His intensity melted my panties as I rubbed against the bulge of his arousal. The feel of my breasts against his muscled chest was heavenly as the heat in my core built to an intolerable level.

Before I knew what had happened, he magically had my bra undone and his hand on my boob.

I'd never done anything remotely like this. I'd never let a guy put his hand up my shirt on the first date before, but here I was letting Charlie not just touch me, but grab me. The strength of his squeeze only spurred me on, and I clawed him closer.

Gerald's proper girlfriend, Danielle, would have screamed to stop. But today I was going to follow Andrina's advice for once. I was going to mark a crazy adventure off my list this morning.

Guys had kissed me before, but never like this. Never had a kiss brought out the animal in both of us the way this one did—not even close. His lips jolted me with unbridled lust. I had no idea how a kiss could convey such passion. All my previous boyfriends had been gentle and subdued. They'd all been too proper, or too properly scared of my father, to be anything else.

Charlie's kiss branded me as his, with heat, lust, and pure intensity. His hand moved to my thigh, up my skirt, and past my panties to enter my slick heat.

We'd gone from a sexual standstill to warp speed in a few seconds flat. It should have had me backing away, but instead, I craved more.

He'd warned me he wouldn't want to stop, and he'd warned me again that there'd be no turning back.

It was decision time. Sensible Danielle would have run, but instead I moaned out the word *more*. I pulled back from the kiss, not to end it, but to get his shirt off. I needed skin contact, to mingle not just breath, but sweat as well.

When he'd challenged that I wasn't ready for his brand of roughness, it had only heightened my desire.

"Are you sure?" he asked, giving me one last chance at escape.

"Try me," was all I said to let the beast off his leash.

He pulled my shirt off, buttons flying. He lifted his shirt over his head and threw it.

I pulled my arms free of my bra and yanked at his belt, but he stopped me.

"No," he said in a stern voice. "Lose the skirt first. Keep the heels on."

I'd put on work heels this morning, mid-height and black.

He stood back, his eyes soaking up every inch of my naked chest. The lust of his stare made my entire body tingle. He moved to cradle the weight of my breasts in his hands and traced hot strokes around my nipples with his thumbs.

The tingles made it difficult to concentrate as I unzipped my skirt and pushed it down. I stood frozen in his glare as he pulled his hands away from my breasts and took me in.

"Now the knickers."

His commanding voice built naughty heat within me. My pussy sizzled with anticipation of what might come next. Sliding the panties down and kicking them aside with the skirt, I was surprised flames hadn't already consumed me.

He made a twist with his finger. "Turn around."

I turned slowly and stopped, facing the counter, wondering what would come next. Would it be a spank, and command to bend over, or—

"All the way."

I'd expected he wanted to take me from behind or something. Instead I felt like a roast on a spit as his hungry eyes devoured me. I pulled my shoulders back, proud to be the object of his desire. I might not be gorgeous, but his eyes said it all. I was what he wanted, what he lusted after, and what he was going to have.

"Beautiful," he said with a growing smile.

A single word of praise had never felt so good. My nipples peaked, and my nerves zinged with impatience as I waited for whatever came next.

"You look beautiful, absolutely beautiful." He pulled me against him forcefully and resumed our kiss.

My breasts pressed to him, and I felt his skin against mine for the first time. The experience of him claiming me took my breath away. I clawed at his neck and laced my fingers through his hair.

Hot trails of sparks followed everywhere his hands roamed my body. He thumbed my nipples, fondled my breasts, traced a finger down my ass cheek, and smoothed his hands over my hips. His fingers went everywhere but to my pussy, where I most craved his touch.

I rubbed myself against the giant bulge in his pants, trying to coax him to give me his cock. I tugged at his belt again.

"No." He pulled my hand away and swatted my ass.

Clearly, I wasn't the one in charge. I might have insisted we start this, but he was going to chart our course.

He lifted me up and set my ass on the cold granite of the island. The man was strong. He'd lifted me like I was a feather, which I clearly was not.

My thighs trembled as he pulled them apart.

A wicked smile came to his face.

I was completely open to him, displayed on the kitchen island with the lights on, not something I was prepared for. Modesty pulled my knees together, but he held them apart.

I gasped and tried again to close my legs as his face approached my thighs, but he was too strong.

In college, I'd been on the giving end of oral sex. But not having been brave enough to ask for it, I'd never been on the receiving end. It wasn't because I was a prude about it.

Okay, I'd pretty much been a prude.

Senior year, Mickie had been willing, twice, but I'd made excuses. *Adventurous* hadn't been a word associated with my sexual experiences. Plain vanilla was more like it.

As Charlie came close, I found myself comparing him to Gerald again. I'd never been on Gerald's menu—not even as a request.

Charlie pushed me back on my elbows before kissing his way up the inside of my thigh.

Trembling, I pushed at his forehead. "Not that, not now. I've never…"

His finger parted my soaked slit, teasing my entrance. "Are you sure?"

Nodding, I managed the embarrassing words. "I haven't ever."

With a slow movement, he lifted me off the granite and pulled me into a hug. "Then not until you beg me." He held me tight.

I slid my hand down to the bulge in his pants. "I still want you."

"Making demands, are we?" he whispered.

"I'm not a virgin or anything." *Just orally.* I stroked him. "I want you inside me." That was as clear as I could make it. I hadn't meant to kill the mood.

He pulled my hand away and cupped my pussy. "Not until you come for me."

I gasped as his fingers slid the length of my folds, parting my soaked lips, teasing my entrance again, and circling my clit. His touch jolted me.

He pushed me back against the island.

I opened my legs wider for him.

Quick, gentle movements built tension in my core. I kissed his neck and pulled his head down, but he resisted me.

His finger circled my little bud. "You're going to come for me, beautiful, but you have to tell me what to do, what you want, what you like."

"This is a good start."

He pulled his finger away. "That's not clear enough."

The loss of his touch was *not* what I wanted. "More, please."

"More what?"

So that's what he meant. "Give me a finger."

He nibbled my earlobe. "I don't understand."

"Inside me."

I trembled as his finger entered me, hooked, and stroked the tenderness inside me.

"Deeper," I said.

He complied.

"Oh, yeah." As he moved his finger slowly in and out, stroking my walls, my anticipation built for more. "Another," I begged.

The second finger joined the first, adding pressure and sensation.

I closed my eyes and enjoyed the building tension.

He kept up the strokes.

With my eyes clamped shut, I imagined his cock inside me.

He breathed into my ear. "I've got two hands."

"My breast," I murmured.

He cupped a breast. "What about it?" He was going to make me explain everything.

"The nipple."

He circled leisurely.

"Now my clit. I'm ready." The heat grew, emanating from my core.

His fingers pulled out to find my clit, with surprising pressure, and held there, not moving.

I caught on to this game slowly. "Now circle."

He did.

With him tweaking my nipple and circling my little nub, the throbbing built quickly.

I gave in to my responsibility. "Lighter...harder."

He followed my words, and I began to get beyond the awkwardness of vocalizing my desires.

"Faster," I panted. "Back and forth." More unfiltered words poured out of me.

As he followed each of my suggestions, more nerves overloaded.

"You need to come for me," he breathed on my neck.

My legs trembled as the tension built. I spread my legs a little wider. "Oh fuck. Harder... A little higher... Shit. Right there." I could only manage the words between moans.

His pressure pushed me back against the island.

"Circle...fuck yes." I could barely hear myself with the blood rushing in my ears. "Lighter." My panting came faster every second. "Fuck, yeah... Faster... Harder... The other direction... Oh shit." I arched my hips into his pressure. "More... Holy fuck."

He pressed harder.

Sparks ignited all my nerve endings, and the tremors took over. My walls constricted, and my clit exploded under his touch. I couldn't breathe. "Holy fuck" was all I could manage.

As the convulsions receded, he pulled his hands away and held me.

I relaxed into him, locking my knees to keep from falling. After a minute I regained some strength and reached for his belt again. "How about now?"

He pulled away to give me room to work. "Now."

Charlie was not a small man, and the same went for the big cock that sprang loose when I got his pants undone.

I wrapped a hand around him as soon as I could, and he groaned a wonderful sound of pleasure. His member was hard, hot, and thick in my hand as I pulled and twisted.

He hopped to the side to pull his leg free from his pants, and I lost my grip.

I glanced toward the full-length windows. "Maybe we should go into the bedroom." After having his cock in my hand, I couldn't wait to have him inside me.

"Scared?" he asked.

I answered quickly. "No way." I'd voted for adventurous instead of scared when we'd started this, and I wasn't going to back down.

"I'll be right back." He moved quickly toward the bedroom and returned a moment later with the little plastic square of a condom wrapper.

The way his cock swung and bobbed as he walked drew my attention, and every second I couldn't hold him tested my patience. I held out my hand for the package.

He tore it opened and passed it to me.

I giggled when his cock bobbed as I knelt down to lick the length of him and suck off the bead of precum. I unrolled the latex slowly, with tiny strokes.

"Faster, baby. You're killing me."

I loved how that rolled off his tongue. I'd been called *darling* a dozen times—*sweetie* even—but the way he said *baby* sounded so much more sensual. I took my time massaging him as I unrolled the protection down his length. He had a lot of that going for him too.

I was barely finished when he lifted me onto the edge of the island again. A second later, his cock teased my entrance with a small push. I was so wet, the tip slid in easily.

His eyes asked a simple question.

I answered with the same word that had gotten us started. "More."

He pulled my legs onto his shoulders and gripped my thighs. In a few quick strokes, he'd stretched me and pushed in partway.

I gasped at the size of him.

He caught me wincing. "Are you okay?"

I nodded and went full Andrina. "I will be when you fuck me properly."

He responded by pulling my thighs close and pushing in to the root, followed by pulling out and plunging back in again.

The pressure, the fullness of it all soon turned exquisite.

As he thrust, one of his hands fondled my breast, and the other pressed and rubbed my clit.

His groans increased in volume. "You are so fucking good. You are so fucking tight…"

I squeezed to give him all the tightness I could as pleasure enveloped me with each plunge of his magic rod.

He was not only bigger than I was used to, but unimaginably hard.

With my legs over his shoulders, he was in complete control. I had no leverage to pull him in deeper. Every thrust brought a new level of fullness and overwhelmed any control I had over my mouth. Danielle wouldn't have dared to say it, but this girl did. "Don't you dare stop. Fuck me harder."

He upped his tempo, and the ferocity that lit his eyes told me the dirty words were what he wanted, what he needed.

I strained to control the sensations, trying to wring every last moment of gratification from him, trying in vain to match his endurance. I needed him to come for me, to repay him.

Still, he drove me yelping toward another orgasm as I clawed at his arms. Shifting to grip the edge of the granite, I finally had a way to thrust my hips into him, matching his rhythm and losing myself in the sensations.

I couldn't hold off my second orgasm for long. I needed him to join me at the edge of the cliff. "Fuck me like you mean it."

Soon I felt him tense up.

"More," I repeated. "Harder, for a change."

With that, our orgasms collided as I convulsed around him.

With a last thrust, he held himself deep inside me as his cock pulsed.

After a minute of me panting with my legs in the air, he let me drop them and scooped me up in his arms. "I think you need a shower before work."

A shower might be what I needed, but more of him was what I wanted. Sex with Charlie had been cathartic. I didn't care that my back was raw from the granite, or that I was too exhausted to stand. I settled my head against his muscled chest and closed my eyes. "I think bed is a better idea."

"Not an option," he said when we reached his bathroom. He set me down. "In the shower, now."

I complied, bracing my arms against the wall, and relaxed under the hot spray.

Now that I knew what I'd been missing, I wasn't going to be content with anything less than Charlie. I needed to make it a verb. I'd been *Charlie'd*, and nothing less would be good enough.

When he joined me, we traded the body wash as I took care of his cock and he washed between my legs. Then, of course, he had to do my boobs, but I wasn't complaining one bit.

"Nice horse," he said soaping my lower back and my strength tattoo. "What's the story behind it?"

I turned to face him. "How are we going to handle this at work?"

He grabbed my breast. "I'm going to handle you as often as I can."

I pushed him. "Stop it. I'm serious."

"How about if we figure it out after lunch?"

# CHAPTER 24

*DANIELLE*

"Chinese or Thai for dinner tonight?" Charlie asked just before we reached the door of the Hawker building.

"Ask me later." After the morning we'd had, I was still processing my situation, and dinner was too far into the future to consider.

"Pick one," he insisted. "That's the way it works."

I didn't understand what *it* was, but obliged. "Chinese."

We passed through the lobby, and Charlie greeted the receptionist, Marjorie, by name. *Interesting*. I hadn't noticed him do that before.

"Are you ready?" Charlie asked as we rode the elevator up to our office.

"Do I have a choice?"

He fished something out of his pocket and offered it—a cardkey. "To the flat."

I slipped it into the outside pocket of my purse.

"You're looking chipper this morning," Abby said as we walked in.

I nodded, assuming it was me she was talking to.

She looked between us for a second and gave Charlie a wry smile.

It couldn't be that obvious, could it?

As I settled at my desk, I heard Charlie set an after-lunch meeting for us with Wroblewski and then warn Abby he'd be out for the rest of the morning.

After my jaunt to fill my mug with coffee, he handed me three sheets of paper. "Circle your choices for tonight."

It was a menu from a Chinese restaurant.

"You do this every day?"

He nodded. "Order ahead? Sometimes. Chinese? No. If you want something else, I've got eight different menus to choose from."

*Interesting.* Takeout every night.

"No, this will be fine." I quickly circled cashew chicken, broccoli beef, and prawn egg rolls before returning the menu to him.

At the door he stopped. "I'm meeting a guy about the two Ts, and then I have a lunch meeting at Taliafaro's."

I nodded. He'd explained on the way here that "the two Ts" was his shorthand for Gerald, Turdball, and Thin Man, who'd followed us before.

I'd written off Thin Man as overactive imagination on Charlie's part, but he didn't agree.

"I'll be back this afternoon," he called to Abby on the way out.

"Got ya covered," she replied.

Mid-morning arrived before I knew it, though boring didn't begin to describe the summary of contract changes suggested by the union. They went on and on, all minor issues. It was a long slog to get through all this in time for our early-afternoon meeting with the HR guy.

Every time I stopped for a second, the throbbing I still felt down below reminded me that I wasn't in Kansas anymore. My life had changed in a big way over the last twenty-four hours, and for the better—not counting what had happened to my apartment, of course.

I wiggled in my chair. I could only wonder how Charlie felt about this turn of events. He'd said we'd talk later.

Gerald and I were over, and the man who'd replaced him was a real man. I had no doubt of that, and I wasn't looking back, not one bit.

I was happy to be Charlie's girl today.

Today? The word sounded too final. Had he put off talking about things because I'd just had my first one-night stand—or one-morning stand—and didn't understand the rules? Did he want to let me down easy?

*Get real, Wentworth. A week ago you couldn't stand the guy.*

That thought gave me a shiver *and* told me something about how I felt. One night, one morning, it didn't matter. It wouldn't be enough.

Yes, but a lot had changed in a week. Pushing Charlie's buttons had become part of my routine since we'd started this venture together.

At first, he'd completely deserved it—not acknowledging to our fathers the role I'd played in securing the deal for this company, grabbing the big office without a discussion, berating me for every little thing.

Had I taken it too far in poking at him every chance I got? Probably. Although getting under his skin had been entertaining, he didn't deserve it anymore. He'd mellowed a bit, actually more than a bit since those first days. It had crept up on me, but it was clear in hindsight.

A text arriving on my phone broke my navel-contemplating session.

GERALD: We still need to talk

I read the text out loud. "We still need to talk." Like hell we did. The words burned my throat as they came out and only made me madder. I was done with him, and he didn't get it. When I'd told him to *get out*, he should have understood that meant *out of my life*. If he hadn't, my kiss with Charlie should have made it plain.

There wasn't anything to talk about—not one, solitary thing. After what he'd done, I couldn't think of anything worse than seeing him, meeting with him, talking to him, being anywhere near him.

I'd dodged a bullet by not staying at that dinner with Gerald. God, I loved Abby's name for him. It summed him up perfectly: a smelly ball of dog shit. Someone who smelled so bad, you couldn't even stand to be in the same room as him.

My terse text reply consisted of only two letters: *NO*.

I deleted his message. If it had been on paper, I would have enjoyed taking a match to it. That visual made me smile. Just like a movie, I'd happily light it and toss the flaming paper in the fireplace.

I went back to my contract work, and he interrupted me by texting two more times and even tried to call once.

I deleted them all and declined the call—not a ladylike response, but that was treating him better than he deserved. "Take that, Turdball," I said to the empty office. I kept my voice low enough to not broadcast my personal issues. Drama was not something I needed.

By lunchtime, his annoyances had come to an end, thank God.

I stood up from the desk and practiced the kick I'd give him if I ever saw him again. I bet connecting with his balls would make me feel even better than sticking pins in the doll had.

Although his messages had stopped, I hadn't been able to entirely rid myself of the recurring images from my apartment. They kept intruding the way a blue jay squawking couldn't be completely ignored, or completely tuned out.

More concentration. That's what I needed. I couldn't allow Gerald to affect me. He was a nonentity, as far as I was concerned. He didn't deserve to be any more than that—a lesson to be learned from, a bad episode in my history, to be eventually as forgotten as the details in my high school history textbooks.

I swung my leg again, practicing my kick.

The sound of tearing fabric wasn't good.

I looked behind me to find the hem of my skirt ripped.

*Crap on a cracker. This is all Gerald's fault. He isn't even here and he's causing me problems.*

Keeping a change of clothes in my desk was something Daddy had taught me, and now I was happy I'd followed his advice.

After changing into a fresh skirt, my thoughts shifted back to the other man in my life, Charlie, and I finally succeeded in putting Gerald out of my mind.

Charlie stirred something in me. His promise of protection made me feel special in a way that gave me goose bumps just thinking about it.

Pulling the apartment cardkey out of my purse, I looked at the small piece of white plastic. For the time being, it represented my future. I hadn't been asked, but I also hadn't declined, and now I was rooming with a man for the first time. Perhaps it was the separate bedroom he'd offered that made it feel safe—less like the scary step I'd always envisioned it would be. But then again, it had only been one night so far—sort of like half a weekend. I'd gone away for weekends before with guys. Even if it was only three times, that counted.

It was temporary, so it didn't count as moving in with a man.

This had all been both sudden and unexpected. Last week I had a boyfriend who I'd thought might ask me to move in with him, but had instead been ready to surprise me with a ring. But it hadn't made me feel... I searched for the appropriate word.

Gerald hadn't made me feel valued or special. And then, to demand I marry him? Where was that on the intimacy scale?

Just because I was cautious about moving in with a man didn't make me frigid or asocial. Cautious was good. Cautious was safe. But I still deserved romance, a connection. You had to live together to get to know the other person more deeply before progressing on to the final commitment of marriage.

Slow was cautious, and cautious was good. That was a fact.

I wouldn't be my father. He'd said his marriage vows many times—too many times. I wouldn't let genetics determine my fate and become a serial wife, a serial liar.

The plastic in my hand wasn't moving in with Charlie. It was for my safety. I hadn't broken my vow to myself to take things slow. The condominium-sharing would be over in a few days when my apartment was put back together. Things would return to normal. Sharing a space for a long weekend—that was the way to look at it. That was a safe step.

I put the cardkey on my desk, picked up my mug, and stood. Caffeine and lots of it—that's what I needed. I'd just made another stupid assumption. Charlie and I hadn't talked. How could I know if I was more than a one-night thing to him? A pity fuck after my apartment disaster.

Traipsing out toward the coffee room, I got the squinty eye from Abby. She'd noticed my change of skirt.

"I didn't feel like black today," I explained on my way past her. It was better than explaining how I'd ripped the other one.

After the machine finished, I brought the mug to my nose and breathed in. The mere aroma awakened me. As a proper British lady, Alicia had converted me to tea in the morning at home, but this machine was changing me back to a coffeeaholic. The mocha I'd chosen was almost too hot, but still delicious. Hopefully the second shot I'd punched up would do the trick and wake me enough to straighten out my thinking.

Walking back to my office, I slowed to take a sip at the corner.

Abby finished touching up her mascara and added lipstick she hadn't worn this morning, followed by a spritz of perfume. She hadn't mentioned a man, but this wasn't the first time she'd spruced up her appearance before going out to lunch. I was curious, but now was not the time for me to ask about the man in her life. I wasn't ready to have that question turned around on me. Was Charlie now the man in my life? I had no idea.

As I approached, she gathered her purse and checked her watch. "I'll be back after lunch."

"See ya," I replied.

The notepad on her desk was almost hidden. It had a single word *Taliafaro's*.

## Charles

After making copies of all the materials I had, I sat in Ben Murdoch's office in the Covington building. We weren't far from Hawker, where I'd left Dani safely on the top floor.

"I'm still checking on your tail," Ben said. "But honestly, we're not likely to get far with just the photo. Our best bet is to catch him following you and tail him back to his lair."

I nodded. *Lair* was a fitting word for the elusive Thin Man's hideout.

"Where was this taken?" Ben asked, holding up a photo I'd given him.

"Eastboro Park on our regular morning run."

Ben rubbed his chin. "We can try that, if you think he'll be there again."

"He'll show."

I couldn't tell if Ben thought my suggestion was a good one. I'd seen my tail more than once at the park, although we hadn't gone this morning.

"Keep it up, then. Text me your timing the night before. We'll try it a few times."

"Okay," I agreed. "Now I have another problem. His name is Gerald Durban." I gave Ben the history as I knew it and forwarded him the Turdball pictures Dani had sent me.

"You said he's a Brit?"

I nodded. "Not all of us are model citizens. I also have a police report number for you on his destruction of Dani's—Ms. Wentworth's—flat." I slid across the copy I'd made of Detective Bosco's card and the case number he'd given me, along with hard copies of the pictures I'd taken last night.

"So they know when it occurred, but don't have a witness to tie this Durban fellow to the crime?"

I'd had to go to the police station to get the report this morning, and I'd noticed the same issue. The neighbor who'd heard the commotion and called the police had been too scared to look outside and see Gerald as he left.

"It was him," I said. "She's only been in town a very short time, and nobody else has a motive."

"What's his?"

"She refused to marry him."

"All this over a girl who broke up with him?"

I nodded. "You'd have to know Ms. Wentworth to understand."

A slight wrinkle formed at the corner of his eye as he appraised me. "Not a great way to win her back."

I couldn't tell if he'd figured out my interest in Dani or not. It didn't matter. "Nope."

He studied the photos for a few seconds. "This is unusual," he noted as he flipped through. "A baseball bat is what it looks like. Right-hand swing. Doesn't help much, but the strength does."

I gave him a quizzical look, not because I didn't know the difference between a baseball bat and a proper cricket bat, but I didn't understand his meaning.

He turned a picture toward me. "See this broken red lamp here?" He pointed.

I nodded.

"Pieces of it are all the way across the room." He pointed again to some red ceramic against the far wall. "That doesn't happen by knocking it over. You have to hit it hard with something like a bat to drive pieces that far away. This guy was pissed."

"You can tell it was a man?"

"Or a very strong woman, based on the dent that piece made in the wallboard." He pointed. "Here."

That only made me madder at Turdball Gerald.

"The detective suggested adding a surveillance camera inside. What's your take on that?" I asked.

"Good idea, and you can get them hidden in books, clocks, stuffed animals—things that blend in."

"She might not like the idea of being watched."

"Someone who does this much damage is dangerous. I wouldn't give her a choice, if it was somebody I cared about. And, it can be set up so that only you and the lady have access to the feed. Nobody will be watching, but if he comes back, recorded video is the way to nail him. The cops eat that up."

"Nobody's watching?"

"Recorded, not monitored, and only you or she can pull up the feed or recordings."

I didn't have to think twice. "Let's do it."

We discussed Ben's observations and questions for a few minutes before I left for my lunch meeting.

Down on the street, I allowed my mind to move to the bigger picture. The union situation had to be stabilized before it got out of hand, and for the life of me, I couldn't understand why it had taken such a bad turn since the purchase. Perhaps Wroblewski would have some new insight today. We could certainly use it. He'd mentioned once that he suspected the union had informants in the company to keep them up to date on what was happening in our building.

He'd used the term *contact*, rather than *informant* or *spy*, but that was clearly what they were.

Another problem to contemplate, and then it was off to my lunch meeting with Vincent Benson. He deserved a proper thank you for the flat *and* the use of his resources.

## CHAPTER 25

*DANIELLE*

THE EARLY-AFTERNOON MEETING WITH CHARLIE IN WROBLEWSKI'S OFFICE WENT by in a blur. I ate the vending-machine sandwich I'd brought along as I sat across from Charlie, prepared to kick him in the shins if he revealed our new status to the HR guy.

Whatever that status was.

Thankfully, Charlie didn't say anything. He also didn't spend a single second looking in my direction. It was as if I wasn't at the table. Did that hint at our status as a non-couple?

*I'm doing it again. Who says this has anything do to with us?*

Of course it didn't say anything about our status. He was being super cautious until we talked. That made sense, even if I did feel neglected.

I swiped that thought away as well. Clingy was not a good look.

Thirty minutes later, Wroblewski's summary of the issues between the union and the company hadn't revealed anything new.

With my sandwich only half finished, Charlie rose to take a phone call. "I have to get this."

He returned a few minutes later. "Thanks for the update, Ron. Seems like we just need to set up that meeting."

"As soon as I can get them to agree to a time, I'll let you know," Wroblewski replied.

"I'll see you back upstairs," Charlie said, looking at me for the first time. A second later, he was walking away.

"In a hurry, I guess," Wroblewski said.

I smiled after him. "Yeah, sometimes he is."

He grabbed Charlie's barely eaten bag of chips. "Want to split these?"

I shook my head. "No, you go ahead."

He smiled. "Don't mind if I do."

Biting into my sandwich, I decided there were worse people to sit with for a snack than this big man.

Eating slowly, I let my mind wander to what might happen tonight—if the anticipation didn't kill me first.

"How are you two getting along?" Wroblewski asked after a moment, going into full HR mode.

I controlled my smirk. "The working relationship is in odd one, and I think it's taking a while for both of us to get used to it."

He nodded, but said nothing more.

When we'd finished, Wroblewski walked me back to the elevator. My mind wandered again to how quickly Charlie and I might dissolve into nakedness once we were alone. My libido had gone into overdrive.

I'd never been in a situation where all I could think about was the next time I'd have sex with someone, and I'd never had a rebound reaction like this. Charlie had woken something in me that I hadn't known was there, and it both excited and scared me.

Was that normal?

Was I ready for *this*?

And, what exactly was *this*?

"If things get too touchy..."

I immediately imagined all the implications of the word *touchy* in this situation.

"...feel free to use me as a neutral arbitrator," Wroblewski continued. "Sometimes the resolutions to problems don't end up being about who's on top."

I successfully avoided laughing at the thought of him arbitrating anything between Charlie and me about who should be on top. "Thanks, Ron. I appreciate it."

"I'm glad things are going well for you two."

Just before the elevator door closed, he gave me what could have been a wink.

My eyes widened. *No.* I was paranoid. That had to be it.

∼

## Charles

After the call from Dad, I went back to the office rather than return to the meeting in Wroblewski's office. It had been essentially finished anyway. And I needed some time to sort through what Dad had told me.

He'd had an offer from Junior to the run the company for us and thought I should send over my list of Dani's deficiencies to get the ball rolling with her father.

He'd spoken rapidly, but one thing came across clearly. He wasn't listening to me. He was hellbent on moving me to Berlin.

It bothered me that Junior was going around us to work our fathers, and I'd have to figure out how to deal with that.

Because he'd scarcely taken a breath during the call, I also hadn't gotten a chance to tell him something odd was up around here. I'd been tailed again by Thin Man today after my lunch with Benson. It didn't make sense now that the purchase was complete for Knightley to still be watching me, but I certainly hadn't imagined it.

∼

## Danielle

Charlie was already in the office when I got back from the meeting.

Closing the door behind me, I started with an innocuous question. "Who called?"

He blinked a few times.

"The phone call…during the meeting?"

"Oh… That was my Dad. He's been calling…to check up on things."

Mine hadn't because I'd specifically limited my updates to him. "Is he concerned?"

"It's nothing. He's just like that."

It didn't sound like nothing, but I didn't push further because it wasn't really what we needed to discuss. The look on Charlie's face indicated that he didn't want to talk about anything right now, but we'd said after lunch, and it was now officially after lunch and the talk couldn't be put off any longer.

Since he wasn't going to start, I did. "We said we were going to talk about this."

He looked out the window. "You're right. Something very wrong is going on with Califano. These delays don't make any sense."

I narrowed my eyes. He wasn't really dumb enough to think I wanted to go over the union issues again.

I walked over and stood next to him. I waved a hand between him and whatever he was looking at to avoid me. "I mean this… us." I motioned between us. "I was wondering how we're going to handle this here…at work."

He stood. "I really don't think I should handle you at work, do you?"

I giggled. It was a good line. The air crackled with tension, and I backed away to keep my brain operating. "You know what I mean… Are we going to be discreet about this, or are we going to tell people?" I waited.

A slow smile grew across his face. "Tell them about what?"

"Us… I mean, us being…" Suddenly I realized this was the wrong discussion. It wasn't what to tell people that we needed to get clear. It was what we were to each other now, if anything.

His mere closeness not only tongue-tied me, I couldn't straighten out my thoughts. I grew wet as his magnetism enveloped me. I couldn't resist the pull this man had on me.

"Did I tell you how beautiful you are when you're flustered?" He smiled, messing with me.

"Cut it out. You know what I mean."

He inched closer.

I backed away, but the wall blocked my retreat.

He placed a hand on either side of me, caging me in.

The only sound in the room was the rushing of blood in my ears as my heart sped up. I closed my eyes and kept my hands at my sides, my only defense against melting into a puddle at his feet, or climbing all over him. Both were bad options.

Leaning forward, he whispered in my ear. "Don't you remember what I said?"

After his chest made contact with mine, memories of this morning further scrambled my brain. I just remembered that we would talk after lunch. "What?" I asked breathlessly.

"That I go all in," he answered. "You had your chance to back out. Now you're mine." He squished my boobs as his chest pressed against me.

My nipples ached. How had it gotten so hot in here?

"Is that what you want to tell them?" he asked.

"What?"

"That you're mine?" He'd known the question all along. "That you woke up next to me this morning?"

How had it taken me this long to figure out he was toying with me? Again Andrina's voice sounded in my head. *"Go for it, girl."* Two could play this game. I opened my eyes, grabbed his crotch, and found the erection he'd leaned far enough away to hide from me.

He gave a quick gasp, but didn't back away.

I rubbed. "You mean you're mine, and you woke up next to me?"

He brought our noses together. "Put it however you want."

Warmth spread through me. "So not just a one-morning stand? Does this mean you'll wine-and-dine me as well?" *Maybe I do have a man in my life.*

He breathed on my ear. "If that's what you want."

He'd given me another chance to back out, to avoid going all in with him, to cut it off. Or, to limit it to casual sex, Andrina style.

It took me no time to decide my answer, but I made him wait a few seconds to hear it. "Yes." The word scared me, but if I was going to meet his intensity, nothing less would do. "It is."

This was way out of Danielle's old comfort zone, and somehow it felt liberating.

He nipped at my earlobe. "Okay. But remember, I warned you."

Now we were back to the original question. "But what do we tell them?" I asked.

"You're not technically my employee, so there's nothing for anyone to complain about."

His cock surged in my hand. I turned the tables on him. "You mean, you're not technically my employee?"

He gave my earlobe a gentle nip. "Against the wall or on the desk, your choice. Yell my name loudly enough, and we won't have to say a thing to anybody. The office grapevine will take care of it. We can't be the only CWBs in the building."

I cocked my head.

"Coworkers with benefits," he explained.

I'd always considered myself a liberated woman, but the thought of how people might look at me after discovering what he'd just suggested filled me with dread—that and learning he'd expected this to be casual all along.

What the hell? I was a modern woman. I could take pleasure where I found it and not get freaked out. *Yes, I can.*

He brushed his lips down the side of my neck. "Or I can be as secretive as the next bugger."

My heart raced, and my brain threatened to turn mushy again as every instinct told me to climb him like a tree and let everybody beyond the door be damned. "I think discreet is best for now." Getting the whole sentence out without tripping over my tongue surprised me.

He pulled back. "Got it. Mum's the word. New rule: no displays of affection at the office."

I instantly missed the warmth of our contact.

He licked his lips. "I think we'd best keep the door open, unless other people are in the room. I don't think I can control myself when we're alone." He kissed me on the forehead. His hardening cock pressed into my hand, proving his words.

Heat raced through my veins as I squeezed his dick.

He moaned. "You're making this difficult."

"Don't you mean *hard*?" I asked. I pushed him back a few inches. "You'd better get out of here before I rip your clothes off and break our new rule."

"Promises, promises," he said as he backed away. He adjusted himself in his pants before sitting behind the desk. "You best open the door."

Checking to be sure my clothes weren't askew, I collected my coffee mug on the way out, but stopped short. "Don't forget you promised me."

He cocked his head. "Promised what?"

They would both be new experiences for me, and today, broadening my horizons held appeal. "Both the wall and the desk."

His eyes went wide with the lust I wanted to see.

I pulled open the door before he could say anything and headed for the coffee machine. The question still hadn't been answered—what we really were to each other—but maybe it didn't matter. *Who cares if this is a rebound?* Hell, maybe I needed a rebound to get myself off the floor after the shit Gerald had put me through. All I knew was Charlie made me happy. For now, that was enough. CWB would do. Andrina would approve.

Abby glanced my way as I passed. Her face didn't show any hint that she knew my new status as Charlie's CWB girl. She would be the hardest to keep in the dark.

Walking toward my rendezvous with the coffee machine, it struck me how natural it felt that Charlie and I had finally connected. How many girls got a chance to come full circle and be with their first crush, even if it was temporary?

Of course it would be temporary. Temporary suited me. It was safe. It wouldn't progress to the danger zone.

Charlie had been my first—crush that is, not boyfriend, at least not back then. He'd been a crush that had ended the day Daddy packed us in the car and cut our vacation short. He hadn't even known how infatuated I'd been with Charlie. How could he?

Daddy had driven us home so abruptly after that terrible night with the stallion that we hadn't even said goodbye to Charlie or his brother, Ethan. Then after that, the feud had made it impossible to even mention their names.

My first crush had become my…what? The heat I felt when I thought of him staring straight into my soul had to mean something. I shook my head. I was his CWB girl. That was enough.

As the machine dispensed my liquid pick-me-up, the steam rising from the cup matched how I felt today. Charlie and I were a team, and we'd figure this out. That's what teams did.

I smiled as I walked back to our office. A casual fling without a commitment—that I could handle. Of course I could. I was a grown woman and in control. No problem.

# CHAPTER 26

*DANIELLE*
*(one week later)*

I WOKE CUDDLED IN WARMTH, WITH A LARGE ARM DRAPED OVER MY WAIST AND breath on the back of my neck. It was Thursday morning, and I'd been staying at Charlie's place a little over a week now.

This was spooning at its best, with a hot man snuggled behind me—and Charlie was hot in all the right ways.

I popped an eye open.

The room was dark, as before, but I'd moved in the clock from my room across the hall. I'd placed a book on the nightstand between me and the clock so the blue digits wouldn't keep me awake.

Andrina had always said sex was the best sleep aid, at least if you didn't stay up all night running on repeat. She was right. After last night's triple-orgasm treat, I'd fallen asleep in Charlie's arms and slept soundly. The light from the clock probably wouldn't have mattered.

After that first night, I'd brought everything over from my apartment, and I hadn't been back since. Charlie had been back there to check on the repairs and told me it was coming along. That would do for now, as revisiting any amount of the destruction I'd witnessed didn't appeal to me. I could wait until it was complete, paint and all. For now, waking up every morning in this bed, with Charlie, suited me just fine.

Reluctantly, I decided to check the time since we hadn't set the alarm. When I lifted my head enough to read the clock, six ten was the answer.

I wiggled my butt and found—ahh, yes—glorious morning wood. "Time to wake up," I whispered.

He groaned like a bear coming out of hibernation.

I wiggled against him again. "We have to get to the park for our run."

His hand captured my boob. "I have a better idea."

It tempted me, but we couldn't miss a morning at the park. "Can't catch a fish without bait."

Charlie fondled my breast, making his desired choice obvious. "I like it here."

I pulled out of his grasp. "You said you wanted to catch Thin Man." Slipping off the side of the bed, I found the light switch.

His hand went immediately to his eyes. "Argh. At least you could warn me before doing that."

"Sorry." I wasn't really. We needed to get going. "But it was your idea to keep up the routine for him."

He'd told me we needed to attract Thin Man so his friend Ben could follow him back to his "lair." And this was the only way to prove one way or the other if Thin Man was a random citizen or the threat Charlie seemed sure he was.

∽

## CHARLES

IN THE OFFICE, THE MORNING REPORTS BROUGHT GOOD NEWS, BUT IT WAS thinking back to earlier that made me truly smile.

Being pulled out of my bed only half awake hadn't been the best way to start the morning, but the run in the park alongside Dani had made up for it.

She was a joy to behold—boundless morning energy and excitement to match. Seeing her enthusiasm in the early light was contagious. Then, of course, there was the added bonus of watching her legs, her ass, her tits... I could go on. Luckily a girl couldn't run in baggy clothing, now, could she? The short bout of shower sex afterward hadn't hurt either.

Ron Wroblewski popped his head inside the door. "Good news, boss."

I waited for it.

Dani looked up from her desk as well.

Wroblewski walked in. "Califano wants a meeting."

I slid my chair back. "Good. But we've been down this road before."

"Do you think he means it this time?" Dani asked.

"He'd like to get together this morning," Wroblewski added.

I looked at my watch. "When?"

"Eleven. At his place," he said sheepishly. "I know it's not much notice."

I waved off his explanation. "That's better than lots of time to cancel. Fallwood?"

"Yeah." He held out a piece of paper. "Here's the address."

"Okay. We'll leave now."

Dani was already up.

Naturally, we had to travel to him, and on zero notice, but that didn't matter. He could have that win in the power dynamics if it got us closer to the contract extension we needed. If every deal had one fly in the ointment, the union contract extension had been this one's.

Wroblewski looked positively relieved that we hadn't balked at the timing.

There wasn't a logical reason for Califano to put it off any longer. Both parties needed contract certainty—our side for continuity of deliveries to customers, and his members needed the continuity of their paychecks. A strike wasn't in anybody's best interest.

∽

DOWNSTAIRS, WE WALKED TO DANI'S CAR FOR THE DRIVE TO MEET THE UNION representatives. She'd insisted her car was more comfortable for the length of the drive.

"I'll drive." I extended my hand for the keys, but she beat me to the driver's side door since my first instinct had been to get in on the right-hand side, the wrong side in this damnable country.

"No way." She opened the door and slid into the seat. "I saw you almost get into an accident the other morning. Kill yourself if you want, but not with me in the car."

"It was the other bloke's fault."

"That's what they all say."

Her stare said it wasn't worth the argument.

Once on the highway, I couldn't keep from looking at her and thinking how lucky I was.

It wasn't long before she spoke up. "You're quiet."

"Just thinking." Admitting I'd been thinking about her wouldn't be manly, so I went with silence.

"About?" she asked.

"Wondering why Thin Man, that guy who was following us again this morning, is back. I'm worried for…"

"Worried for what?"

"When I first saw him, I thought it had to do with the negotiations. Now, with the deal done, I don't know why he's following me." I looked over. She should have asked worried for *who*. Because it was her I was worried about. She was now also in whatever danger Thin Man represented, because he'd seen us together.

Her mobile rang in the center console.

Since she was driving, I picked it up. The screen read *Gerald*. "It's Turdball. Do you want to talk to him?" I offered her the mobile.

"No." Her voice was emphatic.

I clicked to cancel the call and set the mobile down again.

It rang a second time. Turdball again.

"I could tell him you'll call him back later."

"No," she repeated.

"Determined little bugger." I denied that call as well with a smile. It felt good that she didn't want even a single word with that worthless piece of shit.

Then a text arrived.

GERALD: We need to talk

Dani looked over.

"Turdball again," I said.

"And I still don't care."

I composed her message back to him.

ME: And I still don't care

GERALD: You could be in danger

Dani looked straight down the road. "I don't even want to know."

"Okay." I composed one final message to the turdball.

ME: FUCK OFF

"I told him you didn't want to talk," I said as I deleted the text string.

"Good." She took a deep breath and relaxed her shoulders as silence settled between us.

It was another minute before she spoke again. "How do you think this meeting will go?"

"No idea at the moment. Canceling on us the previous times was him exercising his muscle to intimidate us—that and having us come to his house to meet instead of the factory. He might be playing to his internal audience within the union before we settle things, showing them he's not being pushed around."

She nodded. "Or he really does have an issue—one he thinks isn't being addressed by the contract extension."

"If that's the case, why hasn't he come right out and told us? Then we could figure out how to deal with it. Either way, the delay doesn't make sense."

She nodded. "People's motivations can be more complicated than they seem."

That didn't clarify anything. The only reality was that union negotiations were rarely simple, on either side of the pond.

The next bout of silence didn't last long, this time interrupted by the ring of *my* mobile.

"Hi, Dad, what's up?" I answered. He wasn't someone I wanted to talk with right now, but it never helped to put him off for long.

"How are things going out there?" he asked.

"Everything's fine."

"I called about that memo you owe me."

I turned down the volume on the mobile and shifted it to my other ear. This was absolutely not a conversation to have in front of Dani. "We should talk later. I'm driving now."

"I'll be in the office for another half hour. Call me when you get back to the office."

"My trip will take longer than that," I answered.

"Why? Where are you going?" Dad didn't like not knowing everything, and at times like this, it sucked.

I also probably shouldn't have been so specific about our timing. "A trip out to the Fallwood jet-engine facility to look around." It was nearly the truth.

"Why?"

His questions reminded me why I enjoyed being out of the London office. I wasn't a kid anymore, and I didn't need constant supervision. "This is better done in person."

"You should let others handle that."

"This is something I need to do myself."

"Okay, but call soon. I have a meeting scheduled with Wentworth, and I want to get the problem with that girl fixed to free you up for the Berlin operation."

"But—"

"When are you going to send that list? Maybe you don't understand the situation. I can't just pull you out of there and let that girl run Hawker, so I have to get her father to agree to bring Hawker's son back in to run the place for now—at least until we don't have that two hundred million at risk. You know you should never have agreed to that provision."

"I'm not comfortable with that."

"Well, you need to be. Don't keep me waiting forever."

I had nothing else I could say to that with Dani next to me, and the provision he didn't like had probably been the one to seal the deal. So I kept my mouth shut. "Later, Dad."

"By the way, I'm sending you a written offer for the Berlin position. I realize I should have done that earlier. I thought that would make you feel more comfortable about the move."

"Thanks, Dad." A month ago, I would have jumped at this, but not today. I'd need to ease him out of the idea, and that wasn't happening in the car.

We hung up, and Dani looked over. "You haven't told him about the contract problem, have you?"

I pocketed the mobile. "No." It took me a second to ask the obvious follow-up. "Have you told your father?"

Her expression signaled the answer. She didn't look over. "No. It's our issue, not theirs."

"Absolutely," I agreed. "We get it fixed, and neither of them needs to be involved. It would only raise their blood pressure anyway." It could lead to recriminations between the two families as well.

"Yeah. And, they made us the team, so it doesn't concern them."

"That's right. They did." I stopped the discussion at that. We'd agreed, and we were a team. The word *team* was awfully close to couple. Were we a couple as well?

That required a little more introspection. Was there a difference between a couple and two adults enjoying each other's company? It wasn't like me to be concerned about labels. "Are we..." I stopped myself.

"Are we what?"

It would be stupid to ask about being a couple. "Do you think we'll be on time?"

She quickly checked her mobile. "Not a problem."

I settled back in my seat. I wasn't behind the wheel of the car, and I'd almost lost control of my brain-mouth connection. I needed to settle the bloody hell down.

# CHAPTER 27

*DANIELLE*

"We don't need to appear too eager by being early, or disrespectful by being late," Charlie said.

So we stopped and waited a mile away from Califano's address so as to arrive on time. After our pause, when we parked next to the shiny red Ferrari at Califano's house, it was exactly the agreed hour.

After exiting my plain sedan, Charlie peeked inside the low-slung sports car with obvious admiration.

Inside the house, Vinny Stefano, the union's lawyer, and James Bristow, their chief steward, introduced themselves.

"Nice car outside," Charlie noted.

Califano walked up—I recognized him from the photo we had. The picture hadn't included the heavy gold chain he wore around his neck. The other two wore ties, but not the boss.

"Ain't she a beauty?" Califano laughed. "Latest model, and boy, is she quick." He didn't even try to hide the way his eyes lingered on my chest as he extended a hand to me. "And *you*, sweetheart, can call me Tony." He moved a little too close for my comfort as we shook.

His other wrist sported an expensive Patek Philippe watch, I noticed. I only recognized it because Gerald was so proud of his decadent purchase.

Califano was obviously also all about image. I filed that observation away for later in the negotiation.

I waited until he turned away to pull a tissue from my purse and wipe his sweat from my hand.

Charlie wiped his hand against his trousers as we followed the rotund man and the other two into another room.

Stefano began the conversation once we were seated. "We have a number of minor issues we need to discuss." He started through the pages of the contract, ticking off small items.

I took notes, as did Charlie.

Califano sat back in his chair, obviously bored by the details. He played with his watch.

His lawyer finally got to the end and closed up his copy of the paperwork. "We'd like a response on these issues," he noted.

I controlled the gasp I felt coming on. Wroblewski had said everything was settled, and now they had another two dozen issues?

Charlie seemed unfazed. "And if we say yes to all these today? Then what?"

The lawyer looked nervously at his boss.

Califano stopped fingering his watch and shifted forward in his chair for the first time. "How do I know I can trust you?"

He'd aimed the comment at Charlie, but I felt the brunt of it as well. And it certainly wasn't an answer to Charlie's question.

"What makes you think you can't?" Charlie asked.

Califano snorted. "I don't know you, for one. This is the first time we've even met."

I felt like throwing it back at him, pointing out that he'd been the one avoiding a meeting. But this was too important to screw up with impulsiveness.

"And you're not even Americans," he added.

I grabbed for my purse, to locate my US passport. I'd show the arrogant ass.

Charlie put a hand on my arm and shook his head. "And how is that a problem?" he asked Califano.

The union head glanced at me for a second before turning his attention back to Charlie. "I'll deal with Edwin Hawker, but not you. I don't know you, and I don't trust you. Him, I know. It's as simple as that. I don't speak Limey, so tell me if you need that translated."

His lawyer chuckled under his breath.

Even sitting next to him, I could feel Charlie stiffen.

Charlie stood. "Then we have a problem."

Califano stayed seated. "I'd say *you* have the problem." He chuckled. "Why don't you see what the bosses back in jolly old England have to say about the prospect of a strike? Then give me a call when you've hired Edwin back for me to resolve our outstanding issues with. It's that simple."

"We're in charge, and we don't need to check with anyone." Charlie shifted away from the table. "Since you seem to doubt that, it's been nice meeting you gentlemen." He nodded at the other two, without offering to shake their hands.

None of them said anything.

I stood and followed Charlie when he headed for the door. We'd discussed ahead of time how being willing to walk away from a negotiation was a useful tactic. And clearly Charlie was done being insulted.

"I'll be waiting for that call," Califano yelled after us with a laugh.

"What was that about?" I asked as soon as the door closed behind us.

Charlie lifted his chin toward my car. "We should get on the road first."

It wasn't until we were back on the main road that I restarted the conversation. "I guess now we know the issue."

"Yeah. It's just like your situation with your turdball boyfriend."

"Ex," I corrected him. "And I don't see the similarity."

"They both have an odd, sudden obsession with a change that doesn't make any sense. With Turdball, it was wanting to get married instantly. With Califano, it's blowing up the contract extension and demanding we hire back bloody Junior to fix it. Neither of them makes any sense."

I nodded. "There must be an underlying motivation we don't understand."

"Which is?"

"The *we* part of 'we don't understand' means I don't have a clue either."

"Huh." He seemed surprised. Maybe he was surprised I'd admitted I wasn't superior to him in deciphering the union boss.

A minute later I considered another question. "Why Junior and not Senior? That doesn't make sense either." It shouldn't have taken me so long to catch the discontinuity. "Wroblewski said Senior had been the primary contact with them."

He shrugged. "Who knows."

We drove on, and eventually stopped for a fast-food lunch.

Eating hamburgers and fries, our discussion continued on the Califano riddle. Neither of us had any success coming up with a good answer.

We were sharing a basket of fries when Charlie's fingers touched mine as I reached for another. The shock of the contact jolted me once again—or rather, still. How had I lucked into a man that had this effect on me? And it lingered rather than falling away after the first encounter or two.

Every time with Charlie was like the first—not the first bad dinner, but the first good time, when we'd given in to the obvious attraction between us.

"Sorry," he said, pulling back.

Had he felt it too? Was this as special for him as it seemed to me?

A giggle escaped. "There's plenty, and if we run out, we can always get more."

He nodded. "True enough." He grabbed a fry, dipped the tip in ketchup, and lifted it to my mouth.

If this had been a romantic movie, I would've wrapped my lips around the end of the French fry, sucked the ketchup off, and licked my lips seductively. My actions would have communicated how our brief touch had affected me—and perhaps resulted in a quick trip to the secluded spot where we could act on our feelings.

But this wasn't a movie. I bit off the slice of potato and thanked him.

I wouldn't dare tell Andrina how I'd let this opportunity for seduction slip by.

"You okay?" he asked.

I blinked my eyes open. "Just thinking."

"About?" His eyes captured mine.

I was trapped, so I came up with the best lie I could. "Still trying to understand why Junior instead of Senior." But almost immediately, I came clean. He deserved the truth. "I was really thinking about us."

A wonderful smile grew on his face. "Me too." He *had* felt it. "I need to apologize for the way I acted before…when you first showed up, and also for my father."

I turned my hand over to hold his. "Not necessary." In that moment, something shifted in me. "It's okay." The feud our families had started years ago melted away into nothing. I knew in my heart that, in spite of my father's opinion, Charlie Blakewell was a man of his word, and one I could trust.

"Maybe not, but I want to tell you something anyway, because I'm not proud of it. He's been after me to—"

His phone rang before he could finish. It was Ron Wroblewski, checking in.

I only half listened as Charlie told him how badly the meeting had gone.

Instead, Charlie's lips captured my concentration as he spoke. Oh, what those lips could do to me.

"We tried that," Charlie said, clearly frustrated.

Nominally, we were in charge, but there wasn't any other way to look at today than that we'd failed the company by not making progress with Califano.

When he got off the call, I reached for his hand again. "We'll get it done next time."

His jaw clenched. "I should have been able to get to the bottom of it today."

"*We*. This is a team effort."

"Right. We." His face softened.

Looking across the table, as his thumb stroked my hand, I couldn't help feeling that the Charlie Blakewell I'd just shared a burger and fries with was a man I should have spent much more time with over the years. If not for our fathers, I could have.

"What do you know about how the feud started?" It had always nagged at me.

He shrugged. "Well, they don't like each other. We should get back on the road."

# CHAPTER 28

*DANIELLE*
*(one week later)*

AS CHARLIE CLOSED THE CONDO DOOR BEHIND US, MY MIND RETURNED TO A question I'd been pondering for several days now. Did spending two weeks straight at Charlie's condo constitute moving in with him?

If so, it hadn't been anywhere near as frightening as I'd thought. Probably the fact that Charlie had called it *protecting me* instead of *moving in* had changed the emotional equation for me. Two weeks of living with a man for the first time... Half a month, and I hadn't freaked out.

Being his CWB girl meant this was only temporary anyway, and I didn't need to sweat any long-term commitment issues. That had to be it. Another possibility came to mind: maybe Charlie was the difference.

ANYWAY, WAKING UP BESIDE HIM EACH MORNING MADE MY DAYS BRIGHTER. Sharing the bathroom and shower hadn't been the problem I'd always envisioned when thinking about cohabitating with a man. God, I hated that word, *cohabitating*. Instead of being a problem, having Charlie walking around naked every morning had been a treat. And then there was the way he soaped me up in the shower... My skin tingled.

"What are you smiling about?" Charlie asked as he pressed the down button for the elevator.

"Nothing." I looked down at my favorite heels. When he hadn't changed out of his suit as he usually did after work, I'd changed into a fresh dress and these shoes.

"Really? Nothing?"

A subject change was needed. "Where are we going?" I asked again as we waited for the elevator at our building. *Oops.* I didn't catch myself. I'd just thought of this as *our* building, instead of Charlie's building.

The doors opened, and we entered. All I'd gotten out of him earlier was that this was something we needed to do together.

He took my hand. "You're already forgetting tonight's rule." He'd told me earlier to do as I was told and stop questioning things.

I took his hand and silently squeezed my answer.

When we reached the front door, Carl, our doorman, held it open for us. There I went again, claiming this building as my home.

"Your carriage awaits." Charlie pointed to a beautiful horse-drawn carriage out front.

I gasped and pulled on his arm. "For us?"

"Only the best for you tonight."

"Only tonight?"

He swatted my ass lightly. "Stop being a brat. We're not at work."

I held back the argument, because he was spot on. I'd been overcompensating at work, being snarky with him to keep the gang from catching on to our relationship.

The driver climbed down as we reached the carriage and offered me a hand up.

"This is beautiful," I told him.

"Thank you, ma'am."

The carriage had gold trim over glossy white paint, red velvet seating, and bright red blankets for our legs.

Charlie stepped up after I did, and the driver urged the horse forward with a clucking sound. Charlie scooted over and drew me in close. "I told you you'd like it."

I shimmied over without arguing the point. "Just a hint about—"

Charlie put a finger to my lips and cut off the rest of my repeated question. "Patience."

I huffed, but held my tongue. Normally being persistent got me results, but not tonight.

He patted my shoulder. "It'll work out, now that you're my Cookie."

*Wait… what? How did he…* "You knew about that?" I'd kept that name to myself.

"Your brother told me."

*Oops, except for him.* "I'll make him pay." I couldn't believe John had done that. Actually, no. Back then it would have been totally in character for my dipshit brother.

Charlie smiled. "Cookie. I thought it was quite cute."

His use of the term sent a shiver through me, but it wasn't dread—more like delight. I hadn't heard that name since the year I'd turned sixteen. He'd been the one and only boy in my life that summer.

I'd wanted to be his Cookie, because he'd been nicknamed the Cookie Monster for the way he sprinted to the plate of cookies his mother served every afternoon. I'd wanted to be the one he ran to find.

But then we'd gone suddenly, and I hadn't seen him again until coming here to Boston.

I rolled my eyes, but couldn't help smiling. I was his Cookie, the one he would chase after, and that was all I needed to know. It made everything else fade away. I relaxed to the breeze on my face and the clomping of the horse's hooves on the pavement.

We wended our way slowly toward old downtown.

A couple in a Mercedes stopped next to us at an intersection. The woman in the passenger seat looked up with an expression that I interpreted as jealousy.

Her lips moved with a question as she looked up at me. I couldn't hear her words behind the glass, but it looked like, *"Why haven't we ever done that?"*

The light turned green, and they pulled away. I'd never know what the driver's answer was.

We might be going slower, but this was definitely more stylish than driving. However, my attempt to get our driver to reveal our destination didn't get any further than asking Charlie had.

"I don't see how this can have to do with work," I told Charlie.

His smirk didn't waiver. "You'll understand when we get there."

The wait was only another few minutes before we stopped in front of Holmby's.

Charlie grinned when I looked over. "I promised to wine-and-dine you."

"I would have settled for pizza." I actually *had* settled for pizza several times when we'd stayed late at the office. If we made it home at a normal hour, dinner had been whatever he'd ordered for us from one of the many local restaurants that delivered. They had all been delicious.

Thinking back, we'd eaten lunches out together, but not a dinner. I'd thought takeout every night might get boring, but the variety—and not having to cook or clean up—had made up for it.

The hostess escorted us to the same booth where I'd found Charlie that first evening before the Hawker purchase.

He slid in across from me. "I promised to wine-and-dine you, and I thought a do-over of our first dinner would be appropriate since I was such an ass."

"You weren't that bad." He'd mellowed a lot since then, or it was the deal-making Charlie that was the hard-edged man, and since he'd opened up to me, I'd learned the man behind the mask?

He glared at me. "What happened to honesty?"

I shrugged. "Okay, you were that bad. You can make up for it by being nice to the waitstaff for a change."

He didn't acknowledge the comment.

Leo, the same waiter as that first night, arrived. "Good evening, Mr. Blakewell, Miss. What may I start you off with?"

My shoulders slumped. He remembered Charlie. That's how bad an impression we'd made."

"This evening, I think the Cardinelli Cellars cabernet," Charlie began. "And Leo, I'd like to apologize for my behavior the last time we were in."

Leo's smile never wavered. "No need, sir." He turned to me. "Miss?"

"The same." Any wine sounded good with Charlie across from me.

"Thank you, Leo," Charlie said before the waiter departed.

"That wasn't so hard, now was it?" I asked.

Charlie shrugged. "You heard him. I hadn't hurt his feelings."

I sipped my water before throwing it back at him. "What he actually said last time was that you tipped well and that made up for it."

He grinned. "And I do... Tip well, that is."

"Money is nice, but I think he'd also like to have an enjoyable workday. I'm sure his wife would as well."

"And you're sure he's married?"

I tapped my ring finger. "You should pay better attention to the details that tell you the backstory."

He nodded. "I guess that's true. So maybe now you'll tell me what's behind your tattoo."

*Ahh…* He'd noticed my reluctance that first morning in the shower after all. He'd dropped it after a second question the next day—until now.

There was no getting out of this, and the memory of the hooves that night sent a shiver down my spine. "It's a reminder to be strong. There was a time I was afraid of a horse, and like the tattoo, that's now behind me."

"Horses are more afraid of you than you are of them." His eyes betrayed him. He didn't remember what had happened with his family's stallion, Napoleon, all those years ago.

I shrugged to change the subject. "It just reminds me that fear is in my past."

"A good motto," he agreed.

"And it needs to stay that way," I added.

Leo arrived with our wine and took our dinner orders.

I replicated my order from that first night with swordfish, and Charlie did as well, asking for the same steak.

Before leaving, Leo double-checked that Charlie wanted it medium rare tonight.

"Enough about the past," I said as the waiter retreated. "Tell me what Charlie Blakewell hopes is in his future." We had discussed Hawker incessantly, but whenever I'd ventured into more general realms, Charlie always brought the conversation back to our present work situation.

"That my steak is as good as last time." He chuckled.

"I swear, if you send it back, I'm going to kick you so hard—"

He held up his hand to stop me. "I've already promised to behave."

"Good enough." I sipped my wine, waiting for an answer that didn't seem to be coming. "You were going to tell me about what you see in your future. What have you been working toward?"

He twisted his wine glass. "I don't want to jinx it."

"Jinx what?"

"I've had my sights set for a while on a position in our Berlin office."

"What kind of position?" I knew the Blakewell Berlin operation was a large one, but it seemed like many of the positions there would be a step down from what we were doing at Hawker.

"Running it," he clarified. "All by myself."

They shouldn't have, but the words stung.

"I'm sorry," he said quickly. "I didn't mean that I don't like being here with you."

"Of course." I tried to recover the situation. "I wouldn't expect you to aspire to being co-CEO."

He gave the slightest nod, and his lips turned up in acknowledgment.

"And that sounds like a tremendous opportunity," I continued. "Isn't Berlin about three times the size of Hawker here?"

"Yup, and far enough from London to be..." He didn't finish his thought.

"Far enough to be out from under your father's thumb," I finished for him.

He grinned. "A sentiment I'm better off keeping to myself."

I reached across to him. "Your secret is safe with me."

As he took my hand, his eyes conveyed what he didn't say. His gentle touch and the knowledge that I had his trust warmed me all the way through.

"Do you regret taking Hawker on? I mean, it messes up your Berlin plans."

His thumb started gentle strokes of my hand. "No. I'm sure I'll be able to get there expeditiously."

I'd be doing the same, heading to Paris, if I still could. But eighteen months was a long way off.

"In the meantime, I have to get him to back off a bit."

"I have pretty much the same problem with my father," I admitted.

His eyebrows arched as his thumb traced lazy circles on my hand.

Leo interrupted us with our salads, and I pulled my hand back.

I continued after the waiter left. "My daddy wanted me to call him every day about what we're doing here."

Charlie's eyes narrowed.

"But I told him up front I was only updating him every two weeks."

"Good for you."

"It was John's idea." I lifted a forkful of salad to my mouth.

He nodded. "I wish I'd done that."

"Is your dad bugging you?"

"Not every day, but he's persistent about some things."

I sipped my wine before my curiosity got the better of me. "And what do you tell him about our...uh...situation?"

Charlie looked at me over his wine glass with a wicked smile. "I tell him you're the consummate professional and a joy to work with—the perfect co-CEO."

I could tell he knew that wasn't my real question. "And?"

"And that's all. Nothing else about us."

"Are you ashamed to be...?" I had to choose the right word. We'd spent plenty of naked time together, but this was our first actual date—if that was even the right term for this. "You know, hanging out with me?" *Dating* didn't sound right.

He reached across the table.

I accepted his hand.

"Not at all. I've just never confided anything about my personal life to him." He squeezed my hand reassuringly.

In his eyes, I could see the truth. I didn't embarrass him. Actually, I'd been the one who'd asked that we keep our relationship secret. And if that included work, why wouldn't it also include his father?

"Does your family know?" he asked.

"God, no." I wasn't looking forward to the teasing I'd get from John when he found out. And if the feud was only on pause instead of really over, I had no idea how Daddy would react.

"Because of the situation between our fathers?" Charlie asked after a mouthful of salad.

I nodded. "The feud might be over now, but I can't tell for sure. Not knowing what triggered it in the first place makes it hard to tell."

"True, but it doesn't matter." Charlie pointed a finger my way. "Tell me about your time at university."

He'd steered the conversation away from the uncomfortable topic of our families. I smiled, and he returned it. As the meal wore on, every smile he sent my way felt better than the last.

I teased him, and he teased back—in the way I'd seen Alicia and my father act on occasion. This was playful banter I couldn't remember having traded with Gerald or any of the other men I'd dated.

We shared stories of our experiences and adventures. Each story he told had me engrossed and made me realize how wrong I'd been about him that first night here, and how much more of him I saw now.

Even our evenings at his condo had been packed with work-related discussions. Mostly I'd been exposed to the competent, driven businessman, obsessed with accomplishing everything he could to impress his father.

And our times in bed had been so filled with moans of ecstasy that we hadn't slowed down for this kind of casual conversation.

"He was my favorite."

"Who?" I'd totally spaced out and lost track of the conversation.

"Napoleon."

The stallion's name made me cringe, and that night came back to me. The stomping hooves, the incredibly loud snorting, being backed into the corner

—all of it. I clamped my eyes shut and began my breathing. *In, out, in, out. It wasn't real.*

There were no horses here.

～

CHARLES

SHE TURNED ASHEN AND SEEMED ABOUT TO PASS OUT AT MY MENTION OF Napoleon.

"What's wrong?" I asked. I reached over to push her glass closer. "Drink some water."

Her eyes blinked open, but her breathing was deep and labored. "Horses scare me."

I lifted out of my seat and moved around to her side of the booth. In a second, I had my arm around her.

She was shaking.

I pulled her tighter. "You're safe. You're safe here."

"I'm sorry." She sobbed. "It just got to me." She dabbed at her eyes. "It's over. I'm okay now."

"Horses?" I asked.

She nodded.

"That and windows?"

She giggled. "Yeah. Silly, huh? John says I need to face them head on." She picked up the water I'd suggested earlier and took a big gulp.

"You're not going to believe this, but I agree with him for once. You can't let fear rule you. It can be conquered. It can be beaten."

"I know that. It's why I have the tattoo. But every once in a while..."

I rubbed her shoulder. "I'll help you, if you'll let me." I turned her chin my direction. "I conquered my fear, and you can too."

She relaxed under my arm. "What are you afraid of?"

"Was," I corrected her. "And it was flying. It got so bad I wouldn't get on anything except 747s and the like—you know, four engines and all. I was scared of what would happen if an engine quit."

She laid a hand on my thigh. "You know, millions of people fly every day. It's the safest form of transportation."

I shrugged. "That's the rational argument, but fear doesn't reside in the rational part of the brain. I had to confront it where it lives—in the lizard brain."

"How did you manage that?"

The busboy arrived to remove our dinner dishes, and Leo was right behind him. "Would you like something from the dessert menu this evening?"

I looked to Dani, leaving the decision in her hands.

"Dessert sounds good," she answered.

I finished the last of my wine and returned to my side of the booth.

"So? Fear of flying?" she prompted.

"It was my brother, Ethan, who got me over it. It was our mother's birthday, and we were coming home from up north, Manchester, for her party. Ethan got us a taxi to the train station, but the joke ended up being on me."

She sipped her water, waiting.

"Instead of Piccadilly Station, he took me to the airport. He'd chartered a plane to get us home. If it had been anything other than Mother's birthday, I would have refused to board."

"And that was all it took?"

Leo brought the dessert menus.

I sent him away with a request for some time to consider. "There was more to it than that," I continued. "He made me sit up with the pilot."

"Made you?"

"We'd missed the train. He'd taken my mobile and sent the taxi away. I was stuck, and it was that or miss Mother's birthday."

Dani smiled that infectious smile of hers. "I'm glad that got you over it."

"There's more. After liftoff, there was an intervention. I was about ready to pee my pants when Ethan stood behind me and announced that we weren't going to land until I turned off one of the engines and proved we could still fly."

"And the pilot was okay with that?"

"He was in on it, apparently. He explained which lever to pull, and they both just waited for me to do it."

Her mouth dropped open. "Did you?"

"No fucking way. But the pilot did, and after a period of hyperventilating, I realized he'd proved to me that we could fly just fine on one engine. Then, for good measure, he got it going again and made me shut it off myself. We flew the rest of the trip that way and made it to Mother's party."

"You call that confronting your lizard brain?"

I nodded. "You can't talk to the lizard brain; you have to show it."

She cocked her head. "I never would have guessed you have a fear of flying."

"Had," I corrected her. "Past tense. And the same can be true for you. We can get you past your fears once and for all."

Leo returned after a moment, and I was ready. "I'm thinking the chocolate lava cake tonight."

He turned to Dani. "And for you Miss Abigail?"

My stomach twisted.

Her mouth dropped open for a second before she recovered. Instead of answering Leo, she turned to me. "Abigail? As in Abby?"

After a hefty slug of water, I answered. "It's not what you think."

"Sure." That was the only word she said, but her meaning was clear.

Leo waited patiently.

"Nothing," Dani told him. "I think we're done." She squinted pure loathing at me, stood, and walked away.

I threw cash on the table and chased after her.

# CHAPTER 29

*Charles*

I reached her at the curb. "It was—"

She looked up from her mobile. "I asked you that first day what was going on between you and her," she reminded me. "And your words were..." She added air quotes. "'Nothing at all'."

"But—"

"But nothing," she snapped. "You lied to me."

"It's not that simple," I repeated. "I was negotiating to buy the company."

"Deny you lied to me about going out with her."

I shifted my feet without a good answer to that. "I guess, but I didn't mean it that way. There were people around in the office when you asked. *She* was there." It hadn't seemed a big deal at the time, and the truce between Dani and me had been fragile back then.

"She was not. She'd already slipped into Junior's office to console him or whatever. And how far did it go?" She huffed. "Never mind."

"Dinner only, I swear. Nothing happened. I was just learning about the company."

"Using her, then? Like the jerk you are."

I didn't have a good response to that. I had used Abby to learn what I could about the Hawker family.

She scanned the street and then looked back to me. "How many times? A dozen, two?"

"Five, I think."

"You think?"

"Nothing happened. I'm not interested in her and never was. Hell, you know that. You have to."

She checked the screen of her mobile and waved at a Prius coming our way.

"Look, deals require information," I blurted.

Silence was my punishment.

There was nothing left to say. In her book, I'd misled her.

"This is my car," she said when the green vehicle stopped.

"*Our* car," I corrected her. Letting her be alone to stew wasn't a wise move right now.

She shrugged. "Whatever."

She thanked me for opening the car door for her, but other than that, she looked out the window on the entire Uber ride back to my condo.

"Aren't you going to say anything?" I asked as I stepped out.

She shook her head. "Seems to me we've already said enough."

I waved her ahead toward the door Carl held open for us.

Upstairs, I held the door to the condo for her as I always did.

She walked in.

I followed into the chill.

When the door closed, I couldn't hold it in any longer. "I said I was sorry."

"You didn't tell me the truth." Her mouth was a hard, thin line.

"I told you you could trust me, and you didn't."

"I flat-out asked you about her. And you didn't tell me."

"I didn't lie."

"That's not the same thing."

"Yes, it is. And what else haven't you told me?"

"Nothing. Nothing at all."

We were still where we'd started. I hadn't told her when she'd asked, and to her that was the same as lying. I didn't agree, but one of us had to give in if we were going to get past this.

I gathered up different words to apologize again for the misunderstanding.

Then she set her purse on the table and turned back to me. "You're right. I was wrong. You didn't lie, and I should have trusted you."

Surprised, I shelved my apology words for another time. "Damned straight."

She moved to me and straightened my tie. "And, I do...trust you, that is. You'll be happy to know Abby's found another man. At least I think she has."

"Not another," I corrected her. "She never had me."

"Okay, not another. She has a man in her life." She placed a hand on my chest and looked up with soft eyes. "I don't want to fight."

I swiped a tendril of hair behind her ear. "Me neither. Tonight was supposed to be special."

"It still can be. Let me make it up to you." She reached for my belt and knelt down before I realized what she meant.

I pulled her back up. "You're forgetting tonight's rules. You're not in charge."

~

## Danielle

I'D GONE DOWN ON MY KNEES IN AN EFFORT TO HALT THE FIGHT. SOMETHING about this man made me go to extreme lengths to push his buttons, and this evening it had gotten totally out of control. Hell, it was like he'd said—if I thought hard enough about it, I knew I was his girl, not Abby.

And anyway, she had someone else—a man she'd obviously been seeing at lunch. Charlie was all mine, and I wanted it to stay that way.

He stepped back. "Not like that."

I wasn't about to give up. If make-up sex could heal the rift, I was all in. "You told me I'd beg you to...you know..." I could bring myself to say *eat me out* or *go down on me*. I settled for his terminology. "...give me a tongue-lashing." I added my most coy smile.

He cocked his head. "You're begging?"

I'd been the one to ruin the mood tonight, and I couldn't bear to have it end like that. I nodded.

"Turn around." His command was stern. He took my hips and pulled me back against his hard arousal. He leaned over to whisper in my ear. "I've told you before, I always go all in. If we start this, I'm not stopping until you come for me."

I sucked in a breath of courage and twisted around to face him. "Please." I wrapped my arms around his neck and pulled myself up into a kiss to seal it.

He growled into my mouth as his hands found my ass and lifted me up off the ground.

Wrapping my legs around him, I deepened the kiss as my tongue fought for position with his. My sex clenched, and I shivered with anticipation. The magazines said most women enjoyed this. Why should I be any different?

Charlie found the zipper of my dress as he carried me to the kitchen, and I released the lip-lock I had on him to pull at his buttons.

Once he set me down, we began yanking at each other's clothes.

"No. Lose the knickers, but keep those on," he said as I leaned over to unstrap my heels.

Obeying, I slipped my panties down and stepped out of them.

He'd already pulled my bra loose. Bra-hook unfastening seemed to be his thing.

I slid my clothes to the side and helped him with his cufflinks, which were somehow a lot easier to put in than take out. After a few hops to avoid falling over, he'd pulled his legs free of his trousers, and we were down to heels for me and boxer briefs for him.

I reached for his waistband.

He caught my hand. "You first."

"Can we turn off the lights?" I asked, suddenly self-conscious.

He went over to the control and dialed them down, but not off. "You're too beautiful to have them all the way off."

I yelped as he lifted me up onto the island, the same as our first time. The moment of truth had arrived. I clamped my legs together, but it couldn't last.

He pulled at my knees, opening me to him.

I was scared. I hadn't showered since this morning. The TV was full of commercials for products that helped one smell or feel fresher. I didn't use any of them. What if I disgusted him? How horrible would that be?

Neither Gerald, nor Frank before him, had shown any interest in going down on me. What if that was because of how I smelled?

Charlie's smile stretched ear to ear as his eyes devoured me.

It was now or never. "Are you sure?"

The granite was cold, but it was no match for the heat his eyes sparked in me.

"You're beautiful, Cookie, and your pussy is gorgeous."

The words relaxed me.

"Lean back."

I rested on my elbows and closed my eyes as his stubble scraped my skin and he kissed his way up the inside of my thigh.

I spread my legs wider and pulled my knees up, opening myself fully to him.

He blew on my wet lower lips and ran a finger up one edge and down the other, avoiding my most sensitive flesh—teasing, tracing with just a featherlight touch.

Then his tongue delved the length of my folds, reaching my clit and circling the engorged bud. His stubble again scratched against my thighs as he moved. Every breath on me, every slide of his tongue over my sensitive tissues lit sparks that traveled to my core in a way I hadn't imagined.

I wasn't prepared for the sensations as he started his oral sorcery. I hadn't understood how good this could be. Now, I didn't push him away. Instead I speared fingers in his hair and pulled at him for even more.

He lifted up. "You taste fucking fantastic."

So much for grossing him out.

He surprised me as a finger entered and found the sensitive spot deep inside that he'd showed me before. The touch sent my back arching, and I couldn't control the moans as he massaged my G-spot.

He withdrew his finger as quickly as he'd added it, and his tongue resumed its work. He lifted his hand to my face and pressed the finger to my nose.

My aroma filled my nostrils.

He looked up and moved the fingertip on my lips.

I took it in, licking and sucking my wetness off. This unexpected detour took my desire up another notch.

Gripping his hair tighter, I spread wider for more access and rocked my hips into his face. My breaths became short, shallow pants as the sensations became unbearable. Little gasps and yelps I couldn't control were my only communication. With no notice, my toes curled and the brilliant fire of my orgasm overtook me. The spasms rocked me as I pulled his head close. I couldn't contain my screams.

In time, I released my death grip on him, and the post-O relaxation came. "That was fucking incredible," I managed. Why had I put this off for so long? I was ashamed I'd been so stupid.

As my legs fell away, he kissed his way up to my breasts and then my mouth. The taste was me, mingled with him.

He pulled back, and his nose touched mine. "I told you. Nothing to be afraid of."

I nodded. "I was afraid you'd…" It felt too silly to put to words now, so I didn't finish the sentence.

"I told you, you're beautiful all over."

"Thank you," I sighed. "Now, let me up." My butt was sore from the hard stone. "The bed is softer."

He did, and I slid off the island onto unsteady legs.

Seeing my wobble, he lifted me.

I folded my arms around his neck and wondered how I'd gotten so lucky.

He carried me to the bedroom and set me down on the mattress that felt like a cloud after the cold stone of the kitchen.

I lay back and spread my legs. "I think I'm wet enough for you to fuck me properly." My pussy still throbbed from what he'd done. I'd had no idea how his tongue on me could amp up my desire for more of him.

The dirty talk drew out the animal in his eyes the way I'd learned it would.

"You do, do you?" He opened the nightstand drawer and retrieved a condom.

Tonight was a night for firsts. I held out my hand. "Let me."

He tore a side off the packet before handing it over, then pulled off his boxer briefs to let loose the beautiful monster I craved.

Sliding my legs over the side, I sat up and unrolled the latex over his length as he stood in front of me. His breath hitched as I rolled it down, a fraction of an inch at a time.

His hands moved to my breasts and pulled them up and together. "I love these."

That wasn't hard to tell. He'd made a point of thoroughly washing my boobs every morning in the shower.

I rolled the condom down another inch. "I love how hard you are." Moving a hand down to cup his balls, I added, "And these."

His breath hitched again when I caressed them, then playfully pulled on the sac.

"Careful there."

"We could try the shaving kit from the new products team," I suggested, stifling a laugh. "It would make it easier for me to lick."

He yanked on a few of my lower curls. "You're not shaved."

In revenge, I plucked out one of his ball hairs.

"Ouch."

I pulled another short gasp out of him by rolling the condom down farther with two hands. I now knew a trick to get a reaction he couldn't control. "And will you shave if I do?"

"If you wax."

"How about I shave? It's easier." What I meant was less painful.

"Full Brazilian."

"Deal." I knew neither of us was serious.

He reached down to help me roll the protection. "You're taking too long."

I swatted his hand away. "My job tonight." My slowness hadn't lessened his enthusiasm. My man was both big and rock hard.

The words rattled around in my head for a moment—*my man*. They felt good. They felt natural.

"Shaving?" I asked again.

"It would be so hot if you would. I'm going to be thinking about that all night."

He hadn't answered my question, which made his response clear. Real men didn't eat quiche, and they certainly didn't shave their balls. Full stop, as he would say.

So much for that fantasy.

He fondled my breasts again, and I finished my job quickly. The expert way he played with my nipples did it for me.

But thinking back, that was also new. Maybe it had to do with the man as much as the technique. I rubbed my hands down his latex-covered length one more time before I scooted back on the bed to make room for him.

"On your knees."

I grabbed a pillow for my head, pulled my knees under me, and poked my ass in the air. My pussy pounded with the pulse of my anticipation as he climbed up behind me and rubbed his crown up and down my slit a few times.

"I'm wet enough," I reminded him. What I really meant was I didn't want to wait one second longer. I needed him inside me, filling me at this moment, maybe more than his cock longed for release.

He urged me to widen my stance, and I shifted my knees apart. In a moment he pushed inside me, filling me to the limit. This position was so deep, yet so fulfilling.

"My God, you're wet," he said as he continued pushing in. "You're so fucking tight, so fucking good," he hissed as he thrust. "You have no idea what you do to me."

Drowning in my own sea of desire, I wanted him to feel good, great—even better than great. The orgasm he'd given me earlier had been so unbelievable, I wanted to repay him any way I could. As he speared me, I matched his rhythm, rocking back against him. His balls swung forward against me with each powerful thrust.

I reached back between my legs to tickle them as they moved. Listening for the telltale noises, I caught his tiny gasps as I did. Now I had something to add to my repertoire.

He slapped my ass. "Careful," he reminded me between grunts. I'd pulled a little too forcefully. He stopped and pushed my legs together, removing my hand and putting his knees outside of mine.

Pushing my knees together only increased the friction. I thought his incredible tongue work had emptied my pleasure reservoir, but I was wrong. He was so far inside me, and filled me so completely, that each thrust moved me to a higher plane of ecstasy. As the tension inside me built again, I approached the cliff of my release.

His firm grip on my hips pulled me against him with each slap of flesh against flesh as he pounded into me. My toes curled, and he moved a hand to my breast, pinching my nipple. Like a rubber band that had been pulled too far, I snapped, and our orgasms collided as I felt him stiffen and empty inside me with a trembling push. I screamed into the pillow as my inner flesh convulsed around him. He held me back against him, buried as deep as he could go while the throbbing of his cock subsided.

We fell forward, and he spared me the bulk of his weight by shifting off to the side. The occasional throb of his cock deep inside me added satisfaction to what had been a wonderful evening.

After a few minutes of cuddling, stroking my hair, and kissing me, my man went to the bathroom to dispose of the condom.

I'd done it again, thinking of him as my man. When had that changed, and how? But whether my CWB boy toy, or my man, he was mine, and I wasn't letting go.

He returned to bed, and I draped my arm over his chest. Using his shoulder as a pillow, I pressed my breasts up against his warmth, and our hearts beat as one.

I traced circles around his belly button as I looked for the right words. "Thank you."

"For what?" he asked.

I wasn't sure exactly how to answer. For the incredible sex lesson? That wasn't complete enough for how I felt. "For being you."

"You should remember you can trust me."

Without knowing what he meant, "I do," was my answer. If he was referring to the incredible sex lesson, I could've added some banter, but I didn't want to chance that we would return to the dinner argument about Abby, so I didn't.

"Good." He pulled me closer and kissed the top of my head.

## CHAPTER 30

*CHARLES*
*(two weeks later)*

IT HAD BEEN TWO WEEKS SINCE OUR DINNER DATE AND ARGUMENT. I'D WORRIED that the dust-up over me not telling her about Abby might fester and come back as an issue—but it hadn't.

Behind my desk at the office, I again perused the letter Dad had sent a week ago. As he'd said, it was a formal offer to take the Berlin job. Before coming here, I would have accepted in a heartbeat, but now things were different—Dani had changed everything.

Dad had continued to push me toward Berlin, and I'd continued to put him off, but he was as stubborn as they came.

I had to figure out a way to put the Berlin issue to bed without creating a rift between us. Dani and I needed his support going forward, not a fight. I needed an alternative he'd embrace.

My mobile rang, and the screen finally showed the name I'd been waiting for—Ben Murdoch.

"Mr. Blakewell, we have some news," he said. "It's related to your tail."

Dani had gone to the ladies' room. I got up and went to the door. "Great, Ben. Hold on a second."

I made my way to the conference room and closed the door before speaking again. "What do we know?"

"Does the name Phillip Caldwell of Goldwin Investigations mean anything to you?"

It didn't take me long to answer with conviction. "No. Not the name or the company. How'd you get that?"

"Being a PI in this state requires a license, and I have friends with the state police. Once we knew who employed him, it was easy to match the photo to a license."

Amazing. This was one of those times it was more important *who* you knew than what you knew. But just having a name didn't answer the real question. Caldwell wasn't doing this for fun. Somebody was paying the bills, and the man pulling the strings was the one we had to track down.

Ben cleared his throat. "The next step is going to be trickier. I assume you want to know who's hired them?"

"Of course." It was more than idle curiosity. These guys had fucked with the wrong Brit.

"It's going to take a lot of manpower," Ben said. "Both to figure that out, and for your protection."

"I don't need any."

"I wouldn't be so sure about that, but even so, it will still take resources."

I'd expected we'd get to this at some point. I could only go so far in borrowing Ben and his team from the Covington company. "I'll underwrite whatever the expense is." I took a guess. "Do you recommend hiring this out, or do you have people looking for some overtime pay?"

He laughed. "Finding volunteers won't be a problem. I can put as many people on it as your checkbook can handle."

I'd guessed correctly. Money would speed the process. "I need to know who's behind this, so let's get started. What do we do first?"

*Need* wasn't too strong a word for how I felt about it. This situation had progressed from a mild irritant to something more dark. It hadn't been limited to the negotiation, so whoever was behind it had a bigger agenda. Not understanding that agenda made it dangerous.

"*You* don't do anything," Ben said. "I'll handle it, and you don't need to know the details."

His implication was clear. I'd be safer not knowing how he did his job—a bit like sausage making.

"And this firm—"

I cut him off. "What about that other issue?" Turdball was also a high priority. I still wanted to keep tabs on him in case he came back around.

"I'm still working that one. What do you know about his trips to Monte Carlo?"

That question was a surprise. "Nothing."

Ben explained the little he'd found so far about Gerald Durban's employment and travel. "You'll be happy to hear he's not in the States right now. That much I know for sure. I'll have more on his whereabouts later, and we're putting together a timeline of his movements."

"Good."

"Getting back to Goldwin," he said. "That firm usually handles more than simple surveillance."

"I don't understand."

"The scuttlebutt around town is, if you want to apply pressure, they're the people to see."

"What kind of pressure?"

"The kind that made me suggest protection for you and the lady."

That sent a chill through me. Ben thought we were in danger. More importantly, he thought Dani was in danger. I could handle myself, but someone after Dani was another matter.

"I have training."

"What kind?" He wasn't letting me off easy.

"Military. Her Majesty's finest." I wasn't allowed to be more specific. I shouldn't even have told Dani as much as I had.

"And the lady?"

"No."

He sighed. "It's your call, but I'd send her out of town for a while—until we find the man who's paying the bills and neutralize the threat. That's also something you don't want to be a part of. In the meantime, I suggest you get her somewhere safe."

I didn't care for his terminology. "Neutralize?"

"If we find Mr. Big, whoever that is, I can have the kind of talk with him that will get him to back off."

That last part I liked. Ben would take scary to a level the other guy couldn't tolerate. "Nothing illegal, though."

"These kinds of people only operate in the shadows. Since the Covingtons own a local TV station, I can enlighten him as to the consequences of continuing with you and the lady. He won't do anything with the prospect of a spotlight shining on him."

"Keep me up to date."

"I will."

After we rang off, I went back to the office and reviewed Dad's Berlin offer one more time. I didn't have long to consider how to approach it before Dani returned.

"You look concerned," she noted.

I slid the paper into my desk drawer and pivoted the conversation. "I got a call from Ben."

She closed our office door and walked to her desk. "The security guy?"

"Yeah. He tracked Thin Man back to his…to where he works."

She sat. "Okay."

"It's a surveillance firm of sorts."

"So he really was following you."

"It's worse than that. He works for a firm Ben considers dangerous."

She looked away and typed on her keyboard. "He's paid to be paranoid."

There wasn't any way to deal with it except straight on. "He thinks you should leave town for a while. You could check in on your brother."

Her head jerked away from the screen. "That's nuts. He was following you, not me."

"We don't know that for sure."

"And I'm the little woman, so I should go away and hide?" she yelled, too loudly for my taste. "For how long? And why not you instead of me?"

I sighed. This was going about the way I'd guessed it might. "I've got military—"

"Right," she scoffed. "The vaunted SAS training that they don't give to civilians, and you can't admit to or you'd have to kill me."

I nodded slightly, which was more acknowledgment than the Official Secrets Act allowed.

She pointed a finger at me. "Let me say this clearly. No fucking way am I bugging out because you and your buddy are paranoid." She got up to leave and reached the door in a few quick strides.

"Ben thinks it's prudent," I said as she reached for the door handle. It was my last try.

"You should have told him where to stick it." Her shutting of the door behind her was just short of a slam, and made her point.

I wouldn't be passing her exact words on to Ben.

# THE RIVALS

## Danielle

Out the door, I turned left toward the break room and the coffee machines. I hadn't grabbed my mug, so a paper cup would have to do—anything to get out of that room and away from that insulting conversation.

I should turn tail and run? And for what? Because I was the little woman and Charlie was afraid of whoever Thin Man was? The sexist crap stank to high heaven.

I fed the machine a paper cup and punched up an extra shot. While it worked on the brew, I slid over to the candy machine. Behind the glass I spied what looked like the perfect treat to take my mind off of stupid Charlie and Ben: a package of Twinkies.

I took up residence at one of the tables with my sugary treat and my cup of java.

Abby arrived while I was still unwrapping the pastry. She pulled out the chair opposite me. "Want some company?"

I motioned toward the chair. "Be my guest."

"Want to talk about it?"

I shrugged. I probably shouldn't have yelled at Charlie. Or I should've known our office door wasn't as soundproof as it should be. My outburst wasn't great for the united front we were supposed to be showing the employees, and discussing the issues between us wouldn't be the smartest thing to do with Abby.

She pointed at my cellophane-wrapped comfort food. "Whenever I have a bad day, I pull something sweet out of the machine."

I nodded. "Yeah."

"Is it the union again?" Her question let me off the hook.

"Califano is an ass," I snapped. Luckily there wasn't anybody else in the room to hear me bad-mouth the union man. Having it get back to him would only complicate matters.

"That's not exactly news to anyone. So what was the outcome?"

"The long story? Or the short?"

She shrugged. "You're the one doing the talking."

That summed up her purpose here. She thought getting me to open up and talk about my problems would help.

It's what I would've done with a friend who was having trouble, and I appreciated her concern, and her ear.

"He's being obstinate," I started. "He wants to have Junior, sorry, Edwin involved, which doesn't make any sense. But nothing he's doing makes any sense. The contract was ready to go before the purchase negotiations started, and I can't see anything that's changed."

She eyed the sweet treat in front of me.

I pushed it forward. "Want some?"

She shook her head. "No. It seems like you need it."

I took a sip from my cup. "We've already agreed to additional changes they want to make, and somehow it's still not enough."

"Is that what the yelling was about?"

I gave in and took a bite of the first Twinkie, partly to have time to figure out how much I should say. The room was still just us two, so I decided to let my frustrations out.

Who better to vent to than Abby? She could see what Charlie was like.

"He had the audacity to suggest I should leave for a while."

"The company?"

"The country, if you can believe that."

"Why?" she asked. Her eyes lingered on the uneaten Twinkie again.

I took another bite of the soft temptation I held. *Why indeed*. Because he was a chauvinist pig? That wouldn't be good to say.

Because he cared about me? I definitely couldn't say that, and why had I even thought it? He didn't care enough to give me the credit to make my own decisions. *You should do this; you should do that*. It hadn't changed one bit since we started.

I swallowed. "He thinks I'm in danger."

"The apartment?"

I nodded. Going into detail about any more wouldn't be good. "He wants to protect me."

"Guys do that a lot. Hero to the rescue and all," she said before finally taking a bite.

I nodded. *Hero*. Charlie had been that after the apartment was trashed at the hands of my stupid ex, and I hadn't imagined that one. But being followed was passive, even if it was real.

Her phone vibrated on the table. She turned it over and stood quickly after glancing at the message. "I have to go."

The way she'd smiled when she read the message made me again want to ask about the man in her life, but she was already halfway to the door.

I savored the final bite of my treat before picking up my phone.

Abby was gone, and so was Charlie, so it was the perfect time to return Andrina's message. I considered calling, but decided Mena should be involved as well.

ME: Just had a fight with Charlie

Was it really an argument?
It only took a few minutes for the responses to come back

MENA: ??
  ANDRINA: Good for you

MENA: Not good

I agreed with Mena. I didn't see how it could be good either.

ME: How can you say that?

ANDRINA: Can't have make-up sex without something to make up over

It made perfect sense in an Andrina way, but this was different. We hadn't argued about something inconsequential.

ME: This is important

MENA: What happened?

Good question. What had happened? I took a few seconds to compose my thoughts.

ANDRINA: Inquiring minds want to know

Her interruption didn't help me concentrate. I gave them the simple answer.

ME: He wants to send me away

MENA: Why?

ANDRINA: That's not what I was expecting

MENA: Did you have a fight?

Why *did* he want to? Mena's question hit the heart of the issue. I'd reacted because he'd said he wanted me to leave, not to the reason he'd said it.

ME: He thinks we're being followed

MENA: Thinks or knows?

Another employee came in.
I gave a simple wave and kept up my texting.

ME: It doesn't matter - he thinks they're dangerous and wants me to leave

ANDRINA: That's sweet

ME: No, its controlling and he can't just tell me what to do

MENA: Did you agree already?

ME: No way

ANDRINA: That's so sweet that he wants to keep you safe

MENA: You should tell him how you feel

I didn't like that suggestion. Right now it would turn into a yelling match for sure.

MENA: He can't make you can he?

ME: No he can't

ANDRINA: What are you going to do?

I'd answered Mena's question, because I knew the answer, but I didn't know what to say to Andrina's, or what she was implying.

MENA: I say you make him apologize

ANDRINA: Then let the make-up sex begin

MENA: But apologize first

ANDRINA: Of course then make-up sex and bareback

I snickered at Andrina's one-track mind.
Looking up, I found Charlie leaning against the doorframe, watching me.
"Am I interrupting?" he asked as he entered.
I put my phone face down on the table. "Of course not," I mumbled. My phone vibrated with a message and then another.
With a glance at the device he asked, "Can we talk?"
I ignored another buzz from the phone and crossed my arms. "Sure."
He cocked his head toward the office. "Privately."
With a sigh, I followed him and chanced a glance at my phone's screen.

ANDRINA: Waiting. . .

MENA: She's not going to answer us

ANDRINA: Guess not

I only had time to type a short reply.

ME: Later

What was I going to do? I would certainly start by telling him he couldn't order me around, and I wasn't going anywhere.
Abby wasn't at her desk when we passed.
I shut the office door behind us.
Charlie turned and stood dead center in the room with his arms crossed.
If he wanted a battle, I was ready.

## CHAPTER 31

**CHARLES**

I STARTED SLOWLY. "WE SHOULD TALK ABOUT THIS LOGICALLY."

When she crossed her arms, still just inside the office door, her posture said it all. "And you're implying I can't be logical about it?"

This was going to be harder than I'd thought. I opened my stance. "Of course not, Cookie."

She pointed a finger at me. "Don't you dare try that Cookie shit with me." With a hardened face, she moved toward her desk.

So Cookie was out. "Dani, you didn't hear me correctly."

She re-crossed her arms. "Now you're a mind reader and you know what I'm thinking?"

"No," I said calmly and softly. It had been a mistake to let her get away and stew in the break room. Her attitude had only deteriorated. I approached her.

She backed away half a step.

"You're scared to talk about it, aren't you?" I said as I moved closer.

She halted her retreat and straightened her spine. "I'm not afraid of anything. Especially you."

"Is that so?" It was time to shift the dialogue and use her own words against her. "Then go to the window."

"I'm not leaving town."

"Go to the window," I repeated.

"Why?"

"You're the one who claimed to not be afraid."

She strode to the window, but stopped two feet short and turned. "Satisfied?"

I came close to her. "Turn around and put your hands on the glass."

"No."

"You're scared, aren't you? You're lying to me, and to yourself."

She moved her palms to the glass, but didn't put any weight against it. "There. Happy?" She pulled them back.

"Again."

She did.

I moved up behind her and caged her with my arms. "Remember what I said." Her fear of the window was the leverage I needed.

She pushed back against me, but without being willing to shove against the glass, she had no leverage. "Stop it. This has nothing to do with what we were talking about."

"It has everything to do with it. I said trust me, and I'd keep you safe. If you can't acknowledge that, then we have nothing to talk about."

She fought back a bit less. "Let me go."

"You wanted to talk, so talk."

"Why like this?" she asked.

My mobile vibrated on the desk.

I ignored it and whispered into her ear as I pushed her toward the window. "Because until you realize you can trust me, we can't have the right conversation."

She relaxed. "Then why did you tell me you wanted me to leave?"

That was the real question, and the one I was scared to answer. "Because I'm worried about you, and I care."

There. I'd admitted how I felt for once.

"About you," I added, making my vulnerability complete.

She was silent.

"I don't want you to leave. I just thought it would be safer, and I don't want you to be afraid."

"I told you, I'm not afraid of anything," she countered.

"Then let me press you against the glass."

"I don't trust it."

I pushed her closer. "Trust me, not the glass."

She continued to lean back against me and resist.

"I'm going to make you like the window." I rubbed my erection against her.

"Not a chance."

A knock sounded at the door. "Charlie?"

It was Abby. Office sex was going to have to wait.

"The next time you're up against glass like this, you'll be naked and panting." I released her and went to sit behind my desk where I could hide my erection.

With a smile, she straightened her clothes and went to get the door. "I'm staying."

"Of course. How else are you going to experience the window?"

She shot me a glare before opening the door.

"Is this a bad time?" Whitaker asked.

"Not at all," Dani answered. "I was just leaving."

~

DANI WAS GONE WHEN WHITAKER ARRIVED TO GO OVER THE PROJECTIONS WE'D asked for, and I hadn't seen her again all afternoon.

Abby had claimed ignorance when I asked where she'd gone.

On the way home, instead of ordering ahead, I stopped by the Thai place that seemed to be Dani's favorite and loaded up with everything I could think of that she'd ordered from here in the past.

They added six sets of chopsticks and napkins to the huge bag, thinking I was getting food for an army.

When I finally reached the condo, I held my breath and opened the door.

She was on the couch with a book. She shot me an annoyed look before she returned to the pages. "I'm not leaving," she announced as I was closing the door.

"I heard you at work."

She didn't look up. "Good. Maybe if I say it a few more times you'll understand that you can't boss me around."

"I'm..." I stopped myself before objecting to her wording and repeating the same cycle all over again. I held up my bag. "I come bearing a peace offering."

She looked up and sniffed the air for a second. The hint of a smile tried to emerge, but she clamped it down. "That isn't going to change my mind."

Rather than sigh the exasperation I felt, I tried another tack. "It's Thai, but you can only have it if you agree to stay."

Her brows drew together, looking for the trap.

I set the bag down in front of her. "I wasn't sure what you wanted tonight, so I got pretty much everything. I had them label the containers, so if there's one you want to save, we can put it straight in the fridge."

Cautiously she pulled two containers out of the bag, examined them, and then removed two more.

"I'll get plates," I said, heading to the kitchen.

"Bowls and serving spoons too," she called after me.

Finally words that weren't related to our fight.

On my return, I found her typing on her mobile. A slight smile graced her lips as she put it down.

I flicked on the television before sitting. "It's movie night. What would you like to watch?" I handed her the spoons and set the plates down.

She ladled something onto her plate. "Pad kra prow?" she asked, hovering over the second plate.

"I'll have whatever you're having."

Her phone vibrated on the table, earning it a concerned glance.

"Do you need to get that?"

She slopped some of the pad whatever onto my plate. "No, it's just Andrina."

After she'd moved in, I'd learned she still kept in frequent touch with her college friends Andrina Vonn and Mena something.

"Is she on my side?" I asked.

"Of course not," Dani objected with fake horror. Her smile gave her away.

I'd have to thank Andrina when I finally met her. "You still have to choose the movie," I reminded her.

"Bossing me around again?"

I shook my head. "Think of it as me accommodating you."

She scooped from another of the paper containers onto our plates. "I'm still not leaving."

I sat down beside her. "Can you please stop harping on that?"

"I'm just—"

I grabbed her shoulder and put a finger to her mouth to stop her. "I get it. Now stop bringing it up."

∼

## Danielle

Charlie was so sweet after being such an ass at work. The food was perfect, and the gesture made it hard to stay mad at him.

For the movie, I chose Charlie's favorite, *Top Gun*—the original, with Tom Cruise. I'd learned how much he loved it when we'd watched it together two weeks or so ago.

We started out a discreet distance apart on the couch.

Later he reached an arm around me.

I didn't rebel, and as the film went on, I nestled closer to him, drawing comfort from his warmth.

He stayed unusually gentlemanly, not once attempting his signature side-boob thumb stroke.

I missed it.

Near the end of the film, I finally realized why this one resonated with Charlie. The answer was in the subplot of what drove the hero, Maverick.

Mav had a desperate need to prove himself worthy, to show the world he was as capable as his father, able to be the pilot he knew his father had been. Even, in a way, to prove himself to his dead father.

The movie was a reflection of Charlie's life, and Charlie's need to prove himself to his father.

As the final showdown with the enemy jets approached, I snuggled close to my man. Even though I knew the ending, my heart still raced.

Then Maverick refused to run away and rejoined the fight, even against insurmountable odds. I empathized. Today I was taking a stand like Mav, refusing to give up and run away.

I squeezed Charlie's arm and looked into his eyes. "That's me."

He nodded, though he was probably just placating me.

When the final scene ended and the credits rolled, Charlie tightened his grip and kissed my head. "I get it, Mav. Fuck the risks. You're not running away."

"Damn straight," I said, echoing his phrase. "I'm not leaving."

"Uh-huh."

He'd surrendered—sort of.

He clicked off the TV and we sat together, me nestled against him, neither one making the next move.

I gave in. "I don't want to fight anymore. Can we be done with this?"

"Sure, if you can quit harping on it."

As I looked back, even I could see how that would be grating. "I have a different line."

"I said, enough already."

"It's my favorite line from the movie."

He sighed. "Which is?"

Was Andrina right or not? "Take me to bed or lose me forever." I laughed.

He didn't move, not a single muscle.

Andrina had been wrong.

Now what?

I'd pushed too hard, too far, and ruined it.

## CHAPTER 32

*CHARLES*

I SAT STUNNED. IT HAD TO BE A JOKE.

That was the last thing I'd expected her to say after the incessant arguing.

She looked down. "Sorry."

"What did you say?" I asked.

"I'm sorry about today. It just got to me, and I overreacted."

"No," I stopped her. "Before that."

She pulled her knees together. "Andrina said—"

"Fuck Andrina."

"Take me to bed or lose me forever."

In a flash, I scooped her up. "No fucking way am I losing you. You better mean this." I kicked at the partially open door to the bedroom.

"I do," she chirped as I dropped her on the bed. "Andrina said—"

"I said fuck Andrina."

We attacked each other's clothes with a vengeance.

"It's you and me. Nobody else," I told her.

I helped her wiggle free as quickly as I could. She was my prize, and I unwrapped her like a five year old on Christmas morning.

She'd been stroking my thigh as we watched the movie, revving my engine all night. I was hard as steel.

"You have no idea what you do to me, Cookie." I was going to feast on her until she cried for mercy. Struggling out of the last of my clothes, I pulled to spread her legs.

She resisted. "Hold me first."

I settled alongside her and pulled her into my side. Snuggle then ravage, I guessed was tonight's script. "Tell me what you want, Cookie." I was ready to give it all to her.

She drew a circle on my chest. "I want tonight to be special."

"You are always special to me," I told her. "And if you want special, I'll give you a tongue-lashing you won't ever forget."

Her finger circled my nipple in silence.

I hadn't guessed right, so I shut up.

"I don't want..." She didn't finish.

It would be hard. No, it would be insanely hard, but I'd hold off if that's what she wanted. "We can just snuggle then...as long as you want." I could only hope it wouldn't be too long.

"No." The word came out softly. "I want skin."

"You mean no..." I was afraid the argument had put us in the cuddle-but-no-sex zone. At least having her bare chest up against me was intensely erotic in its own way.

"Yes. No condom. Just you." She paused. "I'm on birth control, and I'm safe."

Relief washed over me. "I'm clean, too. But I might not last very long like that."

"Another thing." She rose up and straddled me. "It's my turn to be on top." She tweaked my nipple the way I often did hers.

I could go for that. "It's your night, Cookie." Palming the weight of her marvelous breasts in my hands was one perk of this position. It was nirvana —soft mounds perfect for kneading.

Moans escaped her as she pleasured herself on me. She rubbed her slippery folds over my length, only slowing when her clit ran over my tip.

Shudders I couldn't stop wracked me every time she rode over my sensitive crown. Her wetness gliding back and forth over my length was my new favorite thing.

But it still took all my concentration to resist the urge to lift her up and plunge into her.

She set the rhythm while she vulva-fucked me.

I attended to her boobs, cupping them firmly. Her murmurs of pleasure guided me as I thumbed her nipples.

Her breathing became ragged little breaths that told me she was close to the end of her rope. Her hand clamped over mine, squeezing it against the warm softness of her breast.

Without warning, she lifted up, guided my cock into place, and slid down on me. I slipped easily into her insane wetness, and she took me to the root, lifting up and sliding down—first slowly, then more quickly. She braced her hands on my knees, arched her back, and leaned.

The sight of her breasts bouncing every time she came down on me was almost too much. Clamping my eyes closed, I concentrated on holding off.

Each time, she lifted to tease my tip at her entrance and then slid down fast to take my length, followed by grinding her clit against my pelvis. Each stroke sent a jolt all the way through me.

She reached around and grabbed my balls, and I nearly exploded from her touch.

I retaliated by pressing my thumb to her clit.

She ground forward and back against the pressure of my thumb as short words spilled out between staccato breaths.

"Holy shit... Holy crap...I can't... I'm gonna... Oh God... come... Oh... my God..."

On the next rock forward of her pelvis, I rubbed her clit hard, and she lost it, tensing, shaking, and clawing my legs.

She cried out my name and shuddered—her pussy convulsing around me as she rode the waves down—then collapsed forward on top of me, her breasts marvelously hot against my chest.

"My God," she said several times. "I had no idea."

She rolled off quickly, panting to regain her breath. "Your turn." She put her head on the pillow and poked her butt up. "Fuck me good."

I got behind her and let her position me with her hand before I pushed in —hard.

She moaned and then giggled. "Is that all?"

I grabbed her hips a dug my fingers in, seating myself fully, and held her there. "Is this enough?"

She wiggled her ass. "Oh, God, yes."

I started pulling out and ramming home—all the way home. She was so fucking wet and so deliciously tight that I couldn't hold back.

"Harder," she urged.

Harder is what she asked for, and I gave it to her. I knew she probably said it for my sake, not hers, but it came naturally.

The sounds of slapping flesh filled the room as I thrust home again and again.

She'd been right. The sensations without the latex were better, more intense. The pressure that built behind my balls was quickly too much to hold back. With a final push, I shot my load, tensing up and holding her hips, welding my cock inside her. When the throbbing eased, I pushed us forward onto the bed and lay panting against her shoulder.

"That was fucking fantastic," I managed between breaths.

"Yeah," she replied, angling her head to give me a kiss. "A fantastic fuck."

After a minute, I got up to retrieve a wet washcloth for her.

Curling up behind her, I cradled a breast with my hand. She was mine, and I wasn't letting her go. Not ever.

## CHAPTER 33

*Charles*

My mobile buzzed on the nightstand. The numbers on the clock Dani had brought into the bedroom read four twenty-three.

I shifted toward the noisy device. "This had better be good."

"Huh?" Dani mumbled as her hand slid off my chest.

I squinted and *Ethan* appeared. My stupid brother had a knack for forgetting to check time zone differences before calling. "Bloody hell, Ethan. Do you know what time it is over here?"

"You said to call as soon as I knew something," he shot back with a chuckle. He knew exactly what he was doing, and he was enjoying it.

Dani rolled away.

"Do you want to hear what I have or not?" Ethan asked.

"Of course."

"I could always call back tomorrow with what I found out about your friend Durban."

I jerked up at the mention of Turdball's name. "Now would be better." I'd enlisted Ethan's help in tracking Turdball, with the proviso that he not alert Dad to my relationship with Dani.

"Very well. It turns out your friend has a gambling problem."

The turdball's desire for a quick marriage became clear. "So the proposal was just to get close to Daddy's deep pockets."

"What?" Dani asked groggily.

I laid a hand on her shoulder. "Later, Cookie. Go back to sleep."

Instead, she propped up on her elbows. "Who is that?"

"My brother," I answered as I put it on speaker. "Ethan, you're on with Dani now."

"Hi, Dani, sorry to wake you," he said, more apologetic than he'd been with me.

She sat up. "Morning," she replied with a yawn.

I shook my head. "Just tell her what you told me."

"Your friend Mr. Durban—"

"Ex," she said quickly. "And certainly not friend."

"Right. He has a gambling addiction, I would say, and he hasn't had much luck at the tables recently. He ran up a sizable arrears in Monaco and is now on the no-admittance list there. After that, he decided to try his hand in eastern Europe."

I could guess where this was going to lead.

"There he managed to dig himself an even deeper hole at two more casinos. He has amassed a rather large debt to a Russian fellow by the name of Abramovich. Not a nice chap to owe money to, is what I hear."

"Not my problem anymore," she said.

I circled an arm around my defiant Cookie.

She rewarded me with a smile. "And you think he wanted to marry me for Daddy's money?"

Ethan sighed. "It is one of the oldest reasons for marriage."

Dani laughed into the mobile. "Daddy wouldn't give him a penny."

"But what if his debts put you in danger?" Ethan asked.

Dani shuddered. She hadn't considered that angle.

I pulled her closer and rubbed her shoulder.

"He's booked another flight to Boston, so you might want to be prepared."

"When?" I asked.

"Thursday. I'll let you know if that changes."

"The other reason for my call, brother..." Ethan paused. "Dad is going to be visiting you."

"Here?" I asked. He hadn't mentioned a trip to me. That in itself was cause for concern.

"Indeed. I thought you'd appreciate the warning."

"Thanks. When?"

"Today, tomorrow—I'm not sure."

It wasn't much warning, and I hadn't heard a peep about this from Dad or his office.

"Thanks again."

"TTFN," Ethan said as he rang off.

Dani lay back down. "What do you think he wants? Your father."

The room went dark again as I clicked off my mobile. "To congratulate us on how well the company is running, naturally." That was *not* likely it, but I didn't have a better answer for her. The union situation was getting more troublesome by the day, and he might have heard about it, but that was merely a guess.

She rolled back my direction. "How does Ethan find this stuff out?"

I couldn't answer fully, given the clandestine nature of his status with Scotland Yard. "He has a lot of connections."

"He must."

∽

## Danielle

It was still early morning in the office when I finished my latest text session with Andrina and Mena.

Charlie had gone downstairs. Texting them about life with him was something I had to fit into times when he and I were apart.

I walked to our huge window and looked out onto the city. My phone rang. The name on the screen was almost the last I expected to see—Aunt Emily.

I turned away from the window, selected the "can't talk now" text response, and refused the call. She'd been looking forward to me visiting her in Paris, and now I had to tell her I couldn't. It would be too much of a distraction right now.

I had to stay here in Boston to finish the year and a half I'd committed to. With the Hawker purchase contract worded the way it was, I didn't really have a choice, the financial penalty would be too severe even if I *wanted* to talk Daddy into letting me get started at the Paris office. And anyway, that dream had been my focus before Charlie and I had become…whatever it was we were.

I guess a couple described it pretty well, and almost every morning I woke up with him seemed better than the last. We had something more between us than I'd experienced before.

Sitting down behind my desk, I settled my chin on my clasped hands. Maybe this is what all women felt like after moving in with a man. The physical proximity and simple acts of sharing space and everything from towels to the toaster had to increase the intimacy of the relationship, didn't it?

If so, why had I heard so many complaints? "He leaves his socks around" to the toilet seat left up made it sound like a negative influence on the relationship. They had all seemed like sound reasons to keep separate living spaces and a bit of distance. I mean, not living together prior to marriage had worked forever before the latest century.

But taking that logic was scary as well. It meant that how I felt about living with Charlie was the anomaly. What did that mean? I'd be an idiot to deny that it implied I'd fallen hard for the man. What he and I shared was more than use of the same toaster. My innards tingled at that realization. I could avoid hard issues with the best of them, if I felt like it, and I'd shied away from this one.

He'd said he cared, but that was pretty nebulous, and was it only because he felt responsible for me? You couldn't come out and ask a man, "How do you feel about me?" That got the same response from a man as a puppy—a tilt of the head, sad eyes, and no words. At least none that made any sense.

My phone rang again, pulling me away from my intractable problem. I worked out the Paris time in my head. They still had plenty of daylight left, so putting my aunt off again would only result in a long string of redials.

She wasn't going to give up, so I accepted the call and put it to my ear. "Hi, Auntie Em. It must be getting late there."

"Not at all, dear."

She addressed everyone younger than her as *dear*. She nurtured the image of the sweet old lady, but beneath all that, she was hard as stone when it came to business. The weak-old-lady persona made people underestimate her and regret it later. "I'd like to talk a little further about you coming to Paris to see what it is we do here." Persistence was clearly another one of her traits.

"I'm very tied up here."

"You should still visit," she said, ignoring my comments. "I had a very interesting conversation with your father."

I braced for what might come next. *Interesting* was never a good word in a situation like this.

She didn't let up. "Any time next month would be ideal."
I looked for a different way to explain it to her. "But—"
"Tell me you'll consider it," she said, cutting me off.
"I'll consider it."
"Good. Next month will work perfectly. Au revoir."
What she said took a second to register. "But I'm not certain…"
Silence. She'd already hung up.

# CHAPTER 34

*DANIELLE*

CHARLIE SPENT THE MORNING WITH WROBLEWSKI, COMBING OVER THE LATEST response from the union.

I had the dubious pleasure of going through my copy alone at my old apartment while I waited for a contractor to come fix the sliding glass door out to the balcony. The painters had finished yesterday, and except for Charlie wanting to change the locks to something better, the place was habitable again—or it would be once all the construction dust was cleaned up. It had been transformed enough that fear no longer gripped me when I crossed the threshold.

Lunchtime had arrived by the time I came to the end of my comparison of the new and the old proposals. It was absolutely mind numbing. The contractor also hadn't shown up or answered his cell.

When I turned the last page, I still couldn't for the life of me figure out Califano's objective. He'd insisted on entirely new wording without much in substantive changes. Nevertheless, we had to go through it to make sure we didn't sign up for a hidden gotcha clause somewhere.

Hearing Gerald was coming back to town and having my contractor blow me off, on top of having to deal with this complete bullshit from the union, had made for one shitty day.

∼

A BBY WAS AT HER DESK WHEN I GOT BACK, BUT MY OFFICEMATE'S CHAIR WAS empty.

"Any idea where Charlie went?" I asked. I could use him giving me a shoulder massage at lunch, and maybe telling me things would be better tomorrow.

Abby shook her head and kept typing. "Nope. He's off leash. Maybe he went to lunch."

So much for dining with my man and a shoulder massage. The massage part had to be restricted to when we were out of the office.

I waited until Abby paused, then handed her my marked-up copy of the union papers. "The old is on top and the new on the bottom with my chicken scratch. If you could type up the the new- and old-wording sections I noted, along with the section numbers, that would be helpful."

She took the stack of papers and looked quickly at two pages in the back. "Sure. I'm doing Charlie's now," she said, pointing at her screen. "Bad day?" she asked, picking up on my mood.

"The worst."

She sighed. "Crappy day for the machine to be out of Twinkies."

"You're kidding."

She shook her head. "Wish I was. I had the urge an hour ago, but somebody got there ahead of us."

I backed away. "I'll be back after lunch…with Twinkies."

"You're the best."

In the elevator, I composed a text to Charlie.

ME: Be back after lunch - Abby has my take on the contract

I reached the street, and then my favorite lunch truck three blocks away, without a response.

After munching on lunch from the gyro truck at a table outside Starbucks, I went in search of my sugary snack cakes. I located a store with plenty on the shelves and bought four packages.

I returned to the office, and Abby eyed the Twinkies as I approached. "Success?"

I nodded as I passed by and into my office.

She followed, and after I sat down, she asked, "Want to talk about it?"

It wasn't like I had a ton of choices when it came to people to confide in. "Sure." I pointed to the visitor chairs.

She plopped down in the near one. "Is it the union again?"

"No. It's my ex."

"I thought you told him off?"

"I did." I stretched my shoulders. Just thinking about Gerald made me tense. "But he's coming back Thursday, it seems."

She eyed the unopened Twinkie package. "Why?"

"No idea. We found out he has gambling debts."

"If he's going to ask you for money, I'd tell him to screw off."

"I don't plan on talking to him at all." There wasn't any upside to meeting with him.

"Or you could pepper spray his ass." She giggled. "I had this one old boyfriend..." She bit her lip before continuing. "That got him to back the hell off, and a can is easy to buy."

I laughed at the image of Gerald taking a face full of pepper spray and whimpering off down the street. "That has some appeal, but I think my plan is better."

She glanced at my sponge-cake delights again. "Now that we've solved that problem..."

"Sure." I slid one of the packages her direction and opened another for myself.

The first bite was as good as always.

Abby stood to go after we'd both consumed a pair of the treats. I gave her a second package for later and sent another text to my missing officemate.

ME: At the office - wish you were here

Ten minutes later, when I still hadn't gotten a response, I couldn't take it any longer and decided on a walk.

"I'll be back in an hour or so," I told Abby as I left.

Block after block of walking slowly relaxed me, as exercise normally did. Eventually, the prospect of Gerald coming back bothered me less and less.

I didn't owe him anything. Worrying about him was giving him my time—time and consideration he didn't deserve. On the way back, I started making a mental list of all the ways I was better off with Charlie than with Gerald.

The fifteenth item was that Charlie could watch a movie with me and get it when I made an off-the-wall comment like *"That's me."* Gerald wouldn't have made the connection in a million years.

In the elevator back up, I pulled out my phone again. I hadn't counted, but it had to be the hundredth time I'd checked.

Still no response from Charlie.

When the doors opened on our floor, I put the phone away.

Abby looked up at me, grabbed her mug, and left her desk with a wave.

At our office door, I found Charlie's chair still empty. *Where the hell is he?*

I would have preferred wine right now, but a nice cup of decaf mocha would have to do. Without even stopping to take my purse off my shoulder, I found my mug and followed Abby.

She was waiting for the machine to finish. "Did Charlie say how late he'd be?" I asked.

She pulled her cup out from under the machine. "He's back and with his father. They're discussing something in the conference room."

Relieved, I punched in my coffee selection. Being busy with his father explained why I hadn't heard from him.

"I finished your contract summary." She smiled at me. "You'll find it on my desk under the stuff Charlie wants me to type up for his father." She sat down at one of the tables and started typing on her phone without offering an invitation to join her.

Back at her desk, there was a letter on Blakewell company letterhead and several pages of Charlie's handwritten scribblings.

The letter caught my eye first, and as soon as I saw the words *Berlin office*, I couldn't stop reading.

It was a formal offer of the job Charlie had always wanted in Berlin. And at the bottom, it was signed by his father.

Charlie hadn't told me about this.

The date wasn't today or yesterday, it was over a week ago.

Why wouldn't he tell me about this?

A huge lump formed in my throat at the sight of the handwritten words on the other pages.

    Danielle Wentworth Failings.
    (General) Several emotional outbursts showed a lack of the necessary composure to captain a large enterprise.
    (1)Action: The day of the contract signing, she refused to meet to discuss next steps. Result: We failed to get a running start on any due diligence items.

(2) Several emotional outbursts showed a lack of the necessary composure to captain a large enterprise.

*What the fuck is this?*
It went on with complaints about how I'd handled numerous little things and how I'd made the union situation worse.

He was blaming me?

It was his handwriting, and he'd been doing this since our very first day working together.

The conference room door cracked open.

"Finalize that list of the girl's failings, and you can be in Berlin next week." The voice was loud.

The door opened farther, and Charlie's father stepped out.

*Fuck this.* I threw down the papers. They slid off the desk to the floor. Not caring, I turned for the elevator.

"Berlin is ready for you *now*," I heard Charlie's father say behind me.

My tears started before the elevator doors even opened. I entered and pressed L for the lobby. For me the button meant *leave*, and for the last time.

Charlie's eyes caught mine for the briefest second just as the doors closed.

The whole time, I'd thought he had my back.

"*Trust me,*" he'd said.

How could I have been so stupid?

# CHAPTER 35

*Danielle*

My phone vibrated in my hand again. After I declined Charlie's call a second time, I was able flag down a cab.

"Are you all right, miss?" the driver asked as I got in.

"No... Yes, I will be as soon as we get out of here." I pulled tissues from my purse and dabbed at my eyes. They came away with the black evidence of my crying.

"Right," she said as she pulled away from the curb. "I hope you gave him a good kick in the balls."

"Huh?"

She passed a package of makeup wipes over the seat toward me. "Sister, whenever a woman gets in my cab looking like you do, it was a man who did her wrong."

I opened the package of wipes. "Thank you."

"Well, did ya?" she asked again.

"That'll have to wait till later." I worked on cleaning up my eyes and passed the wipes back to her when I'd finished. The mirror in my purse now showed red eyes, but at least no more telltale makeup issues.

The trip wasn't a long one, but it felt that way this afternoon. I shifted in my seat as anxiety ate at me. I needed to move, run, walk, or maybe punch something. Anything but sit.

When we reached the building on Tremont Street, I thanked the driver and handed her an extra-large tip. The world needed more kind people like her in it. And certainly fewer deceitful assholes like his lordship Charlie fucking Blakewell.

Our doorman, Carl, gave me his usual salute when I entered, and I returned a smile.

Too late, I caught myself. I had to stop thinking of this as *our* place, Carl as *our* doorman, or anything as *ours*. There was no more we, us, or anything like that—there couldn't be after what he'd done.

"Carl?" I said. "I'm going to need some help getting things down in a little while."

He moved inside with me. "I can't leave the door, but I have something for you." He opened a door and wheeled out a hotel-style luggage trolley. "Will this help?"

"Sure. Thanks." I wheeled it to the elevator.

I should have known better than to move in with Charlie and get close as we had. This was another lesson in why it was better to be alone. Getting stabbed in the back by a coworker, I could handle. That sometimes came with the territory. But by a man I'd been living with? Sharing showers and a bed with? Unacceptable.

Upstairs, I located the bags we'd used to bring my things here from the apartment, along with my original suitcase from London, and started packing. *Packing* wasn't really the right term. I decided to borrow two garment bags Charlie had hanging for some of my things. As for the rest, *stuffing* was closer to it because I was in a hurry. All they got were plastic bags.

A third call from Charlie made me punch the decline button so hard the polish on that nail chipped. *Damn him.* Now I had to redo it.

With every article of clothing I shoved away, my anger grew. I didn't deserve this shit. I didn't deserve to be treated this way.

The pile I'd created by the door wasn't everything, but it was enough to start with, and as much as I could carry in one trip. The rest could wait.

My next stop was his liquor stash. I chose the most expensive bottle of scotch—the Macallan 25.

Charlie had bought it for celebrating signing the union contract, back when we'd foolishly expected it to be imminent.

I broke open the seal. When the first gulp of the smooth amber liquid hit the back of my throat, I added more to the glass. This was seriously good shit—not the kind of indulgence I ever bought for myself.

The second glass burned less than the first and settled my nerves. I poured a third and slipped the bottle into my bag. I deserved it. He could buy another.

What I had to do now was wait for the fucker so I could tell him exactly what I thought of him. I wasn't one for violence, but the Uber driver's advice seemed more appealing by the minute. One quick kick ought to get my point across. But looking down at my heels, and their pointy toes, I backed off of that thought as perhaps too extreme.

A good slap would have to do.

∽

## CHARLES

THE LOOK I'D GOTTEN FROM DANI AS THE LIFT DOORS CLOSED HAD BEEN ODD. It wasn't until I saw the papers on the floor by Abby's desk that I realized why.

Somehow both Dad's offer letter regarding Berlin and my old, handwritten list about her were there.

She'd seen them, and that pained look could only have meant that I had some explaining to do. I cursed myself for not destroying that list weeks ago.

After getting Dad on his way, I summoned an Uber.

Dani had ignored both of my calls, which wasn't a good sign, so I asked the driver to stop off in front of a florist and wait while I bought something. Flowers had to be a better way to apologize than merely words.

"I'll be right back out, if you wait."

He shrugged. "You in trouble?"

"I hope not." That hope was a long shot.

Inside, the flower shop only had six red roses left, and that was clearly not enough, so I had the man make up a bouquet of a dozen white ones. When that didn't look impressive enough, I had him add a dozen yellow, because the yellow were so perfectly formed and large. Two dozen was clearly a better display than one.

Getting back into the car, the driver looked askance at me. "White and yellow?" he asked.

"It was all they had in quantity, and I don't want to show up empty-handed."

"I hope you know what you're doing."

I didn't. I was in uncharted territory here and had zero idea how many roses were appropriate. Should I have gotten a third dozen?

Apologizing to a girl had never been my strong suit, and I hadn't done it in years. My work had always come first—they all new that—and it provided the necessary explanation for any screwup I made.

The few times I'd tried apologizing while at university, it hadn't gone well. Perhaps my technique needed polishing. Flowers would be that polish, but polish needed a base to rest on, and I hadn't figured out the words that would be that support. Smooth words weren't my forte either.

After I decided on an opening line, I dialed her mobile again. Once again, she didn't answer.

As we drew closer to my building, a nervous jitter began in my leg and wouldn't stop. I hopped out and managed to walk fairly normally to the entrance.

"You're home early," Carl, our doorman, said as he held the door for me.

"True."

"Birthday or something?"

I shook my head with a sigh. "Something."

Thankfully he didn't ask anything more. I didn't have a good explanation.

Upstairs, outside the door to my flat, I took several deep breaths to calm and prepare myself, then inserted the cardkey.

When I passed through the door, the site wasn't as bad as I'd imagined.

Dani leaned against the couch, glass in hand, with something indiscernible in her eyes. "You're home early."

Maybe it wasn't so bad after all. I drew a relieved breath. "I was worried about you." I held up the vase of flowers. "I got these for you."

She sipped again. "Yellow roses, how thoughtful." She held the tumbler high enough that I couldn't make out her expression.

The words gave me optimism that I'd overreacted. Maybe she hadn't seen the papers. "For my Cookie, always." I kicked the door shut behind me.

"Did you have a nice chat with your dad?"

I started toward her with the vase. "I guess."

She pointed at the entryway table. "You can put them over there."

I retraced my steps to set them down.

"Did he want to talk about anything special?" She moved toward the window.

I walked to join her. "No. He's being a pain in the ass."

She looked out at the city. "Berlin? My shortcomings?"

My blood chilled when she turned around. Cold eyes and a sneer said she'd *most definitely* seen the papers.

"When were you going to tell me?" she asked.

This was bad. "I thought we'd talk about things tonight."

"You're a lying piece of shit, Charlie Blakewell."

I closed the distance between us. "It's not what you think."

She raised a hand and pointed her finger at me. "Don't come any closer."

That was a bad sign, and we were just getting started.

"How could you?" Her voice broke.

"You have to let me explain."

She gritted her teeth. "I don't fucking have to do anything. You want to know what the hardest thing was?"

I stayed silent.

"I actually thought you cared for me." She sniffled.

"I did—I do. None of what you read is really how I feel."

"Right," she snarled before taking a sip of her drink. "So, answer me this. The offer letter your father gave you for Berlin—did that come today?" She sniffled again. "And try being honest for a change."

"I've always been honest with you," I shot back.

"Like when you told me there was no history between you and Abby?"

I sucked in a breath through closed teeth. "We've been through that." I breathed slowly. "There never was anything *going on* between us, which was your real question."

She lifted the glass to her lips and took a sip. "You see, that's the difference between us. If you ask me a question, I answer the question you asked, not the question I expected you to ask or wanted you to ask."

"You know what I mean."

"Do I? Does anybody? Let's go back to when I asked you if there was anything else you wanted to tell me when we were having that discussion about you and Abby." She took another sip.

I braced for another assault. "Can we just sit down and talk about this?"

"We are talking. So, when I asked you if there was anything else you needed to tell me, do you remember your answer?"

It was getting warm in here. I loosened my tie and stayed silent, sure I was about to get lectured.

"*Nothing*. That's what you said." She added air quotes. "Absolutely nothing. So tell me, Lord Blakewell, while you and your father were scheming to get rid of me and you were keeping notes about my…deficiencies?" She added air quotes again. "Was that what you call absolutely nothing?"

With a dry mouth, I started to explain. "My dad—"

"We're not talking about your father, goddammit. We're talking about you. Did you write those things? That's all I need to know."

This couldn't get any worse. I sighed before nodding. "But it's not what you think." I needed a chance to explain it logically, a chance to explain Dad's pressure.

"I've heard enough." She put the glass down and started toward the bedroom. "You're an asshole."

I moved to block her path so we could talk some more.

She stopped. "Don't you dare," she hissed.

I raise my hands and backed away. "You have to listen. There's more to it."

She walked around me to the hallway and a pile of things there. She started laying garment bags over her shoulder. "No. I don't, because I don't care."

That was the hardest to hear. "You can't leave without talking this out."

"Watch me," she snarled.

Ten seconds later, she'd gathered up the pile of things and was gone.

Watching her leave was like having my insides torn out. The sound of the door slamming hurt the most.

When I sank into the couch, I knew I'd lost her, and for once in my life, I had no plan. No way forward. No clue.

Glancing at the amber liquid in her half-finished glass gave me my first plan: dull the pain. I went to the liquor cabinet and poured a full tumbler of the first bottle I pulled out.

~

## Danielle

I slammed the door behind me, closing off that failed period of my life.

Downstairs Carl ran up. "Let me."

Glad for the help, I handed over half the bundles.

Even loaded down, he got the door for me.

My anger had kept the tears at bay so far, and I wouldn't cry in front of anybody who knew Charlie and have that get back to him.

"Should I hail you a cab?" Carl asked, setting things down.

I sniffed. "No. I'll get an Uber. Thanks." Pulling my phone out, I tapped the keys to call one. The cabs weren't always clean.

Why did all the Ubers have to be Priuses? When the little car pulled up, I knew with all my stuff, I'd be forced to sit up front with the driver. But sending him away and waiting for another risked having to face Charlie again if he came downstairs.

I kept my face pointed toward the window, and the ride back to my apartment was mercifully quiet. The driver even offered to help me lug everything inside to my door, which I accepted with a nod and a grunt.

I forced out a pleasant, "Hi, Mrs. Blanchard," when we encountered my neighbor and her scrawny dog at the base of the stairs. At least the dog didn't growl this time.

"I guess the workmen got it all fixed up for you," she said as she went around us.

"Yeah," was all I could manage.

"Welcome back, dear."

I nodded and continued upstairs. The place smelled like fresh paint when I opened the door, and handing my driver a twenty for his help completed my escape from Charlie's palace in the sky. This place was small, but it was mine, and only I had the key—just the way I liked it.

An hour later, the warm water sprayed over me as I sat on the tile floor of the shower with my expensive bottle of scotch. I wouldn't finish the bottle tonight, but I'd made a dent in it. Sitting was safer than standing after all the alcohol I'd consumed.

A hot shower had always been my retreat after a shitty day.

My tears had already washed down the drain, and all that was left was self-pity. I was such a loser.

Looking back, I had to admit that I hadn't sought refuge in the shower since moving in with Charlie. He'd made me feel so good, so often. But that was before I knew the real Charlie.

"Charlie Blakewell, you're an asshole," I yelled at the wall. "Charlie Blakewell, you're an asshole," I yelled even louder. Taking a breath, I thanked Abby again for teaching me this. It helped, and I wasn't done yet.

He'd brought *yellow roses*, of all things. Yellow roses were for friends, not the lovers I'd sensed we'd grown to be. That proved we'd only been fuck buddies all along. I'd been an expendable sex toy to him.

Had any of it been real? From my side of the bed, it had seemed that way. From his side, obviously not.

I yelled at the wall again. "Yellow roses? Are you kidding me? You bring me yellow roses? You're an asshole, Charlie Blakewell."

Reading people had always been a skill of mine. How had I gotten him wrong? What signs had I missed? Had I been so infatuated with him that my judgment had been impaired?

The only answer had to be yes.

When I started to stand, the shower stall tilted on me, and I fell against the wall. Steadying myself with a hand against the tile, I shut off the water.

Maybe drinking in a slippery shower hadn't been the best idea after all. But the hot water had sure washed away some of the anger—that and Abby's yelling trick. Either way, I felt better.

Once I made it out of the shower without stumbling—a major victory—I toweled off.

The state of the bedroom told me maybe I should have gone to a hotel. The bed wasn't made, and the sheets were in a pile, just as we'd left them the night of the break-in, except with a layer of construction dust added.

But in my current state, I didn't trust myself to make it to a hotel for the night. And the condition of my bed meant sleeping in sweats, wrapped in a blanket. My life sucked.

## CHAPTER 36

*Charles*

The next morning, a hammering headache woke me.

My conscience said I shouldn't have gotten so sloshed.

I knew that.

*And you should've drunk some water*, it reminded me.

I knew that too.

*And eaten something.*

I was zero for three on those.

This called for an extra-strength dose of painkiller. But the need to pee almost doubled me over when I climbed down off the mattress, so that took priority.

Waking up in a bed was a refreshing change, at least. The last time I'd tied one on this badly, I'd woken up half off the couch and drooling. I wiped wetness from the side of my face. One thing hadn't changed.

But I hadn't wet the bed. Hooray for minor victories. After taking care of my bladder, the childproof cap on the ibuprofen became my next enemy.

An hour later, my headache still wasn't great, but the pills had allowed me to deal with the morning light. The strong coffee and breakfast burrito I'd had delivered had helped as well.

When my mobile vibrated on the counter, I lunged for it.

I'd been hoping for a return call from my Cookie, but no luck—it was Abby.

"Are you almost here?" she asked.

"No," I croaked, holding the phone a little farther from my ear. Why did she have to shout at this time of the morning?

"What shall I tell the cosmetics group? They're here for the nine-thirty meeting, and Dani's not answering her phone."

"Shit." I'd totally forgotten about anything and everything work-related. "Let's cancel that meeting for now."

The mention of Dani's name didn't help. Last night I'd been trying to formulate a plan to get her back, but this morning I couldn't remember if I'd figured one out. Another reason to stick to wine maybe.

"I'll tell them... And?" Abby prodded.

It took a few seconds for me to catch her drift. "What else do I have on the schedule?" My mind was too fuzzy to recall.

"You also have a one o'clock and a three thirty."

"Let's put off the one o'clock. I should be in by the later meeting... Oh, and if you hear anything from Dani or she comes in, please let me know."

"What happened?" Abby's words were thankfully hushed. Having the employees learn of our altercation wouldn't be good.

"I'll be in after lunch." The phone slipped from my fingers and clattered on the floor. I picked it up. The call was still active, and the screen was intact—my first good break.

"You okay, boss?"

"Sorry. You can call me butterfingers this morning. After lunch, I promise."

I set the mobile down and grabbed another glass of water with the intention of sweating out the alcohol with a good run. It'd help me in the past, although my brother, Ethan, insisted there was no scientific proof to back up my claim.

An hour later, I found myself in Eastboro Park, same place Dani and I had run so many mornings. I could hope, but at this hour I didn't stand a chance of seeing her here. Still, it seemed like the appropriate place—good memories and all.

Only, by the second lap I'd realized running here might not have been a great idea. Every time I passed the tree where we'd kissed, I was reminded that it might never happen again. Each step I took, not being able to look over and see her running next to me, was worse than the last.

As I came up on the parking lot again, I veered off the path. I was being such a freaking idiot. Giving up wasn't in my nature, and time was running out. I needed to talk to her before her position solidified.

She'd said it was over, but that didn't have to be true. We could still talk it out. I could still get her to see the truth of the matter. It had to be possible.

I couldn't let it end like this—on an untruth.

~

## Danielle

I woke up to the sound of Mrs. Blanchard's yappy little mutt. From the sound of it, Rufus was out on her balcony, which adjoined mine, and was not happy about someone down on the street.

Pulling the blanket over my head didn't help, but swearing at him miraculously did, and after a moment, it was relatively silent again.

Getting up, I noticed pink stains on the mattress. I scratched at one and confirmed—just as I thought, it was nail polish. Another reminder of that terrible night.

Why did Gerald have to be such a destructive dick? I would never understand that man, not that it mattered. He was somebody else's problem now. It was just too bad that other person wasn't a prison warden.

Two glasses of water and a generous dose of Advil later, I was in the shower and working hard to not play yesterday through again in my head.

The question of understanding Charlie, instead of Gerald, occupied my thoughts. Charlie had turned into such an enigma—gracious, funny, understanding, until I learned he was a liar, just like all of them.

It wasn't worth worrying about.

In the kitchen, I rummaged around until I found a can of chili. It wasn't exactly a breakfast burrito, the way Charlie had taught me, but it was the closest thing I could find. After a minute and and a half in the microwave, it smelled enticing. After I added some shredded cheese from the refrigerator, it wasn't that far off.

*Thank you, Charlie.* Just as he'd promised, the food helped.

Why had I done that? Thinking good thoughts about *him* was not right—not after yesterday.

What I needed was a good run to get my head on straight. Exercise always grounded me.

Instead of going to Eastboro Park, where Charlie and I had run every morning, I decided on the path by the Charles River basin. I might have to dodge a few bicycles, but at least there wouldn't be any cars to deal with. Best of all, no Charlie.

Things were fine for the first half mile, but then I saw them—a couple running together the other way. They were talking as they ran, and they both smiled. The picture tore at my heart, because that had been us, Charlie and me.

We'd been happy running together, hadn't we? I searched for a reason to think that wasn't true, but I couldn't come up with one. It had been an enjoyable way to start the day, running with my man by my side.

Just the words *by my side* got to me. We been running side by side, working side by side, living side by side, and sleeping side by side. The times had been good, only they'd been a lie. The whole time he'd been scheming to remove me from the company.

And I'd never seen it coming. When had I actually felt better about being with a man than I had with Charlie?

I dodged right onto the grass to avoid a bicycle coming the other way. Back on the path, I couldn't answer that question, because there hadn't been a better time.

It should have been clear in all the times I'd compared Charlie to Gerald. Before Charlie, I'd considered Gerald to be a pretty good guy. But that had been because I hadn't been around a man as good as Charlie to have my yardstick properly calibrated.

The path curved right around a bench. A man in a suit sat there, reading a stack of papers in his lap. That brought me right back to where I'd been yesterday, after reading the awful things Charlie had written about me.

I guess I hadn't known him as well as I thought. The words he'd written on those pages for his father proved that. I was deficient at this and deficient at that. The taste of bile rose in my throat.

"Fuck you, Charlie Blakewell," I said softly.

I wasn't the problem. He was.

"I hate you, Charlie Blakewell," I chanted as I ran—pausing, of course, when I encountered others. I didn't need to look like a deranged idiot to everybody around. I was merely angry, as much at myself as him.

I turned around when I reached the Longfellow Bridge and out of habit checked the time. But the time didn't matter. I didn't plan to go in to work, at least not today.

On the return leg, the cycle repeated itself. First, I saw a happy couple that reminded me of the good times with Charlie. Then I had to bring myself back to the reality of how he'd betrayed me.

When I toweled off at my car, I was more determined than ever to not stray from my course. Good times that had been a mirage were no reason to stay with a liar. Fairy tales didn't exist.

Charlie had totally messed up my mind. He couldn't be both a good man and a bad man. It had to be one or the other. Like a chameleon, he'd fooled me as to who he was. It had made me miss the warning signs.

Every time I started to think about those warning signs I'd missed, my mind dredged up a good memory instead. But the Cookie Monster was indeed a monster, I assured myself. Black-and-white words on paper didn't lie. No amount of chameleon makeup or ninja mind tricks could change what I'd read.

∽

CHARLES

A LITTLE BEFORE LUNCHTIME, I'D MADE UP MY MIND, AND I PARKED MY CAR outside Dani's apartment building. It made sense that she would come here, and her car on the street confirmed it.

I'd found her. Now the only question was what to do—how to approach this. Fuck it. There was only one way, and that was straight on. I had to get inside and talk to her.

She'd understand the logic once I explained it. Well, maybe that was true, but what made her good at this job was the fact that she could read people. She'd for sure understand that I was telling the truth. She knew me by now, and she'd have to understand that I meant what I was saying.

I marched inside. Using the key I had from overseeing the reconstruction of her apartment would be stepping over a line, I decided. So instead I knocked lightly on the door and listened.

Nothing.

I knocked harder and listened again.

Sounds of somebody shuffling along the floor came from behind the door, not loud, but clear enough for me to know the place wasn't empty.

"Dani?" I called.

Silence.

"Dani, we need to talk."

Still no response.

"Danielle Wentworth, stop being childish. We need to talk."

"We've already said enough," she said.

At least she'd acknowledged me. "Not until I've had a chance to say what I want to say." The words weren't elegant, but they were the fact of the matter.

A sniffle. "No. Go away."

I took the sniffle as a good sign. "You know you want to talk to me, because it's the right thing to do."

"Back to mind reading now? You're not very good at it."

"I'm not leaving until we talk." I slid my back down the door and settled on the grungy carpet. "I'll just wait here until you're ready."

"Suit yourself."

The sounds of her walking away from the door made it clear this wasn't going to be easy.

Ten minutes later, the door to the next apartment down the hall squeaked open. An elderly lady came out with her little dog on a leash. The look she gave me was more quizzical than concerned.

"Morning," I said with a wave, trying to make it seem normal that I would be sitting leaned against my woman's door like a vagrant.

She nodded. "Morning." She yanked the little dog back when it decided it wanted a closer look at me. "Now, Rufus, you never mind him." The pair trundled off toward the stairs.

The kid who walked toward me wearing a Burger King uniform was so engrossed in his phone, he almost tripped over me. "Sorry, man." Then it was back to his phone again.

The girl with the blue stripe in her hair and eyebrow piercings noticed me as soon as she came out of her apartment. Her hesitation made it clear I scared her.

"Just waiting for Dani," I told her, without any idea if she knew Dani's name or not.

She seemed to relax a bit but still gave me a wide berth as she walked by.

By the time Rufus and his owner returned, I'd tried twice more to get Dani to open the door for me, without any luck.

"You might try flowers," the old lady suggested before she disappeared back into her apartment.

That hadn't gone well for me last night, so I needed a different approach. Standing, I knocked on the door again. "Dani, I know you can hear me."

Still silence.

"I'm going to go get you lunch. I'll be back. We can talk then." That was my presumptive close, something all salesmen were taught, and I hoped it worked.

"Knock yourself out," she said, apparently not far from the door.

*Progress*, and I'd take it. Rubbing my sore ass, I left to get her favorite.

It took me almost an hour round-trip to get her preferred lunch from the Royal Gyros food truck near work. There'd been a long line.

Since I didn't know if she preferred lamb or chicken, I'd gotten her one of each. Three rounds of knocking on her door and calling her name got no answer.

I tried again, louder.

The neighboring door squeaked open, and Rufus's owner came out. "She's not there. She left ten minutes after you did." The woman blocked Rufus's escape with a leg.

My shoulders fell. *How could she?* "I brought lunch."

"After the fight you two had this morning, yes you should."

"I wasn't here this morning. I only just arrived around eleven."

"You weren't here early this morning?" she asked.

"Sadly, no."

"Good thing I didn't call the police, then."

When I gave her a questioning look, she tapped her ear. "Thin walls. Oh my. She's mad at you. You should have brought flowers. And before you ask, I have no idea when she'll be back."

I lifted the bag of food. "At least I won't go hungry while I wait."

"Nonsense, young man." She waved me over. "Mrs. Sumter will have a fit if you're still in the hallway when she comes home. And she's the kind to get the police involved."

My choices seemed to be leave or visit with this lady while I waited.

"Thank you. That would be lovely," I said, leaning heavily on my British accent.

"Rufus, get back." She swung a foot at the little thing, and it obeyed. "Do you like dogs?" She held the door open for me.

"Who doesn't?" I managed a smile.

"His name is Rufus, and I'm Doris. Doris Blanchard."

"Charles Blakewell, Mrs. Blanchard." I entered her flat, which Rufus decided deserved a few barks.

Despite the musty smell, it was cozy.

I took a seat on the couch with its smattering of dog hair. Dozens of pictures of a couple documented a life of travel. Rufus kept a wary eye on me. I stared him down.

Over the next hour, I was fed sugar cookies and milk while I learned more than I cared to about Doris's travels with the late Mr. Blanchard.

It turned out, Doris had met Dani on a few occasions in the parking lot or the hallway, and liked her. And, Doris had been the one to call the police when Gerald ransacked Dani's flat. It was a pity she'd only seen the man from behind at a distance. She would be no help in nailing Gerald for the destruction.

## CHAPTER 37

*DANIELLE*

It had taken several minutes of pacing and two bouts of kicking my defenseless coffee table while swearing at Charlie to come to my senses. I'd packed clothes for several days and decided to leave for the hotel. That would be a good place to get my thoughts together and figure out how to explain this to Daddy.

Then a phone call from Abby had interrupted my progress. In desperate need to talk through my predicament, I'd agreed to meet for lunch. Escaping the apartment before Charlie got back meant I wouldn't have to face the challenge of keeping the door between us closed as he argued from the hallway another dozen times that he needed to see me. The man had a magnetic pull on me that I couldn't explain. Being in the same room with him again couldn't lead anywhere good. I'd made my decision, and I needed to stick with it. That's why I was here now.

Abby scanned the menu for only a second. "I'll have the chicken pomodoro with angel hair, please," she told our server as she picked up her iced tea.

I hadn't been to an Italian restaurant before that didn't have even a single alfredo dish, but I should have expected as much from The Tomato Factory. "For me, I think the spaghetti with meat sauce."

The server scribbled on her pad.

*Maybe more protein would be better.* I raised a hand. "I changed my mind. Instead, I'd like the chicken parmigiana."

With a sigh, she scratched on her pad and wrote again.

*What's the big deal about changing an order?*

Abby cast her a glance.

"No, sorry," I said. "Baked lasagna." That seemed like the most comfort-food-type dish here—hefty and filling.

The server eyed me and didn't write down what I'd said.

I answered the implied question. "I'm sure this time."

She turned on her heels and left.

"Frazzled a little?" Abby asked.

"I didn't sleep well," I admitted, staring at my water glass. I couldn't make up my mind about a simple lunch order. No wonder my feelings about Charlie ping-ponged from one end of the spectrum to the other. I hated him—I loved him.

Time out.

Did I just think that? I loved Charlie? The man who'd been betraying me this whole time? The man I'd told to fuck off this morning? As nonsensical as it sounded, I didn't know the answer. What was love if he didn't return it? Could love exist amid the lies?

Abby put her tea down. "I asked how you're feeling?"

Her question brought me back to the moment. I shrugged. "Crappy. I mean why did he have to…" I couldn't even finish.

She sipped her tea. "I didn't know what he'd asked me to type up until after you left. I thought it was the union contract notes." She stirred her glass with the straw. "I'm sorry. What he wrote was so mean."

I picked up my water and tilted my head, unsure how to respond to that—shake, nod, shrug.

Our tiny salads arrived, and I busied myself forking one piece of lettuce after another into my mouth. I'd thought I wanted to talk to Abby, but I couldn't bring myself to start.

She broke the silence. "Was that offer for him to move to Berlin real?"

I nodded. "Getting that job has been his dream for a long time." After a bit, I added, "I like your hair."

She pulled a few strands out to the side. "You don't think it's too short?"

"No, of course not."

Thankfully, our conversation stayed on simple, mundane things for a while. Then our food arrived.

She used her fork against her spoon to twist up a mouthful of noodles. "How's your lasagna?"

"Great. Just what I needed."

"Have you talked to him?" she asked, getting back to the elephant in the room.

I nodded just before stuffing lasagna into my mouth.

"And?" She wasn't letting me stay in my shell, which was probably good.

"I yelled at him." I couldn't think of anything else to add. We hadn't settled anything other than the fact that he was an ass.

"Did you move out?"

My mouthful of food almost ended up on the table as I coughed. After swallowing, I said, "You knew?"

She didn't look up from her food. "I work for you. It's my job to know."

I brought the napkin to my lips. "Does everybody know?"

"I wouldn't say *everybody*." Her eyes met mine, and she shrugged one shoulder. "It's no big deal. I mean, office romances happen all the time… close proximity and all."

So much for our attempt to be discreet.

"So did you? Move out, I mean?" she repeated.

"Yeah, I'm back at my apartment." I cut some more of my food and got back to eating.

"Give me a sharp knife. I'd slice off some of his dangly parts," she said matter-of-factly.

"That's a little extreme."

She lifted her glass toward me. "Do you think what he did to you was fair?"

"Of course not."

"There you go. Extreme assholeness deserves extreme measures." Her tone was cold.

Outside of work, she was probably not someone you messed with.

"I guess."

"Did the yelling help you? Me and my ex would sometimes get into real knock-down drag-outs. I always found the yelling emptied out emotions and cleared things up between us."

"I don't think so."

"You can always resort to sharp implements." She laughed.

I shrugged, not wanting to even talk about going down that path, and wondering if her boyfriend understood how dangerous it would be to piss her off.

She looked me square in the eye. "I assume we're having lunch because you want to talk about it."

*Did I?* I'd thought I did, but this might be a conversation better had with a practical joker like Andrina than with Abby and her knife fetish.

When I didn't answer, she scooped another mouthful of pasta.

Keeping it in was too hard. "He didn't tell me about the Berlin offer when he got it, even though he had told me it had been his dream basically forever."

"That's tough." She nodded.

"And then those things he wrote down for his dad about my *deficiencies*..." I put air quotes around the word. "The whole time I thought we had a good working relationship." I stopped for a sip of water. "I mean, I've contributed plenty to the partnership."

"Typical guy," she mused. "You gotta watch them like hawks." That statement obviously came from experience. "So what are your plans?"

At least this was something I thought I knew the answer to. I took a breath. "Depends on what he does."

She gave me a questioning look.

"If he goes to Berlin, the way he'd planned, I'll stay on here and do the job without him. It'll be easier that way."

"I thought you had your eye on something in Europe as well?" she asked after swallowing.

"I did—I do, in Paris."

"It seems far enough from Berlin that you could both go to your dream jobs."

"I can't." I told her as I pushed my plate away. "I promised Derek, Sr., that a member of one of the families would stay here to run Hawker for eighteen months."

"I still say you should take the job you want. The Paris one."

I closed my eyes for a moment and imagined the view of the Eiffel Tower, the office I would have, if I went. "It's not that simple. I made a promise."

She shook her head and sighed. "How could you not go to Paris?"

"It was a promise." I'd already answered the only way I knew how.

When we left, my stomach was full, but it wasn't any more settled.

For some reason, the conversation hadn't helped as much as I'd hoped it would. Perhaps a group text with Andrina and Mena was in order. I'd get to that this evening for sure. But I was beginning to think this was just one of those problems that didn't have a good solution.

It had clarified one thing for me, though. I knew I had to stay if Charlie left, but if he stayed, my Paris dream might come true. It was a silly thought. Why would he want to stay? He'd said before that he thought Berlin was far enough away from his father. Had that changed?

The ball was in his court. Was he going to take the Berlin position or not?

Only after I knew Charlie's plans could I understand my path forward.

∼

## Charles

I ARRIVED AT THE BUILDING ALMOST IN TIME FOR THE AFTERNOON MEETING upstairs. Walking through the lobby, I half tripped as I forced a smile and a wave toward Marjorie.

She didn't smile back.

If the news of my fight with Dani had already traveled downstairs to reception, then probably everybody in the company knew. Marjorie's lack of a smile also indicated what version of the story she'd heard, and it didn't paint me in a good light.

Maybe that was as it should be. My petty scribblings had precipitated this. I should have shredded them weeks ago.

Upstairs, Abby checked the time and gave me the squinty eye as I approached. "They're waiting in the conference room."

I set my bag inside my office.

"You don't look good. Maybe you should splash some water on your face before going in," she said.

"Huh?"

"You asked for honesty. You look like you didn't sleep a wink."

"Right." I shrugged and turned around to follow her advice.

The face that greeted me in the mirror was every bit as bad as Abby had said. The water on my face barely helped before I hustled in to join the meeting. "Sorry I'm late," I said as I closed the door.

The marketing update went by in a blur, because every minute in there was another minute away from regaining my woman.

"Good work," I said as I brought it to a close. I'd done more nodding than listening and surely more hearing than understanding. But it would have to do for now.

Pradeep Chopra, our strategic marketing VP, looked around the room. "I guess that's it until next week."

His group nodded.

"Yeah, next week," I echoed.

As they departed, I opened my bag and looked over my desk for things I could take with me to work on at home.

Abby came in and closed the door behind her. "Leaving already?"

"I'm calling it a day for now."

"I saw the offer letter," she said. "Is it true. Are you leaving Hawker?"

"You didn't see my signature on it, did you?" I instantly regretted my tone. "I honestly don't know. I have to get some time to talk to Dani first."

"So you really haven't decided?"

I shook my head. "No."

∼

BACK AT MY FLAT, I WALKED OVER TO THE FULL-LENGTH WINDOW. FROM THIS vantage point I could see so much of the city, but not the one thing I wanted.

It was getting dark already, and Mrs. Blanchard hadn't called, as we'd agreed she would, if she heard anything next door, which meant Dani most likely wasn't returning today. Not returning today could turn into not returning tomorrow, and not returning forever. That only twisted the knot in my stomach tighter.

How had I managed to screw up the one good thing in my life? I was such an imbecile.

I pulled the mobile out of my pocket. Still no call. The saying that a watched pot never boiled might or might not be true, but I could attest that a watched mobile never rang. I set the phone down on the table by the window and walked to the kitchen. Maybe more space would do the trick.

Abby's question weighed on me. *Was I leaving Hawker for Berlin?* I used to want the Berlin job, but now I craved Dani. *She* was all I wanted. The Berlin operation paled in comparison.

Maybe I would leave Hawker. If Paris became Dani's destination, perhaps I'd find an opportunity there.

Whichever way it went, Dani was my future, and my task now was to convince her—to deal with what was driving her away. If it was the writings I'd done for Dad, she'd come to her senses once I explained it. If there was anything else, I'd slay that demon as well.

# CHAPTER 38

*Charles*

The next morning, I drank a glass of orange juice in front of the windows, looking out over the city with the same question on my mind: *Where are you, Dani?*

I almost dropped the glass when that wonderful ring of my mobile finally sounded. Rushing over, I was disappointed to find the name on the screen wasn't Dani *or* Mrs. Blanchard.

"I have an update for you, boss," Ben Murdoch said.

"Yeah?" I said.

"I think we've traced the guy paying for your tail."

"Who?"

A few days ago, finding out who was paying Thin Man to follow me would've been wonderful news, but it wasn't at the top of my list today. Maybe I could add finding Dani to Ben's list... He'd probably locate her quickly, and waiting wasn't ideal.

"Wanna guess?"

His words brought me back to the problem at hand. "I don't pay extra for drama," I said dryly.

He laughed. "We had to go to indirect surveillance to catch this guy."

"What does that mean?"

"All of the sudden it looked like he'd figured out we were watching him, so we had to give him the dumb-bird routine. That's where we plant some electronic tracking on him, along with an obvious tail, and let him lose us right away. Then, after he gets comfortable—a couple miles from where he started, probably—we can pick him up with another looser tail."

I didn't have the patience to listen to this. "I hope this is leading somewhere."

"I'm not an amateur. I wouldn't call otherwise," Ben said.

"Sorry, Ben. I'm expecting an important call."

"So," he continued. "We tracked this guy to the western part of the state, twice. Both times he met with a fellow we didn't think was important—that is, until we figured out he's the head of the union at your Fallwood factory."

I almost dropped the phone. "Califano?"

"That's the guy. Anthony Califano."

I clenched my teeth. "That son of a bitch."

"You know him, then?"

"Unfortunately. He's been creating problems for us ever since we bought Hawker."

"Like I said earlier, the kind of people paying for this firm don't want their business publicized. I could have a talk with him."

"Not yet."

That had sounded better the first time he'd suggested it. Now that I knew it was Califano, it made sense to figure out his game plan before confronting him. We'd have to continue dealing with him, and a pissed-off adversary with his power was not a pleasant thought. Up until now, I'd considered the strike threat to be a bargaining tactic, but embarrassing a man in his position could result in a labor strike as a revenge tactic.

"Okay. I'll be available to have that talk with him when you're ready."

"Sure, Ben, and thanks for the good work. I sincerely appreciate it."

"Just pass that along to my boss when you talk to him."

"Will do." For a moment I considered bringing up locating Dani, but I decided it was still too soon.

"Now that we've traced Mr. Big, do you want us to continue to shadow this guy?" Ben asked.

The daily expense was substantial—nothing I couldn't easily afford, but I had been brought up to not waste money. The question was, where was the payoff now that I knew Califano was behind it? When I couldn't answer that, I told Ben, "No. That's good enough on him. We still do have the Durban issue, though."

"We'll be ready for him when he shows up Thursday."

I thanked Ben again before we rang off.

Scanning the cityscape again, I voiced the question out loud this time. "Where are you, Dani?"

After calling again and getting her voicemail, I composed another text.

ME: Please call - Looking forward to talking with you

It was the fourth message I'd sent. Sooner or later, her inclination toward politeness would override her anger and she'd call. I'd give her another day or two before sending in Ben.

∽

## DANIELLE

I'D SPENT THE NIGHT AT THE PARK PLAZA, THE SAME HOTEL I'D STAYED IN WHEN I'd arrived in town. Just because I didn't want to stay in the apartment didn't mean I had to find a fleabag place to escape Charlie.

The sheets weren't as silky soft as Charlie's, but that wasn't the reason I hadn't slept well. When the clock next to the bed read eight o'clock, I gave up the battle and dragged myself into the shower.

I knew I had to talk to Charlie soon. It wasn't something I could avoid forever, but I still dreaded the meeting. How was I supposed to sit across from him, or be anywhere in the same room with him, and resist the pull he'd always had on me? I needed more time to build up the anger that would propel me through the meeting to the end. Otherwise I might give in to the dangerous temptation to forgive him and go back.

As I dressed, I concentrated on the awful words he'd written down. Those would propel me out of his orbit and keep me safe.

I left the room, and the experience of walking into the hotel restaurant downstairs was reminiscent of before. The petite hostess took one look at my face and her brows gave her away. Last time it had been the stain on my clothes. This time it was likely the no-sleep-for-two-days bags under my eyes.

The breakfast menu in front of me was surely the same as before, but somehow it didn't seem as appetizing as my first time here.

"Did the darts help?" I looked up to find Lisa, the waitress who'd been here when I'd first learned I was assigned to work with Charlie.

"Uh...yes and no."

"Is Dart Man still driving you crazy?" she asked. "Or again?"

It made me smile that she remembered our previous dartboard conversation. "It's complicated."

"It always is with men." She held her pencil over the order pad. "What can I start you off with?"

"I'd like a small orange juice, but what I really need is some strong coffee."

She smiled. "We've got a pot of what we call *morning triple* for a few of the regulars. Three passes through the machine—strong enough to wake up your dead uncle, if ya know what I mean."

I laughed. "Sounds perfect."

"Just don't blame me if you get the shakes. It's strong stuff."

I nodded, and she was off. Lisa's brand of humor was a welcome break.

I soon discovered she wasn't wrong about the coffee. Even after I stirred an extra packet of sweetener into the cup she came back with, it needed more.

Over my oatmeal and fruit, I checked the text that had come in while I was showering.

DADDY: Just checking in. Call when you can.

Daddy was another complication. I couldn't go long without talking to him, but what would I say? I didn't have an answer to that, so I put the phone down.

Calling Daddy without a plan was a horrible idea. I was still his precious little daughter, with the emphasis on *little*. He'd be on a plane to snatch me up before the day was out, and then he'd be utterly clueless when I protested that I wasn't still five, or eight, or ten.

No. I wasn't leaving or communicating until this issue was settled and I had a plan mapped out. I dialed Abby.

"Hi," she answered. "Are you on the way in? Wroblewski has been up here twice looking for you."

"No, not today."

"Tomorrow?"

"I'm not sure... I need you to cover for me if my father calls."

"Oookay." She paused. "What should I tell him, or not tell him?"

I'd thought this would be easier. "I'm off-site at a meeting—that kind of thing."

"In other words, duck the call like nothing is off."

"Yeah." I sighed. It was lame, but necessary.

"You're going to have to talk to Charlie to resolve this. You said he has to make a decision, but he's not going to do that until you two talk things out."

"He said that?" I knew it was a silly question as soon as the words left my mouth. She worked for both of us; of course she'd talked to him.

"I wouldn't be surprised if he's outside your door right now waiting for you."

"It doesn't matter."

"I could suggest it," she said. "That way it's not you asking him to come over."

"Maybe later."

After one more reminder to call Wroblewski, we got off the phone.

What I'd told Abby was the truth. If Charlie left for Berlin, I'd need to fulfill our promise to Derek, Sr., and stay here. But if Charlie wanted to stay, I couldn't—just another reason to face him and get the situation resolved once and for all.

*Charlie, what are you thinking?*

Almost as if we'd been telepathically connected, my phone rang with Charlie's name on the screen.

It took a few seconds to decide, but I declined the call—again. Just as with Dad, I needed to be prepared for the talk, and I wasn't. Not yet.

The text arrived a minute later.

CHARLIE: Please call - Looking forward to talking with you

I didn't answer that either.

I couldn't avoid everybody—two men at once was about my limit—so of the three, I dialed the easy one, Wroblewski.

"I have a note for you," he said as soon as we passed hello.

"From Califano?" I guessed.

"It's important."

I'd learned a non-denial in HR speak was most often a yes. Another set of demands wouldn't be surprising at this stage.

"Is this strike deadline?" That was the one thing Charlie and I had been dreading recently.

"I'm just the messenger."

"Leave it with Abby, and I'll get it later."

"Where are you so I can bring it over? I need to hand deliver this."

That was a twist I hadn't expected. Unwilling to give up my comfortable hiding location, I lied. "At the apartment."

"I'll come right over. What's the address?"

The man was certainly persistent. Checking the time I answered, "Make it ten thirty, and Abby has the address." Curiosity won out. "Are you going to at least tell me what it is?"

"Above my pay grade," he replied. "Like I said, I'm just the messenger."

He was hiding something. It had better not be a ruse to show up with Charlie in tow. That would suck.

All this was taxing my brain, so I did what any rational woman in my position would do. I added more sugar to my oatmeal. Without any Twinkies nearby, it would have to do.

Lisa returned. "Can I get you anything else?"

"Naw. I'm good."

She pointed the eraser end of her pencil at me. "Dear, I've seen good. And it don't look like you. Stop obsessing about Dart Man. None of them are worth it."

"Right," I agreed.

"I'm serious. Go get a mani-pedi—pamper yourself, and send him the bill."

I nodded again. A spa day might help.

She was about to continue when my phone rang, saving me from more advice.

The surprise came when I turned the phone over to find Andrina calling.

The name sent a shiver down my spine. She never called. We were always very good about keeping to texting so all three of us could be in on the conversation. This had to be an emergency.

"Are you all right?" I asked as I answered.

"Yes, I'm fine. But I won't stand by and watch you wimp out again without saying something."

For a moment, words failed me. I was the one having a bad time, and my friend was supposed to be helping me instead of ranting over the phone.

"You're doing it again, girl, and you have to own up to that."

"Own up to what?"

We'd had a marathon texting session last night, and I'd thought her messages were supportive.

"I reread everything from last night and before, and you're back to your pattern."

"I don't have a pattern," I snapped. "And why are you yelling at me?"

"Simple. Because I'm your friend, and you need to stop ruining your life."

I had no idea where this was coming from. "I'm not ruining anything."

"Your letting your fear of commitment drive you away from this Charlie guy, just like you always do."

"I do not, and besides, I didn't do anything except find out he'd been lying to me."

"And what about Lawrence?"

Things had been fine with him—for a while. "He lied to me about where he was going."

"Drinking with the guys. Big deal."

"But he lied," I protested. "He said he was going bowling." I was right. Lawrence had lied to me, and nothing she said would change that.

"And then there was Jerome, and Randolph, and Frederick."

I gritted my teeth. "None of them were good for me," I growled. Her tirade was getting to be too much.

"How would you know? You broke it off."

"I knew it was wrong. That's why I broke it off." Her stupid question answered itself.

"With each of them, as soon as things got serious, you found something to complain about and ran away."

I didn't answer that. I hadn't gotten far enough to move in with any of them and take it to the next level.

"Your pattern is clear as day," she continued. "Things get the slightest bit serious, and you bail out of the relationship."

"They weren't right for me," I repeated.

"Maybe they were, maybe they weren't, but you never got to know. And, you've never gushed about any of them the way you have this Charlie dude. Look, girl, I've always had your back, and I love ya to death, which is why I have to say I think you're being an idiot by not giving this one a chance."

"I did."

"Stop being afraid of becoming your father. It's okay to get serious with a guy. You'll never know if it can work out until you try."

The comment about Dad hurt, because not being a serial marriage artist like him had always been important to me.

"Nobody's perfect," she continued. "Stop trying to put everything on him by finding some fault. At least be honest that you're scared. Start there and talk to him about it. Listen to what he has to say."

I didn't know what to say. Getting serious with a guy made me uncomfortable, that was true. *But they had lied.*

"Just think about it before you throw away the best guy you've met yet—and those are your words."

That hit me in the gut. I *had* said that about Charlie in a text last week. "Andi, I gotta go."

"Sure thing. We can talk later."

*The best guy I'd ever met*—it was true.

Was I overcompensating to avoid being like Dad? Was there another side to this story with Charlie?

# CHAPTER 39

**CHARLES**

I WAS STILL ON MY MORNING WALK WHEN MY SECURE SECOND MOBILE VIBRATED IN my pocket.

It was Ethan, and if he was using this phone, it wasn't just to check in. The street noise was heavy enough, and the foot traffic light enough, to allow for private conversation. Stopping by a tree, I accepted the call. "Hello?"

"Charlie, Durban is on the move."

My stomach tightened. "Where to?"

"I only just found out, but he boarded a flight to Boston first thing this morning. He's traveling British Air, arriving at eleven forty-five your time."

I checked my watch to make sure I had the right day. "I thought you said he was coming Thursday?" This was a day early.

"That was the plan, dear brother, but he changed it, probably due to his little mishap."

I could tell I was going to have to pry it out of him. "And what mishap would that be?"

"He's one-handed today." Ethan laughed. "It seems the poor chap was tying his shoes when his left hand got run over by an automobile."

I tried to imagine how that was possible. "His hand was run over by a car?"

"Absolutely. The hospital photos even show the tire treads."

He clearly wasn't telling me everything. "What's the real story?"

"That's what he told the coppers. His hand got run over as he knelt down to tie his shoe. And, of course, the perpetrator got away. Also, he was too distracted to notice the make of the car or get a look at the driver. The poor bugger's going to have to learn how to write with his other hand, probably forever."

I still didn't understand. "I don't get it. What does this have to do with him getting on an airplane to the States a day early?" It didn't make sense to travel directly after getting broken bones.

"I told you Abramovich wasn't a nice man to owe money to."

*Ahhh.* The injury wasn't actually an accident.

"Durban will be a desperate man when he reaches you," Ethan continued.

*No shit, Sherlock.* Turdball had to be in fear of his life, and that made him dangerous.

"Do we know anything else?" I asked.

"He booked a hotel in Salem. Is that near your lady friend?"

I blew out a breath of relief. "No. Pretty much the opposite direction." *Why Salem?*

"That's all I have for now. Good luck with the bugger. I'll text you the hotel details I have."

"Thanks for the heads-up, brother."

"Sure. That's what brothers do—tell each other important things when they come to be known." He was back on our Covington connection again.

"I was sworn to secrecy. I couldn't tell you; you know that."

"You didn't think I'd want to know about another branch to the family tree?"

"It's not like that, and you know it. I would've told you if I could." I'd said this before, and he never believed me.

"Well, I know now, and the world hasn't ended. So what would have been wrong with telling me earlier?"

I shifted to my other foot. This wasn't the time or the place for this again. "I know I owe you, and I haven't forgotten."

"Good." This had all been about reaffirming that I owed him a favor. "Now, go protect your girl from this Durban bloke. I understand the Americans have a liberal view of self-defense."

"I hope it doesn't come to that." Gerald deserved to have his face bashed in, but avoiding a battle was always better than having to win one.

"The man just had his hand crushed. He won't be in a good mood... TTFN." He rang off.

Ethan's comment worried me. After an encounter like that with his loan shark, Gerald was likely to feel the world closing in on him, and like any cornered animal, he would be irrational and dangerous.

With extra adrenaline in my veins, I rang Ben Murdoch.

He picked up after the second ring. "Mr. Blakewell, if you're calling to ask if we're ready for tomorrow, the answer is yes."

"Durbin changed his itinerary," I blurted. "He's arriving at Logan today on the eleven-forty-five British Airways flight from Heathrow."

"Shifty little bugger, huh?"

"Can you handle it?" That was the important question. The alternative was for me to throw Dani over my shoulder and carry her out of town.

"Do we know where he'll be staying or any other information?" Ben asked.

"Yes, he's booked a hotel in Salem. I'll forward the address."

"Anything else?" he asked.

"He had a serious altercation with his loan shark and has a bandage on his left hand."

"That should make him easy to spot. We'll use the same plan. You go tell the lady, and we'll follow him from the airport with backup."

I thanked him and rang off without explaining that *the lady* and I weren't on speaking terms right now. It wasn't a detail he needed.

With a little luck, this would be the final showdown with Gerald that would get him completely out of Dani's life.

Turdball needed to understand that he was Dani's past, and I was her future. Full stop. End of discussion.

After pocketing the secure phone, I turned back toward the flat to change.

∼

### Danielle

I waited at the apartment for Wroblewski and his all-important note. Personal hand delivery—it was like something out of a spy novel.

Why the union boss thought he had to communicate via written note instead of a simple phone call or meeting was beyond me, but there were a lot of things about Califano and his actions that didn't make any sense.

A half hour later, the knock at the door was Wroblewski, and I let him in.

"How you doing?" the big man asked.

I pulled the door closed behind him. The question wasn't unexpected, but I still fumbled the answer. "Just fine."

"Right." Of course he knew better. He held out a large envelope. "I promised to deliver this in person."

I accepted it. It was plain manila, with no writing on either side. "Any thoughts on why Califano is communicating this way?"

The big man chuckled. "This isn't from him."

When he didn't elaborate further, I tore open the envelope and pulled out the piece of paper.

"He faxed it to my office this morning," Wroblewski explained.

My breath hitched. The handwritten note wasn't signed by Tony Califano. Instead the name was Derek Hawker. "Hawker, Sr.?" I asked out loud without meaning to.

"He wanted you to have it as soon as possible."

"Thank you. You've done your duty." I nodded toward the door.

"I'll wait 'till you're done."

"Okay." It didn't make any sense that Derek, Sr., thought I wouldn't read it. But if he wanted the theater of it, I could go along. I sat on the couch and started reading at the line above my name.

> Although we never got close enough to use shortened names in our meetings, I'll use Dani, since Ron tells me you prefer it to Danielle.
>
> Dear Dani,
>
> The day we concluded the sale of the company, I was grateful for your help in coming to the quick solution that we did. The terms you proposed allowed me the unusual opportunity to spend additional time with my dear wife, Leslie. These past few weeks with her on the boat have been a godsend, and only now do I realize how big a debt of gratitude I owe you.
>
> Before you ask, yes, Leslie is doing well, and she very much looks forward to visiting the Galapagos Islands next week.

With wet eyes, I looked up to the HR man. "How long does she have?"

He took the chair across the coffee table. "Three to six months is what the doctors say."

I went back to reading.

I've been happy to hear how well the people at Hawker feel they've been treated by you and Charles. For that, I thank you.

I know it's not considered good form for your generation to take advice from oldsters such as myself, but I have a few things to convey, and I hope you will take these to heart. First, please excuse Ron for keeping me abreast of developments at the company. I made him promise me he would do so.

So, Ron had been a spy this whole time for the old man. I squinted up at him "Spying?"

He shifted under my gaze and shrugged. "Keeping him informed. He made me promise."

I nodded and went back to the letter.

I understand that you and Charles have been a very dynamic team and have gotten along quite well together until just recently. And I've also learned that a certain document prepared by Charles may have caused you to doubt him.

I looked over to Wroblewski again. "You saw what Charlie wrote about me?"

He sucked in a breath and nodded.

He'd been at the desk when I saw those and threw them down. "And the offer letter?"

He nodded again. "Yes."

"Does everybody in the company know?"

He shook his head vigorously. "You, me, I assume Abby…" He lifted his chin toward the letter. "And Mr. Hawker. That's all, I swear."

"And Monica?" I asked, referring to his assistant.

"I said nobody else."

Slightly relieved, I went back to reading.

You may know what was written, but I have something to add that may enlighten you as to why. It wasn't more than a day after the close of our transaction that I received a call from Charles's father. He didn't ask my opinion, but told me he planned to bring my son into the CEO role at some point after he convinced your father it made sense. With what Ron has told me, it seems clear that the elder Mr. Blakewell precipitated this whole episode. Now, it is your right to feel badly about what was written, but I'd suggest you consider the circumstances before rushing to judgment on young Charles. We all make mistakes. I certainly have made my fair share. One of those was rejecting my Leslie when I was younger. We parted ways, and it was my exceptional luck to get a second chance with her. For that I will always be grateful. Not many people get a second chance with the one that got away. I am one of those few.

The fact is, all men make mistakes, even the best.

Please accept this advice from an old man. Have courage. Look into his eyes and judge the man separate from the mistake. You both deserve that. You may not get a second chance. If farther down the road he turns out to not be the man you see in his eyes today, so be it. But you can't know without being brave enough to accept that risk.

Leslie and I thank you for the precious time together your efforts have afforded us. Every day is a blessing, and none should be wasted.

I wish you the best.

Have courage.

With many thanks,

Derek

I dabbed at the tears welling in my eyes.

"The old man sure can turn a phrase, huh?"

I nodded between sniffles. "But…" I wasn't sure where to start my argument that he didn't understand the whole story.

Ron leaned forward. "It's not my place to argue one side or the other, but if you want someone to talk to, I'm available."

I nodded again. "So you know we've been… We were…" I didn't know how to say Charlie and I had been sleeping together.

He smiled. "It's a small company. It's my job to know."

I sat silently, trying to absorb it all. Derek, Sr., had written things that echoed Andrina's rant. They were both telling me to not be a fool.

Wroblewski stood. "You let me know if you'd like to talk."

I sniffled again and thanked him before he left.

A lot of things needed to be considered. It was all so complicated.

I poured myself a glass of water, and drank it slowly. An hour later, I realized this wasn't complicated at all.

I'd claimed that my tattoo meant my fears were behind me. Now, I'd be the one who was a liar if didn't face my fear and take the leap. I had to believe it wouldn't turn me into my father. Failed relationships didn't have to be genetic.

It was time to end this and resolve the open wound between Charlie and me. I needed to look him in the eye and judge the man.

Since it wasn't a phone type of conversation, I sent him a message.

ME: We need to talk

His response was quick.

CHARLIE: Where are you?

ME: Apartment

CHARLIE: I can be there in twenty

His reply was just what I should have expected. Telling him I was here had been a mistake.

ME: Not now

I thought for a second.

ME: Could you meet me in the park at 1:00?

CHARLIE: I'll be there

That would give me time to get my head on straight and come up with more words than merely *I'm sorry*. The park where we'd had our first kiss always brought back that memory. It was a fitting place for this talk.

I needed the words to make him understand how hard it was for me, and how scared I'd been—how scared I *was*, and would remain. But I would let him explain what had happened, and I would look in his eyes for the truth as he did.

Derek, Sr., had written that I needed the courage to judge the man separate from the mistake. I knew in my bones that Charlie was a good man. Today I'd choose the hard path and stick it out, come thick or thin. I'd be his woman and get past this mistake.

Andrina's accusation had been spot on. I'd been the one to pull the ripcord on each of my relationships when I felt threatened. I'd told Charlie high windows and horses were my two big fears. How had I been so oblivious to the fact that my fear of commitment topped them both?

## CHAPTER 40

*Charles*

I checked the text messages again.

DANI: Could you meet me in the park at 1:00?

Then I checked my watch for the twentieth time.

She was five minutes late. There must've been traffic. But it wasn't like her to be late and not let me know. She hadn't said exactly which park, but this was the only one that made sense. It was the only park we'd gone to.

Sure, we'd walked in the Common across from my building, but if she meant that, she would've said the Common, wouldn't she?

There was a park closer to her flat, I remembered. Would she have meant that one without mentioning the name?

Pulling out my mobile, I rang her number again. No answer, which wasn't any different than it had been the last few days.

Maybe I shouldn't have overridden my impulse to go straight to her flat the moment she'd gotten in touch. But I was a gentleman above all else, and she'd asked for this place, so here I was, stupid or not.

The jitter in my leg wouldn't stop. The tension and lack of sleep had made me a complete wreck. All I wanted to do was get her back in my arms. Then things would be right again.

Mentally, I'd kicked myself a dozen times for not shredding those pieces of paper when I should have. I'd known for a long time that I wasn't giving any of it to Dad to use against her.

I jumped when the mobile rang.

Finally.

Unfortunately, the screen showed Ben Murdoch.

"Blakewell here," I answered.

"We lost the subject," Ben confessed.

"Lost him? How?" This day had just gotten monumentally worse. "You said you'd have him covered."

"There was an accident in the tunnel. My guy lost him, and we didn't get phone reception back until just now. These things can happen."

"So now what?"

"What I need from you is a list of places he might go. I've already sent a man to the hotel in Salem. Where else should we cover?"

I thought back and only came up with one suggestion. "The last two times I saw him were inside and outside the Hawker building."

"Then I'll have my airport guy cover that and send a separate one to cover your lady friend, if you tell me where to find her."

"She's meeting me here at Eastboro Park, and I can handle things."

"You sure you don't want me to send somebody?"

I shook my head. "No thanks, and I'll be taking her back to the flat." I fully intended to sling Dani over my shoulder if I had to. The Tremont Street building was the one place I knew she'd be safe from Turdball.

I tried her phone, and once more got no answer.

∾

## Danielle

The knock called me to the door. "Who is it?" I asked as I squinted through the peephole.

"Flower delivery for Wentworth." The guy was facing away from the door and adjusted his cap.

The roses were red this time, but I didn't want roses. I wanted to talk.

Grudgingly, I unlatched the deadbolt and opened the door. "Just a sec.

Let me get a tip." I turned to get my wallet. When I turned back, my heart stopped.

"Say a word and you're dead." Edwin Hawker, Jr., held a gun on me as he kicked the door closed behind him. He dropped the flowers on the floor.

I gasped. "What do you—"

He raised the gun toward my head. "I said not a word." His voice was cold, menacing.

I froze.

He glanced around before waving with the gun. "Over there. Sit in the chair."

I moved to the chair Wroblewski had vacated earlier and sat.

Daddy had once sent John and me to a kidnapping-survival course that I'd thought was a total waste, but it didn't seem so now as I dredged my memory for the rules.

*If there's an exit, yell, kick, hit, run like hell for it*, I remembered. If not, I should comply with all orders and make myself as compliant and unintimidating as possible.

A minute later, I had tape across my mouth, and my arms and legs were taped to the chair.

"Now we wait for your boyfriend."

"No," I screamed into the tape.

"Quiet." He slapped me hard.

I tasted blood and shivered as the ugly revolver came up.

He pushed the barrel against my forehead. "Quiet or die. Your choice, bitch. Nod if you understand."

Blinking to clear the tears, I nodded. *Compliant and unintimidating*, I repeated in my head.

He paced while we waited.

*Why me? Why was Junior here? What did he think he could force us to do?* The questions rattled around without answers.

Then the scary questions started.

*Would I survive this?*

*Would I get the chance to tell Charlie I loved him?*

In my mind, the words came so easily. Why hadn't I told him before?

*Why?*

*Why?*

∼

## Charles

I surveyed the parking lot one more time to be certain she wasn't here, sitting in a car waiting for me.

She wasn't.

Not answering my calls had become the norm since she'd left my building, but being twenty minutes late to a meeting she'd set up was not her style. Punctual with a capital P was one of the things I admired about her.

Having Turdball Gerald loose in the city made me antsy.

I checked my watch again and decided this was the least likely place for her turdball ex to come. There wouldn't have been any way for him to know Dani planned to be here. He did, however, know where her flat was and could be headed there right now.

Jumping into my car, I was careful this time to take the right-hand side of the road. Even if she'd decided against meeting me in the park, I needed her to answer the door when I knocked. Why would she have decided against meeting me and not texted? One answer to that involved Turdball, and it wasn't good.

~

## Danielle

Edwin paced back and forth like a caged animal, watching the door and glancing back at me occasionally.

I started the technique they'd taught us in the kidnapping class and prayed it would work. Wheezing loudly as I breathed through my nose, even I thought I sounded like I'd die if the tape stayed on my mouth.

After a minute of it, he stomped over. "One sound out of you..." He stuck the barrel of the gun against my nose and pushed my head back. "And I decorate the wall with your brains," he hissed. "Understand?"

I nodded as much as the gun shoved up my nose would allow.

He ripped the tape off and moved back.

Gasping for air, I took a number of deep breaths, the way they'd taught us. The hyperventilating made me nauseous, but score one for the class.

"You and your fancy terms," he spat, waving the gun around. Drops of his spittle landed on my legs.

"If you'd just left well enough alone, I'd be CEO now." He checked the door before continuing. "It says Hawker on the building for a reason. The company should have been mine. It's my birthright. You and that English dick have no right to be sitting in my office." An evil smile grew on his face. "But we're going to fix that. You won't be setting foot in my office ever again."

The man was delusional.

"When your boyfriend arrives, we're going to have a little party." He waved the gun around. "You two will be together in the great beyond, and I'll get the office I deserve."

I bit back my thought that the police would see right through whatever he had planned. *Stay calm, and don't rile or argue with the kidnapper* had been one of the primary lessons. I had to survive this.

The knock at the door sent a lump to my throat. It couldn't end like this.

He checked the peephole and unlocked the door.

As soon as it was open a crack, I yelled, "Run, he has a gun."

The door opened fully, and Abby walked in.

"Tape her mouth shut," she told Edwin.

## CHAPTER 41

*DANIELLE*

"WHAT?" I GASPED.

It couldn't be.

I blinked several times, but it was still Abby standing there.

Edwin raised the gun before I could get out another word. "Shut up." He closed the door behind her. "She almost suffocated."

"I don't care. We follow the plan," Abby said. "And we can't have her yelling."

The way she said *the plan* made it sound like she was in charge of this insanity. It didn't matter, they were both dangerous nuts.

She kissed Edwin, pulled a knife from her purse, and unfolded it. Cold, dangerous light glinted off the blade as she handed it to him.

I'd had a bad feeling when she'd talked about knives before, and this was the reason.

"And cut her loose," she said. "I gave you the statistics. They're never tied up. This needs to fit the profile. He'd just shoot her."

Sensing a possible way out, I ignored the teacher and spoke. "They're not going to believe it. He's not a violent man."

"Sure they will," she shot back. "Especially after I tell them about the threats I heard him make at the office."

The tape went back over my mouth, and Edwin laughed. "I definitely like her better quiet."

Abby stepped closer. "It happens every day. Woman rejects man. Man tries to get back together. Woman rejects man again. Man kills woman, then man kills himself—a cruel, Romeo-and-Juliet-style ending. The scenario fits perfectly." She laughed. "And everyone knows Englishmen are crazy."

I hadn't heard her laugh before. It was more a witch's cackle than a laugh.

Edwin cut my feet loose first and pulled away the tape before undoing my arms.

Now at least I had a slim chance of escape if the right opportunity presented itself.

Edwin waved the gun in my face again. "I know what you're thinking. You're thinking you can jump up and outrun a bullet." He grinned, and one eyebrow lifted. "Should we test that?"

The training took over. I shook my head. *Don't argue with them.*

"Cut it out, Eddie. We need the sequence to be right."

He stood up. "Just making sure she understands."

Abby looked my direction with icy eyes. "Oh, she understands. Don't you?"

She truly was a witch. I nodded slowly.

Edwin checked his watch. "He's late. What if he doesn't show?"

"He'll be here. What choice does he have?"

This was one time I hoped Charlie didn't do what was expected of him. Closing my eyes, I tried the telepathy thing again.

I repeated it over and over in my head: *Charlie, please know I love you and don't come.*

~

## CHARLES

I DROVE AROUND THE SLOW TRUCK. I JUST HAD TO REMEMBER TO CRANK THE wheel right instead of left when the oncoming traffic honked at me. Dying in a twisted heap of metal was not my future today.

*She'll be safe*, I told myself. The way she'd refused to open the door for me would keep Turdball at bay if he came knocking before I got to her.

My plan might not be the best, but at least it was simple. I was going to grab Dani, hoist her over my shoulder if need be, and take her back to Tremont Street. She wasn't leaving until she heard me out. End of plan.

Of course carrying a screaming woman through the lobby of my building might not fly, but I'd figure that out when I got there. Carl could probably open the back door and freight elevator for me. That could work.

Dani and I were going to be together—at least long enough for her to see beyond my last name and judge me for who I was, not as my father's son.

The family feud had to be the core problem, didn't it? Dani still had the Blakewell hatred baked into her brain from her father. She'd never known the truth about the night it started.

After parking, I strode with purpose, but I didn't run. I took the stairs one at a time.

*Calm*, I reminded myself.

Showing up at her door panting like a raving lunatic wouldn't get me inside. Calm, cool, and collected.

I reached the door and raised my hand to knock.

## CHAPTER 42

*DANIELLE*

Concentrating on my mantra, I had no idea how long it had been when a knock did sound at the door.

Abby jumped to her feet and unfolded the knife again.

Edwin tiptoed to the door.

I tilted my head away when Abby poked her weapon in my ear.

"If you make a sound, you'll find out it takes less than ten pounds of pressure for a knife to penetrate the brain through the ear canal."

I gave the slightest nod.

After checking the peephole, Edwin nodded toward Abby before pulling open the door and leveling the revolver. "Inside. Now."

It was Gerald.

Gerald's eyes went wide, and his mouth dropped open. His left hand was covered by a huge bandage. A second later, he slumped to the floor without a word.

"Huh." Edwin stuffed the gun in his belt, grabbed Gerald's good hand, and pulled him inside before closing the door. "I don't believe it. He fucking fainted."

I stretched my neck after Abby pulled the knife away.

She looked at me and giggled. "You were going to marry this stiff? He peed himself."

The wet spot was obvious, and them laughing was almost enough of a distraction, but I didn't have enough separation from them to try anything yet.

*Wait for the right moment*, I told myself.

With Gerald on the floor, their words clicked. By *boyfriend* they'd meant Gerald, not Charlie. I still had a chance.

It was worth a try. Closing my eyes again, I started a different telepathic message. *Help. I'm in danger*, I repeated silently, over and over.

"What the fuck?" It was Gerald.

I opened my eyes.

Edwin waved the gun at him. "Quiet."

Gerald looked at me. "You said you had money for me?"

I knew better than to respond to anything he said.

"You're too easy, Durban," Abby said. "I borrowed her phone to send that."

"No money?" he asked incredulously. He looked ready to break down crying.

Edwin kicked his leg. "Shut up."

Too stupid to obey, Gerald asked, "What's the meaning of this?"

Edwin kicked him harder. "I said shut the fuck up."

Abby brandished her knife in his direction. "You'll do as Eddie says, if you value your dangly parts." She pointed the tip at his wet crotch. "Here's the deal. Your girlfriend here wasn't smart enough to leave after we trashed this place." She looked at me. "Nice job cleaning it up, by the way."

I didn't respond.

"We needed a different way to get rid of her. That's where you come in." She pulled my phone from my purse and typed.

Gerald's phone dinged.

Abby wiped the phone off and replaced it where it had been. "She just told you there is no money, and the joke's on you."

"This is where it gets good." Edwin laughed. "What kind of gun is this?"

Gerald blinked a few times. "A Webley. I have several."

"Exactly," Abby replied. "You brought one of your guns along, and in a rage, you shot your ex-girlfriend here."

"I couldn't have brought a gun on the plane."

That was the first smart thing Gerald had said.

"But you did overnight several packages to yourself yesterday," Abby noted.

Edwin grinned. "I helped you with that."

"And paid a shill to pick them up for you," Abby added. "Whole guns might not get through, but gun parts are another matter. And after you shoot her, you'll find you can't live with yourself and blow your brains out."

"I'll not be a party to that. You'll have to shoot me in the back." Gerald tried to get up, but Edwin put a foot on him.

"Or, she shoots you in the crotch two…no, three times and watches you writhe in agony for an hour or so before putting a bullet in your head and taking an overdose of pills herself," Junior suggested. "Either way, it works."

Abby lifted a couch pillow. "In case you're thinking it would be too loud. Think again."

"Yeah, think real hard," Edwin echoed.

Footsteps approached, coming down the hall.

"Quiet," she said as she moved toward me with the knife.

Edwin pressed the gun against Gerald's crotch.

The footsteps receded.

"Tape both their mouths until I get back to the office and call you." Abby said softly.

"Over by her," Edwin ordered Gerald. He handed the gun to Abby while he taped us.

Just like that, both Gerald and I had tape over our mouths and around our heads. This wasn't coming off with a quick pull.

Edwin took the gun back and waved us to the couch.

∽

## Charles

Something told me to pull my hand back instead of knocking.

Retreating a door away, I pulled out my mobile and located the email from Ben with the link. My finger hovered over it for a second. I'd only pressed it once before to check that the camera in Dani's flat worked.

Right now I needed to know—if she didn't answer the door, was she inside or not? If she was in there and didn't answer, it was over and I wouldn't stoop to begging. If we had a chance, if we had had a future, she would have come to the park.

Before I'd summoned the courage to click the link, the door behind me opened, and Mrs. Blanchard peeked her head out. "Back again?"

I nodded.

"Where are the flowers? I told you two, three dozen red roses. Nothing less."

I didn't need flowers if she wouldn't answer the door. I clicked the button. My mouth dropped open, and my heart almost stopped.

A man had a gun on Dani and some other man. I couldn't see any of the faces, just my woman's.

I looked to Mrs. Blanchard and back to the screen, stunned.

"Don't give me that look, young man. You know what I'm talking about."

"Inside." I lifted a chin toward her door. "Can I come in for a second?"

She forced Rufus back and opened the door for me. "I only have two carnations on the table. You need a florist."

I shut the door behind me, still watching the screen.

She walked toward the couch. "You young people need to put those things away and learn the basics, starting with flowers and compliments."

I put a finger to my lips. "Quiet. I have a problem."

"I'll say you do."

I pointed the screen toward her. "There's a man with a gun next door."

She gasped, and her hand went to her chest. "You need to call 9-1-1."

My SAS training went through my head in fast-forward. Rule number one of hostage extraction was surprise. Any sirens suggesting help was on the way and the enemy would use the hostages as shields, making the whole operation seven times more likely to result in injuries to the hostages. They'd actually run the numbers.

"No time," I said, putting a finger to my lips. "We need to stay quiet."

Her eyes bugged and the blood left her face, but she stayed silent.

Then it came to me. The back door out to the balcony still didn't lock.

Quickly I slid open the door to Mrs. Blanchard's balcony and slipped out. I was in luck. The partition between the units would be easy to get around.

Looking back at the screen, I still couldn't see the gunman's face, but he'd shifted to the side, and now I could see the other man more clearly. Gerald the fucking turdball. But the bad guy had his gun on both of them.

I left the balcony door open and went back inside. "I need your help to get Dani out safely."

"Me?"

"What would you do if someone threatened Rufus?"

"I'd kick him in the jewels so hard they'd hear the scream in New York."

"That's the spirit." I pulled out my secure mobile and dialed it from the mobile I held. Once they were connected, I muted mine and put the secure one on speaker at full volume.

She looked on, puzzled.

I handed her the secure one. "Put this on the floor right in front of her door. Knock once, hurry back here, and lock the door."

## CHAPTER 43

*DANIELLE*

ANOTHER KNOCK SOUNDED AT THE DOOR.

Edwin looked over at us and waved the gun with a finger to his lips.

With the tape on my mouth, there wasn't anything else I could do.

He approached the door.

"Dani, are you in there?" The voice from behind the door was Charlie.

I shivered with an instant chill.

Abby flushed the toilet.

"Dani?"

Edwin leaned against the door, looking through the peephole.

I had to do something, but he had a gun. I stood up, grabbed the closest thing—a book—and threw it.

Edwin turned back.

In a flash, the man ran by me and slammed into Edwin with a thud.

It didn't make sense. It was Charlie. He'd come in from the balcony behind us.

Gerald slid to the corner.

Edwin turned and growled, but a punch to the throat and the gun clattered to the floor without another word. Several punches and slaps to the head, a knee to the groin, and Edwin doubled over.

With a swift kick and twist of the arm, Charlie took him to the ground. Edwin screamed in pain as Abby bolted from the bathroom. "Eddie?"

As soon as she saw the scrum on the floor, she unfolded her knife and started toward me.

I grabbed my purse and hit her square in the face with the pepper spray.

This time Abby screamed as she clutched her eyes. "You bitch." She swung the knife wildly.

I stepped back just as Charlie grabbed her wrist, spun her around, and kicked her in the back.

She hit the wall with a thud and slumped to the floor like a rag doll.

"Abbs," Edwin shrieked.

Spinning back to Edwin, Charlie pulled the gun from his belt and leveled it. "On the floor or else."

Edwin lay down.

Gerald cowered in the corner.

It was over, and it had only lasted a few seconds.

My heart was thundering a thousand beats a minute when Charlie slipped me his phone. "Dial the police for me."

I did, and I put it on speaker for him, laying it down so I could work on the tape wrapped around my head.

~

*Charles*

A LITTLE WHILE LATER, THEY'D FINISHED QUESTIONING MRS. BLANCHARD and let her go back to her flat.

"Flowers," she'd whispered to me on her way out.

I kept my arm tightly around Dani as I explained how things had gone down to Detective Bosco.

He'd tried to separate us, a common interrogation technique, but I'd refused. I wasn't letting go of my woman again.

"And you decided to try this crazy stunt alone instead of calling us?" he asked. "You could have gotten everybody killed."

"I'm trained," I told him.

"Yeah? By who?"

I wasn't allowed to say, so I stayed mum.

"He can't tell you," Dani said. "Official Secrets Act, you see."

"That doesn't cut it here in the colonies," he said.

I shrugged. "I'm not at liberty to say."

The detective shook his head and moved on. "And all this has to do with the company you run?"

"Apparently." I nodded. "They thought that with Dani out of the picture and me headed to Berlin, Edwin there would get to run the company."

"And the one-handed man over there is just a victim in this as well?" Bosco asked.

"He was going to be the patsy," Dani explained. "They thought they could make it look like a murder-suicide."

Just the sound of that made me cringe. They'd come too close.

"Isn't he the one you think trashed this place before?" the detective asked Dani.

"He was," she said. "But they admitted to doing it."

"You're going to pay for this," Abby screeched as they led her out with her broken nose bandaged.

"You're the one who told me to get pepper spray," Dani shot back.

## DANIELLE

Two hours later, the door closed behind the final police officer.

We were finally alone.

Charlie pointed at the wall Abby had landed against. "I don't know if the cleaning crew will be able to get that out or not."

A pool of blood from her broken nose had soaked into the carpet.

"And the pee," I pointed to the wet spot near the door.

"Who?" he asked.

"Gerald," I sighed.

"I don't know what you ever saw in that wanker."

"Me either." In retrospect, I'd probably seen a sense of safety, in that I knew deep down we'd never progress as a couple.

I walked to the fridge. One of us had to break the awkward silence. "We should talk."

Charlie came up behind me. "Let me go first."

I pulled out a water. "Want one?"

"Sure."

He took the one I offered, and I grabbed another one. For a moment, the crackling of the plastic as we twisted the tops off was the only sound in the apartment—that and my heart thundering with fear.

I turned to face him. It was now or never.

He took a quick sip. "Listen, I told Dad I'd take the Berlin assignment—"

"I'm sorry," I blurted. My eyes started to water, and I looked down. I'd screwed this up. There it was. I'd waited too long and pushed him away. I couldn't even look at him, I was so embarrassed.

He set his water on the counter and took mine from me.

A second later I was in his arms, sobbing. "I'm sorry. I'm sorry," I repeated. "I should have listened to what you wanted to say."

He pulled my chin up to force me to look him in the eyes. "You didn't let me finish. I told him I would take the job, *if* things didn't work out with you."

I sniffled. "You want to try?"

He pulled my head to his chest. "Cookie, I've never wanted anything else."

I hugged him tighter. "When Junior held the gun on me, my greatest fear was that I'd never get to tell you I love you, Charlie Blakewell."

He tightened his grip and kissed the top of my head. "Cookie, I love you too."

Derek, Sr., had said I needed to look into his eyes and have the courage to judge the man separate from the mistake, but he'd been wrong. With Charlie, I had no need to look into his eyes to know the man he was.

I took a breath. "It's hard to admit, but I was scared, and I still am. I've never—"

"I know," he said. "You've never done it on a tabletop or in the woods." He laughed. Even now, he was trying to make it easier for me. "Don't worry. We'll get to all those positions and then some."

I pushed at his shoulder. "I'm being serious. I need to say this so you'll understand."

"I understand enough," he said. "To appease my father, I wrote things about you I shouldn't have. Mean things. Things that never should've been written. And they weren't even true. I'm sorry I hurt you. You need to know that."

"Now you're the one not letting *me* finish."

"Okay. I'm listening."

I nestled into the safety of his shoulder. "I have a third fear, beyond high windows and horses. A bigger one. I'm afraid of following in my father's footsteps. I'm afraid of committing to a relationship and having it fail. You know how many times he's been married?"

"Stop it. You're not him."

"What if it doesn't work? What if we can't make it work?"

He pulled my chin up to look at him again. "Listen to me. Everybody has that fear. We just take it one day at a time. That's all we can do. You're overthinking it. You don't know the future any more than I do, or anybody else. We start the journey together with faith in each other. That's all we need."

"But—"

He silenced me with his thumb to my lips. "It's true for all of us. We have nothing to fear but fear itself."

"Quoting Roosevelt now?"

"No. Churchill."

"I'm pretty sure it's Roosevelt."

"They call it the English language for a reason. I'm English, so I'm right."

I laughed at that, and continued laughing when I figured out what he'd done. He'd pulled my attention away from my fear on purpose. I said the one thing I knew to be true. "You're a good man, Charlie Blakewell—strange, but good."

"Maybe so, but I love you, Dani Wentworth, and that's all I need to know. I don't know where the road of life will lead us, but it's certain to have potholes along the way. We'll work through those things. I'll make a mistake here and there, just because I'm human. But I don't want to give up all the good days I know we're going to have together just to avoid a bad one."

I sniffled again, realizing how close his words were to the sentiment Derek, Sr., had tried to convey. *Don't let the good one get away.*

"You know me," he said. "I'm all in. You're mine, Cookie. And I'm not letting you go."

I knew I loved him, but I still had to suck in a breath of courage. "Okay. One day at a time."

He squeezed me in a bear hug. "That's right." He released me and pulled me toward the door.

I resisted. "My water."

He let me go. "Bring it then. I'm ordering Thai. But first we're hitting the tattoo parlor."

"No way."

He lifted my wrist and traced along the inside of my forearm. "Right here. So you don't forget, it's going to say *Charlie loves me.*"

"I won't forget." I put my arm down.

"Okay, no tattoo parlor. So we go straight to new experiences." He pulled me to the door again. "Come with me. Tonight you get the tabletop."

Strange but good. That was my Charlie.

# CHAPTER 44

*Charles*

***(one week later)***

Dani and I were on the way to meet Califano at his house again. The scenery outside the car was lush and green, but it didn't make up for the fact that she was driving.

I hated not being in control. "I'll drive on the way back," I announced.

She didn't even look over to deliver her rebuke. "My car, so I drive. I'm not taking any chances after your fender bender."

"It was just a minor prang. Nobody got hurt. And it was the other bloke's fault anyway." It'd been two days ago, and the shop said I wouldn't have my car back until next week at the earliest. A whole week in the passenger seat would be agony.

"We call it defensive driving over here. You need to learn."

I looked out the window. Arguing wasn't going to get me anywhere, and I had another solution in mind anyway. "You remember the script for how we start?"

"Yeah, it's real hard," she scoffed. "Look pretty and be quiet. Act like I'm too stupid to understand when he dumps on me."

I rolled my eyes. The *be quiet* part might actually be hard for her.

A mile later she announced, "Here we are." She turned into the drive that led to Califano's house.

I pulled out my mobile and sent the text I'd already prepared.

ME: We're arriving now

The reply was immediate.

BENSON: We'll be waiting.

"I'd sure like to be driving that," I said as we passed Califano's Ferrari. It was a beautiful car that begged to be driven fast. Even parked, it reminded me of a greyhound waiting to be let off the leash.

"I'll bet you would, but the company doesn't have the budget for something like that."

"This will be fun," I told her as she shut down the motor. "But I wish we weren't going so easy on him."

"Simple human dynamics. We need to do them a favor now—"

"To get them on our side for later," I finished. "I get it." I opened my door. "That doesn't mean I have to like it." I knew she didn't like it either, but we'd agreed it was the best solution for us.

She exited before I could get around to open the door for her. Her rebellion against my impulse to be a gentleman was a small price to pay for having my woman by my side.

I took her into my arms. "Have I told you I love you today?"

"Let me think." She scrunched up her face. "Three times, I think."

"It was four," I corrected her. "Or five. You always forget about the shower."

"When the word *love* comes out of your mouth and you have my boobs in your hands, it's hard to tell who you're talking to."

I looked her in the eyes. "Don't let him get under your skin. Remember our objective." Nailing Junior was what mattered.

"It won't be a problem." She undid another button on her top.

As before, Stefano, the union's lawyer was at the door to greet us before anyone else. Bristow, the chief steward, was just behind him, followed by Califano.

"If it isn't the Limey again. How ya doin'?" Califano asked as he shook my hand. "We weren't scheduled to meet again until next week."

"We have something important to discuss," I replied.

His gaze shifted to Dani. "And I see you brought your pretty assistant. Sweetheart, you can call me Tony."

Of course his eyes drifted down to her chest.

"Thank you," she said sweetly.

I wiped my hand on my trousers while he wasn't looking. The man was a pig.

"You're American, right?" he asked.

Dani nodded. "Why yes, I am."

"When you get tired of working for the Limey here, you come work for me."

"Thank you. I'll remember that."

She hadn't broken character, but this had to be killing her.

We were ushered into a room with the table where we took seats opposite the three of them.

Califano's gaze stayed on Dani, and not her eyes.

I didn't waste any time pulling the contract extension out of the folder I'd brought in and sliding it across the table. "We brought this for you to sign."

Stefano flipped through a few pages. "This is several revisions old."

"Exactly," I said. "It's the same one you agreed to just before we started negotiating for the company."

Stefano closed the document. "We didn't agree to anything back then, and we certainly didn't sign."

Califano looked bored. "No still means no." He shifted to Dani. "You got that down, sweetheart?"

She didn't bat an eye. "Sure, Tony. No means no."

"If the word is too difficult for ya," Califano told me, "check your American-to-Limey dictionary."

I smiled at her, proud that she'd kept her mouth in check. We were almost to her turn. I turned back to the arsehole. "Her name isn't sweetheart."

He smirked. "Seems to me we're done here." He put his meaty hands on the table and pushed his chair back.

"This is a one-time offer," I said.

"Then I should only have to say no once."

"It's your only chance to shave off five years," I told him.

"Off what?"

"Your prison sentence."

"Don't you fucking threaten me," he shot back before looking to his lawyer. "Don't we have laws against shit like that?"

The lawyer stayed silent.

Califano put his finger on the papers. "Why do I have to repeat myself? I'm not doing this piece of shit."

His chief steward didn't seem amused.

Califano pointed his pudgy finger at me. "You, I don't trust. I said I'd only deal with Derek Hawker, Jr., and I meant it."

As we'd hoped, he hadn't heard of Junior's arrest yet.

I opened my mobile and sent the message I'd cued up.

ME: Now

I turned the show over to Dani. "Why don't you explain it to him?"

∽

## Danielle

I'd seen Charlie send the text, and it only took two seconds for the sirens to sound. "Thank you, Charlie. I'd love to."

The three across from us focused on the sounds coming from the main road and getting closer.

I hesitated as they looked back and forth between us and the door. "What you hear is the FBI arriving."

"What kind of game are you playing?" Califano demanded.

I savored the moment before answering. "No game, Tony. They're here to arrest you." *Take that, you pig.*

"You can't fucking arrest me. I ain't done nothin'." The look in his eyes said otherwise. He was scared and ready to lash out.

Stefano put a hand on Califano's shoulder. "Don't say any more, Tony."

"They got nothin' to arrest me on," Califano complained as he swiped the hand away. "Nothin'."

"Shut up, Tony," Stefano told him. He turned back to me. "What's this about?"

The sirens came closer, and Califano glanced toward the door again.

*Sweetheart my ass.* I couldn't help but smirk. "Tony took bribes from Derek Hawker, Jr., and conspired with him to hold up this contract extension so Mr. Hawker could get the CEO position at the company."

"I never took no money. Not a penny," Califano blurted. "I ain't even met with him in over a year."

"Not another word, Tony," Stefano hissed.

I pulled the paper from my portfolio and slid it to the lawyer. "You and I both know Mr. Califano doesn't pull a large enough salary from the union to afford the Ferrari outside. This is the purchase contract for the car, paid for in cash by Mr. Hawker. The same car he then transferred to Tony."

Califano slumped slightly and for once didn't have anything to say.

"They record VIN numbers, even for cash transactions, and it matches the car outside. Then there are the statements a Mr. Caldwell is willing to make about the arrangement. He was the go-between so they didn't meet face to face."

"That fucking rat," Califano sneered.

Stefano glared at his client, just as the pounding on the door started.

"FBI. Open up. Anthony Califano, open the door."

I looked at the lawyer and nodded toward the door. "Either you open it or they break it down."

Stefano waved Bristow to the door. "Let 'em in."

"And you stay quiet," he told Califano before standing. He rounded the table and intercepted the agents just inside the door. "I'm Vincent Stefano, Mr. Califano's attorney. I'd like to see some identification."

I turned to watch Ashley Benson and John McNally present their credentials.

Ashley was a senior FBI agent in the Boston office, and very conveniently for our plan, the wife of Vincent Benson, who lived one floor above us in the Tremont Street building. It was Benson's company, Covington Industries, that Charlie rented the condo from. Like he said, it was good to know a guy.

We'd met Ashley and her partner, John, the day after my harrowing kidnapping. The fact that stupid Gerald was a British citizen had gotten the Boston PD to call in the FBI.

To my chagrin, I'd learned that no ransom demand meant it didn't rise to a federal kidnapping case. Still, Califano was about to learn his fate, and that made me smile.

Ashley handed Stefano a piece of paper. "We have an arrest warrant for your client."

The lawyer moved aside and refolded the paper after reviewing it briefly.

Ashley didn't mince words. "Stand up, Mr. Califano. You are under arrest for criminal conspiracy and racketeering."

Califano stood. "But I didn't—"

"Tony," the lawyer said. "Stop talking and go with them. I'll arrange bail."

The sound of the handcuffs clicking closed was music to my ears.

Charlie laid a hand on my thigh with a gentle squeeze.

I smiled back and listened to the Miranda warning they read the jerk. It was straight out of the cop shows on TV, only more ominous in person.

Califano's bluster wilted into slumped shoulders.

Ashley then handed Stefano another sheet of paper. "A court order to impound the Ferrari outside, pending possible forfeiture proceedings."

Stefano merely nodded and handed back the paper.

McNally led Califano to the door.

"Counselor," Ashley said, pointing a finger at us, "I suggest you listen to these two." She added to me, "We'll wait outside for you."

After Califano was led out, and the door closed behind the trio, the lawyer sat. "Listen to what?"

Charlie patted my leg and sat back. "Go ahead."

"Two things." I pulled out the Assistant US Attorney's card. "AUSA Gordon will be handling his case. You have twenty-four hours to agree to a plea deal for a reduced sentence in exchange for testimony against Mr. Hawker, Jr., and Mr. Califano will be barred from future leadership in any labor organization."

"That's ridiculous," Stefano objected. "I haven't seen one iota of evidence against Tony."

We'd expected that. I slid over the rest of the statements I had. "These are from the go-between, Caldwell, detailing his several meetings with Mr. Califano and Mr. Hawker. The conspiracy case is clear, as you'll see."

"I doubt that." Stefano's bluster was obvious. "And why do you care?"

"Hawker, Jr., held a gun on me, that's why." I'd recovered enough that I could discuss the event without reliving the fear.

"I see." Now he was connecting the dots.

"The second item," I continued, "is that we have certain evidence we haven't shared with the FBI yet. It indicates that your boss was acting in his official capacity as a representative of the union in this whole scheme."

"That's not possible," Stefano complained.

Bristow merely shook his head.

"If you two convince the executive committee to accept the previously agreed contract extension…" I pointed at the stack of paper still on the table. "…by tomorrow, we won't share that information with the FBI."

"We're only two of seven," Bristow said, finally finding his tongue.

"It's just a question of being persuasive, then. The Justice Department is full of zealots when it comes to unions and racketeering. You'd be much better off if this prosecution was limited to Tony personally, rather than dragging the union in as an organization. We'd like to think this stunt didn't go any further than Tony." I looked to my side. "Right?"

Charlie nodded. "Exactly. We'd like to put this behind us and get back to business."

"I never knew a thing," Bristow said.

Breathing a heavy sigh, Stefano added, "I don't expect a problem with the executive committee. We should be back with you before the end of the day, don't you think, Jim?"

Bristow nodded. "I know the guys on the floor would feel good about having the stability of an extension."

Once we were outside, I whispered to Charlie. "Do you think they connected the dots?"

"No doubt about it. Didn't you see Bristow's eyes light up when you mentioned no more labor roles for Califano? He sees a promotion in his future. Those two will convince him to cooperate, and Junior will be looking at a very long stay behind bars."

Charlie's words filled me with relief, and his arm around me reinforced it. Junior would get what he deserved.

Agent McNally was standing alone outside. The black SUV he and Ashley had been in was gone. "Done?"

"Yup," I said.

Charlie held out his hand to me. "Keys?"

Not feeling like arguing, I fished them out of my purse.

He released me and tossed them to McNally.

"What the..." I ducked a set of keys McNally threw back.

Charlie caught them. "Thanks. See you back in town."

McNally walked to my car and opened the door. "Remember the Pottery Barn rule," he called before climbing in.

"Right." Charlie veered left, pulling me away from my car to the Ferrari.

"How?" I asked as he opened the passenger door for me.

"It's not what you know, but *who* you know."

Shaking my head at the absurdity of this, I slipped down into the low-slung, red beast.

Once we were buckled in, Charlie pressed start and the engine roared to life with a mechanical symphony of sounds. He blipped the gas pedal a few times like a teenager, and his grin grew.

"Ever drive one of these?" I asked.

"Can't say that I have, but how hard can it be? Point and press the throttle to the floor."

The way he drove the car gingerly down the drive relaxed me.

We turned onto the main road, following McNally in my sedan.

"What's the Pottery Barn rule?" he asked.

I laughed, realizing he'd pretended to know what McNally was saying. "You faker, you. You're the one who agreed to it." I was in luck because there was one about two miles ahead.

"And what is the rule?"

"If you see a Pottery Barn, you have to switch drivers," I deadpanned.

He glanced over. "No. What is it really?"

"If you break it, you own it. It's yours."

He laughed. "I like it. I'll have to remember that one." He downshifted and floored it.

I braced my feet against the floor and held on to the door.

With a roar of what had to be a thousand horses behind us, we passed McNally in a flash.

"You know we have speed limits in this country?"

He slowed from Mach one to a merely fast pace.

Once on the turnpike, Charlie guided the car with precision.

The faces of the people we passed were filled with envy. They probably thought I was lucky to be riding in this red rocket. They didn't realize my real luck was being with the man next to me.

I looked over and extended my hand over the center console. "Thank you."

He glanced my way and took my hand. "For what?"

"For making me face my fear and say yes."

"Yes to what?"

I reveled in the warmth his hand transmitted to mine and rubbed my thumb lazily back and forth. "Yes to being with you, to being your girlfriend, to taking a chance on our future."

The squeeze of his hand said more than words could. "Hang on, Cookie. There's more fear-facing to come."

I knew in my heart that being with him would give me the strength for that.

I pointed. "Watch out." A pothole the size of Detroit loomed ahead.

He torqued the car hard right and then left, missing the Grand Canyon in the pavement. "I told you there'd be potholes along our path, but we'd get past them."

I huffed. "I thought you were speaking metaphorically."

"I was, but you survived, didn't you?"

I nodded. I was more than surviving. Thanks to him, I was living.

# EPILOGUE

## "I BELIEVE THAT EVERY SINGLE EVENT IN LIFE HAPPENS IN AN OPPORTUNITY TO CHOOSE LOVE OVER FEAR." – OPRAH WINFREY

**DANIELLE**

It was Saturday night, our game night.

Charlie opened the condo door and turned the lights on low. "Stop right there."

Shivers ran through me as I froze. I'd been wet since before we left the restaurant, unsure what his choice of game would be tonight.

His conversation all through dinner had been full of sexual innuendo and suggestive comments. He had a knack for getting my motor running ahead of time with his words as much as his touch.

"Go to the center of the room and turn around," he said.

When I turned, he eyed me hungrily. Tonight he was the predator, and I was his prey. So long as it involved getting naked, I was all in for this game, and I had a surprise of my own.

He walked to the controls and turned on soft music. He twisted his finger in the air.

Slowly, I twirled around.

"You're a fucking beautiful sight to behold." He swirled his finger in the air again.

I turned another time.

"Dance for me, and lose the dress."

I did my imitation of a hip-swaying striptease as I unzipped the dress and let it slide down to puddle at my feet. I stepped out and kicked it to the side.

He adjusted the lights lower. "Now the bra."

I undid the hooks and slipped off one strap then the other, holding it in place with my elbows before finally letting it drop to the ground. A striptease wasn't something we'd done before, and I got goose bumps—not from the temperature in the room but from excitement.

His finger asked for another turn, and I obliged, taking my hands up to my breasts and squeezing them together.

Even in the dim light, I could see his eyes bug out. He adjusted the bulge in his pants.

I leaned over to undo the straps on my heels.

"No. Keep them on."

It didn't surprise me. Sex with me in nothing but heels turned him on. And I needed him turned on. I needed him to need to touch me, to lick me, to kiss me. We'd only gotten halfway through dinner before I'd needed him to bring me home and fuck me senseless. This was taking too long.

His finger twirl asked for another turn, but I didn't. Instead, I did something I knew would drive him over the edge. Still gyrating to the music, I slid a hand down inside my panties, ran a finger along my slit, and brought it to my mouth.

His eyes were ravenous as I sucked my own wetness off my finger.

"Turn around and walk to the window," he commanded.

I did as he said, continuing my dance as I went and stopping three feet short.

He turned up the lights.

I stopped dancing and covered myself with my hands. A striptease for him was one thing, but not the whole city. I turned back. "They can see my boobs."

He'd pulled his tie off. "Turn around."

I did, but covered up.

He brought the tie around my head. "Close your eyes." He tied it behind me as a blindfold. "You can't see them, so they don't exist. Put your hands down."

"But they can see."

"You are stronger than the fear." This had been his saying for a while.

I concentrated on relaxing and finally dropped my hands to my sides. "Satisfied?"

I heard his zipper, and then his clothes falling to the floor. The next thing I felt was his cock against my ass, his chest against my back, and his hot breath on my ear. "Remember Churchill's saying."

"All we have to fear is fear itself," I finished for him, even though he still had it wrong and those were FDR's words.

He pushed me forward, toward the window I could no longer see.

I resisted.

"Put your hands against the glass." He pushed me harder.

I had no choice but to touch the glass, though I leaned back against him as hard as I could.

"Scared?"

"You have no idea."

"I'm going to fuck you right here up against the glass where everyone can see."

"But—"

"No, not in the butt, unless you ask for it."

The laugh his line forced out of me helped me to relax a little—but very little. "What if there's a crack in the glass?"

He nipped at my ear. "Would I put you in danger?"

That question crystallized it for me. "No."

Charlie had rushed a mad gunman to save me. He was the one person in the world I knew would never put me in danger—not ever.

He kept me pressed forward to the point that I had to hold myself away from the glass. "Then decide if you're going to let the fear control you for the rest of your life or not."

"But—"

"But nothing." He stepped back. "You decide. Have courage or be afraid forever."

For several seconds I was frozen in place, in total darkness from the blindfold. I was able to step away from the window if I wanted, but I wished for the courage not to.

"You decide."

I wanted to live. I wanted to be proud of taking charge of my life. I pushed down the panties and kicked them aside before easing my breasts against the cold glass. I said the hardest words. "Fuck me against the glass already."

He urged my legs apart and brought his hand around in front of me, finding my surprise. "You shaved?"

"Waxed. You said full Brazilian." I giggled, still up against the window. "So now you have to shave for me."

He pulled his hand back and grasped my hips. "Real men don't shave their balls."

"We had a deal. Real men honor their word."

He growled but didn't argue. He knew I had him cornered. His hands left my hips and retraced the route to my slippery folds. "But you have to keep up the waxing."

His touch was like a thousand volts of electricity as his finger slid along to tease my clit, pressing me harder against the glass for the whole world to see.

He nipped at my ear again. "Tell me what you want, dirty girl."

"They can see us." It wasn't an answer, but the words came out anyway.

"Only if they know where to look, and we're too high for them to see anything."

His words eased my anxiety. We were an anonymous couple doing it against the window.

He entered me suddenly with his fingers before retreating and playing over my swollen clit. He continued to nibble on my ear, kiss my neck, and generally drive me crazy, brushing his chest against my back.

He pulled my hips back and ran his cock along my pussy, past my entrance and over my hypersensitive bud several times, guiding himself with his hand. His fingers took turns teasing the tiny bundle of nerves.

I arched my hips every time he brought himself forward, trying for more friction, more pressure, needing more everything—most of all, more him.

"Take me already," I pleaded.

Spreading my legs farther, I stuck my hips back and guided his tip into my heat. A burst of pleasure was my reward as he finally slipped inside.

He seemed hesitant at first, moving slowly, gently. "You're so fucking wet, so fucking tight." He groaned as I took him in. "Unfuckingbelievably good."

I panted from the sheer pleasure of him inside me where he belonged. It melted away my thoughts of the glass. His cock was what I'd needed to relax tonight, and I should have known it.

His hand returned to my aroused bud as his thrusts grew deeper, and I bucked my hips against his rhythm. The other hand came around me. I pushed away from the glass to give him access to my breast. He teased my nipple, fondled and squeezed and teased some more. His tempo increased, the thrusts gaining strength as I took him in all the way.

"How many people do you imagine are down there watching us?" he asked.

Adrenaline surged through me with dread of being seen like this, doing this.

"How many?" he repeated.

"I don't know," I panted. What if one of them was catching us on a cell phone, ready to blast it across the Internet? What if it was more than one?

Charlie's breathing came faster. His moans said his release was approaching as I rocked against him, taking him in again and again.

The hot, liquid pleasure of him filling me washed over me in waves. My orgasm built so quickly that its arrival surprised me. The tremors took over as I clenched around his cock. My legs weakened but didn't buckle.

He released my breast and took my hips with both hands. Moments later he pounded out his own release inside me.

The fear-induced adrenaline made my legs jittery. Panting, with my face against the glass, I pushed the blindfold up over my head. I squinted.

A single figure walked by on the sidewalk below. Was he looking up, or she? I couldn't tell anything from this distance. There hadn't been anyone watching, and I didn't care anymore.

I was naked, plastered against the window I'd always feared, and all I felt was satisfied—that and happy my man was as well.

*"Fear is natural, but you need to channel it and control it rather than let it control you,"* he'd told me a dozen times.

Charlie had helped me once more to deal with fear, and he'd channeled it to give me my quickest orgasm ever.

He truly was my man.

His fingers slid over my bare pussy. "I like you waxed."

"You still have to shave."

He growled again.

~

DANIELLE
*(two weeks later)*

THE MESSAGE CAME IN AFTER LEAVING HEATHROW AS WE TRAVELED DOWN the M4.

ANDRINA: Can't make next week. Jordan has been shot

I sniffled as I reread the message. The terrible news about her sister clearly overshadowed the reunion she, Mena, and I had planned.

ME: Will she be okay?

ANDRINA: They think so. She's in surgery. I'm sure she will

I sniffled again.

ME: Let me know if there is anything I can do

ANDRINA: Thanks

Charlie glanced over. Being back in the UK, it was safe to let him drive. "What's wrong?"
"My friend Andrina. Her sister's been shot."
"That's terrible. Will she be all right?"
"She thinks so."
"Any idea how it happened?" he asked.
"Jordan is a cop." I didn't need to say more.
"That's a tough job."
I nodded, and except for a few more sniffles, we drove the rest of the way in silence.
"We don't have to go through with this," Charlie suggested as he opened the car door for me.
I'd slowly given in to his insistence on door-opening chivalry, as archaic as it was.
We were outside Daddy's house.
"It would break his heart if I didn't come," I explained.
"You've been a wreck the entire trip over. Maybe we should turn around and visit another day."
I had been fidgety. Daddy had summoned me—us—and normally I wouldn't have hesitated, but it was the timing that shook me. Yesterday had been five years. Five years since he and Alicia got married.
I shook my head. "No. This is something I have to do."
Alicia and Daddy had been so loving that day, and I'd cried tears of

happiness for them. But since Mother died, five years had been Daddy's limit to hold on to a woman.

I liked Alicia much more than the stepmothers who'd preceded her, and I feared the announcement Daddy would make.

I stepped close to Charlie and wrapped my arms around him, nuzzling into his shoulder. "I love you."

He held me tight and rubbed my back.

Why did this trouble with relationships have to be in Daddy's genes? And the darker question, one that had haunted me for years—what did it mean for me?

Charlie had made me question that suspicion and shelve it away, but was our clock ticking down? Was the number of hugs I'd get from my man limited by the passing of time?

He kissed my head. "If your fear is correct, it's just another pothole in life's journey. Tomorrow the sun will rise on a new day."

"Tomorrow will be a new day," I repeated, for him more than me. I'd been through these before and cried each time I'd lost the stepmother I'd thought would stick.

Charlie released me. "Dad."

I turned.

"I didn't expect to see you here," Charlie said.

Charlie's father, the duke, walked over from the doorway. "Jarrod told me you were coming back, and I didn't want to miss my chance to meet your girl here." A second later he took my hand in both of his. "My, Danielle, you've grown up to be a lovely woman."

"Thank you, your grace." I hadn't seen him since the feud started, since I was a teenager.

"Now cut that out. It's Carter, please. Especially now that your father and I have settled things." He leaned closer. "Until it's time you call me Dad."

I blushed at the implication.

"Stop it," Charlie cut in. "I won't have you embarrassing her."

Carter pulled back and turned to Charlie. "Your mother couldn't make it today. It's her turn to host the bridge group, and you know how she is about that. Perhaps you'll be able to stop by before you go back."

"We'd love to," I answered for him. It was the courteous thing to do, and family was family.

Although Daddy and Charlie's father had agreed to have both of us stay working at Hawker, Charlie had been worried that his dad would take this opportunity to try to talk him into moving to Berlin.

"Splendid. Shall we?" Carter motioned to the open doorway.

I followed, not eager for this. "What's settled?" I asked Charlie when we were far enough away.

"The family animosity."

"I never understood it."

Inside, his smirk gave him away.

"You know, don't you?" I asked.

Our conversation was interrupted as Alicia gathered me into a hug that seemed overly joyful for the occasion, as did Daddy's.

A little while later we were eating snacks Alicia had prepared, along with Daddy's favorite hard cider, when my brother John came down from upstairs. He still had a bit of a limp from the accident and used a cane.

Charlie eyed him cautiously. "You're looking good."

There was an issue between them Charlie wouldn't address.

"You're looking good too, Blakewell. You must have gotten some plastic surgery."

Charlie glared. "Too bad the chicks don't dig a walking stick."

John lifted it a few inches. "It's only so I can beat you if you mistreat Dani."

I slapped his shoulder. "Stop it."

"It's a shame what happened to what's-his-face made you take up with this clown," John said.

"Now cut it out. Both of you. Charlie treats me better than you ever did."

John put his hand over his heart. "Ouch, sis."

Charlie wrapped an arm behind me. "Yeah."

I wiggled free. "I mean it. The first one of you who starts anything gets a kick in the you-know-whats."

John put his hands up, fully aware that I meant it. "It's just a little fun."

"And it's over," I told him.

"I take it you're coming back for the trial?" Charlie said, pulling me to his side.

"Of course."

The police had found video of Thin Man—Caldwell—exiting the car that had forced John off the road and put him in the hospital.

Thinking nobody knew, Caldwell had neglected to include that in his immunity agreement.

In a bit of retribution for Caldwell giving testimony against him, Junior had provided a statement about paying Caldwell to get John. That, along with the film tying Caldwell to the car and paint on the scrapes that matched the car John had been driving, made it seem like Caldwell wasn't getting away without some prison time.

"Did you see anything more on Gerald?" I asked Charlie when we had a minute off to the side.

"No," was his curt reply.

Gerald had left Salem on a one-day sailing trip shortly after the whole kidnapping incident with Junior. They found the dinghy adrift, an empty life jacket, and some debris. The search had been called off after a few days. "Shouldn't have gone out alone with only one good hand," a local fisherman had told the news after he'd gone missing.

Although I certainly didn't love Gerald, I still felt sorry for him. Lost at sea was not a good end for anyone. The thought of being thrown into the water with sharks sent a chill down my spine as bad as my horse nightmares.

"You okay?" Charlie asked. His eyes were kind with true sympathy, which only reinforced my feelings for him.

I nodded. "Just thinking about poor Gerald and sharks."

Charlie sucked in a breath. "Yeah, that should have been Junior. He's getting off too easily."

"It's still sad."

"You know one of the things I love about you?"

I shook my chest. "I have two of them."

He chuckled. "That, too, but you don't have a devious bone in your body. I can think of another scenario that doesn't involve sharks if an angry Russian was after me."

I nodded. He thought Gerald had staged it.

John returned, and Charlie went over to talk to his dad.

Junior had accepted a plea deal and gotten twenty-five years. Abby's sentence was ten years shorter. For cooperating, Califano only got six months, with five years of probation and a ban from labor organizations. Assuming Caldwell's trial went as expected, this would be behind us soon, and we wouldn't have to deal with any of them again.

After the union agreed to the contract extension, a lot of things had fallen into place at Hawker. Spirits in the building had been especially lifted by the news last week from Derek, Sr., that his wife, Leslie, had gone into remission. The doctors wouldn't speculate on how long it might last, but the news was still fantastic.

Seeing Daddy and Charlie's dad laughing in the corner brought back my question about the feud Charlie had adeptly sidestepped earlier, so I left John to peel Charlie away from our fathers and get to the bottom of it.

"What?" he asked after I got him into the kitchen.

"You told me you didn't, but I can tell you know about the origin of the trouble between our families."

Since he wouldn't lie to me, his silence was a clear indication he was holding back.

"Out with it," I half yelled. I was through being the only one in the dark.

He backed up. "Want some more cider?"

"Tell me," I demanded.

He sighed. "It has to do with your tattoo, your fear of horses."

"What?"

"He shouldn't have let you go down to the barn that night," Daddy said from behind me.

I turned. I hadn't noticed him come in. Daddy had refused a million times to discuss it, but now he was ready? "What do you mean?"

"With mares in season," Daddy said, "stallions can become unpredictable, even mean."

I blinked away the memory of the *very* mean horse I'd encountered that night.

"He shouldn't have let you go to the barn. It was completely irresponsible of him. You could have been hurt."

This wasn't making sense. "This was all about that night?"

"I couldn't have you kids put in such danger."

"But—"

Daddy cut me off. "When I confronted young Charles here, he admitted it. He let you go down there alone, and he knew better. He knew the danger. That set me off, and it just snowballed from there."

"But he didn't *let* me go down to the stables."

"Quiet, Dani." Charlie reached for my hand. "It's over. Let it be."

I huffed and pulled away. "Daddy, he warned me not to go, but I snuck off and went anyway."

Puzzlement crept across Daddy's face."

"Let it be," Charlie repeated.

Daddy was incredulous. "He told you it was dangerous and you went anyway?"

"I was sixteen. I was stupid. I admit it, but it wasn't his fault."

"Incredibly stupid." Daddy shook his head and walked off.

I made a move to follow him.

Charlie grabbed for me. "He'll get over it. Just give him time."

I turned on my boyfriend. "Why did you do that and set our fathers at each others' throats for years?" He'd caused the entire problem.

"He was in a mood to lock you up for a year."

"What?"

"He was set on punishing you for getting into the stables. I couldn't let that happen. I just couldn't."

It finally dawned on me. Even back then, Charlie had been protecting me, and my hardheadedness was the true cause of the rift between our families. "You took the blame for me?"

He drew me into a hug. "Any time, any place."

In that moment, against the warmth of his chest, I knew our connection hadn't just begun. It had started years ago and only been put on an extended hold. "You're a fool, but I still love you."

He held me tighter and rocked us. "A fool in love with you."

Our embrace only lasted a minute before Alicia broke it up. "It's time, you two."

How she could sound so cheery about announcing her impending divorce I didn't understand. Maybe she'd negotiated a generous prenup, but knowing her, I doubted that had ever been her mindset.

My phone vibrated as we were called to the kitchen. I pulled it out for a quick peek.

ANDRINA: Jordan is out of surgery. She'll recover

Charlie glanced over.

I put the phone away. "Andrina. Her sister will be fine."

"Good news."

I nodded. "Yeah."

After we all gathered in the kitchen, and the glasses were refilled, Daddy stepped forward.

I tightened my grip on Charlie's hand and braced for the inevitable.

"As you know, it's been five years since Alicia and I said our vows." Daddy tipped his glass toward her.

She smiled and nodded.

This is exactly how the last two of these speeches had started. I closed my eyes to hear the horrible news again.

"Alicia and I," Daddy said, "would like this group to be witnesses as we renew those vows in the back garden this afternoon."

I blinked my eyes open to a joyous scene of congratulations going around in all directions.

Alicia beamed like a blushing, first-time bride as she came over. "Sorry for keeping you in the dark, dear, but your Daddy insisted."

I hugged her tight. "That sounds like him."

Later in the garden, as Daddy and Alicia repeated their vows, Charlie held my hand and whispered, "That's beautiful."

Charlie had been right. Genetics didn't have to determine my father's relationships, or mine.

He leaned close. "I love you, Cookie."

I squeezed his hand. "I love you, too, Cookie Monster."

He'd given me the strength to face my fear and give us the chance we deserved. I turned to him and saw love in his eyes that told me everything I needed to know.

I had found my love, my protector, my everything.

~

THANK YOU FOR READING CHARLIE AND DANI'S STORY.

To learn what happens to Andrina's sister, Jordan, after she is shot in the line of duty, you can get Temptation at the Lake on Amazon. The following pages contain an excerpt of the book.

(Case and Jordan's story) Getting back to one hundred percent was supposed to be hard, but she didn't count on the irresistible Casey becoming the devil pushing her to the breaking point. A fling with this devil becomes complicated when she gets pulled into the dangerous town feud.

# SNEAK PEEK: TEMPTATION AT THE LAKE

# CHAPTER 1

*Casey*

The Monday night crowd at The Peanut Barrel was louder than usual.

My brother, Waylon, was in the bathroom looking for his phone again. There was a reason his wallet was on a long chain attached to his belt. He could lose anything.

As the door to the bar opened, I twisted on my stool and squinted at the outline of the new arrival.

"Who ya waitin' on, big guy?" Sonya asked from her perch behind the bar.

"Pris." My sister was late, as usual.

"Don't bother checkin' the door, then. You'll hear her as soon as she shows."

I lifted my glass in acknowledgment of Sonya's wisdom and downed the last gulp of my beer. Studying the bottom of my glass didn't produce an answer to my dilemma. "I'll take another."

"Bad day?" Sonya asked.

"No." I twisted up my face. "Just thirsty."

"You don't fool me, Case. If you have more than one, something's wrong."

I squinted my best evil eye at her. "Are you going to serve me or not?"

Fifteen glorious seconds of silence was followed by my beer arriving.

Sonya waited in front of me. She fancied herself the town shrink, but this wasn't a problem I would mull over with her.

"Thanks." I could still be a proper gentleman.

"Be that way." She huffed and left me alone.

The full glass didn't give me any more inspiration than the empty one had.

A slap on the back woke me out of my trance.

"It wasn't in there," Waylon said. "I'll have to retrace my steps back to the house."

"That's just an excuse to avoid Pris." Our little sister could be a handful.

He shrugged, not denying it. "I'll handle Lee. You got Pris."

So far his method of handling Lee had resulted in bruises all around, but no movement on the issue.

"Sorry about the punch," he added. "You shoulda ducked." He waved at Sonya and left.

I went back to staring into my glass.

"Your problem is different than you think." Rose Seneca's voice drifted over my shoulder a second before she climbed onto the stool next to mine.

"Or not," I replied. I hadn't voiced the problem, but Rose had a way of guessing things that baffled me.

She pulled a basket of peanuts closer and shelled one before waving Sonya over. "A chardonnay to go, please."

Sonya crossed her arms. "Rose, your tab is full up."

Rose hesitated before reaching for her purse.

I pulled my wallet out and threw two of my three twenties on the wooden surface. "The lady asked for wine."

Sonya swiped up the money. She gave me an eye roll Rose didn't see and marched off. Sonya, like a lot of people in town, had Rose pegged as odd, which was spot on, only they couldn't see past that to the intuitive girl underneath.

"Thank you. You didn't need to," Rose said, looking up from the purse she'd opened.

"True enough, but I felt like it."

She chewed another few peanuts while waiting for her wine.

Sonya dropped off the plastic cup and added a straw without Rose having to ask for it this time.

Rose thanked her, and a handful of peanuts later, she was on her way. Wine to go in a plastic cup with a straw. Odd was just the beginning.

## SNEAK PEEK: TEMPTATION AT THE LAKE

A half dozen rowdies having a loud argument parted to give Rose and her flowing, purple skirt a wide berth as she made her way to the door.

The last guy who'd hassled her in here had run his truck off the road that night. He'd claimed the steering failed. At the shop the next day, the mechanic couldn't find any problem. None of the guys had messed with Rose after that. Superstitions ran deep here.

I turned back to my beer, still with no idea how to make this situation with my sister right. My jaw hurt from the punch my brother Waylon had delivered an hour ago. Breaking up fights came with risks.

He and Lee Pollock had been going at it in the middle of the street over my baby sister, Pris. Their previous altercations had been verbal, but this time Waylon had bloodied Lee pretty good by the time I got involved. We'd both hightailed it out of there when the siren got close.

Pris was way too wild for her own good, and Waylon was just as determined to keep Lee away from her as Lee was to see her. With the history between our families, this was not going to end well. It had been a long time since we'd had a murder in town, but Waylon might just change that.

The door opened, and I listened instead of looking.

"Hey, Rusty," Pris said loudly enough for me to hear across the room. "Where's my twenty bucks?"

I looked back and raised my glass to my sister.

Rusty's lame excuse didn't carry to my ears.

"Do you reckon he'll pay up anytime soon?" I asked Sonya.

"Naw. He likes her chasing him too much."

Pris punched Rusty in the shoulder. "That's for being late." Then she turned toward me and smiled.

I looked beyond my sister to see Rusty's face more happy than scared. In my book, he was playing with fire, and that wasn't particularly wise with my sister.

Pris took the stool next to me. "What's so fucking important that I had to rush over?"

Delaying didn't seem like it would help. "I think you should cool it with Lee for a while."

She punched my shoulder. It was her thing. "Not you too. Ever since I grew boobs, you guys think you can run my dating life."

I'd figured it would go like this, so I let her vent some more and avoided getting punched again.

"You didn't listen to my warning about hooking up with that skank Ella-Mae, so no fucking way am I listenin' to y'all," she spat.

A lot of glances were coming our way now. She was loud—too loud. Par for the course with my sister. I hadn't prepared for her throwing my mistake with Ella-Mae Forrester back at me, but I held my tongue.

"Did you get warts? Or was it sores? No, let me guess, warts and sores. Are the antibiotics helping? I hope so, cuz I hear some of those things are antibiotic-resistant these days. You know Leroy left town right after a week with Ella-Mae. I heard it was cuz he caught somethin' and his noodle went limp. But maybe he didn't get the right pills and you'll be okay."

When she finally shut up, I said, "That's not the same."

"It never is with you guys. But I'm not a little girl anymore. You can't tell me what to do."

I faced her head-on. "I'm not telling you. I'm suggesting."

She glared back. "Then thank you for your very kind fucking suggestion, and I love ya to death, Case, but the answer is still no goddamned way am I takin' orders from any of you."

I sighed. It was the way Waylon had said he'd kill Lee if he ever came around Pris again that scared me. If looks could do the job, Lee would already be six feet under, and Waylon wasn't one for idle threats.

I stared into my glass. "This could be dangerous for both you and Lee."

That stopped her mouth for a second.

∼

JORDAN

WHEN I TURNED OFF THE HIGHWAY AT THE SIGN FOR CLEAR LAKE, THE CURVY, two-lane country road brought back memories of a better time—carefree summers. A time when Dad had been alive. A time before Stan, and a time before the shooting.

Pain shot through my leg as I shifted it. Bad idea. The throb intensified from dull to I-want-to-scream for a moment before dying down enough to be tolerable. Maybe I should have taken some Tylenol before leaving.

No, that would have interfered with my plan to treat myself to several stiff drinks tonight. The unopened bottle of rum in my bag would see to that. This would be my first taste since the *incident*. That was the word the news whores used for it, because I'd shot back and the other guy died.

The ugly envelope taunted me from the passenger seat, peeking out from under the McDonalds bag that had sufficed for lunch and dinner on the way here. The awful letter was the last thing I'd thrown in before starting out. Stooping down to drag my purse off the floor and put it away would have hurt too much, so I'd thrown it on the seat before limping around the car.

At the first stoplight in town—actually the only one, as I remembered—I shifted into park.

I blinked twice to be sure he wasn't an illusion.

A bearded man on the tricycle pedaled slowly across the intersection with the sign suspended above him that read: *Tonight's Boathouse Special: pot roast.*

Things certainly were different here.

Unbuckling, I leaned over to the passenger side and snagged the handle of my purse. "Fuck." Swearing took my mind off the pain. In this position, the evil writing on the envelope was too big to ignore.

It was addressed to A. Jordan Vonn, but the printing in the upper left corner was the problem.

> Lt. Ivan Edmonds
> Richmond Police Department, Internal Affairs

Ivan Edmonds could go fuck himself. He wasn't called Ivan the Terrible for nothing. His shooting review board was akin to the Spanish Inquisition these days. My partner, Bryce Shepherd, had joked that it seemed like the only time Ivan thought we were allowed to shoot back is if we were already mortally wounded. That way he wouldn't have any paperwork to do because we'd be dead.

I'd only had one drink before I'd been called to the scene. Because I was in plain clothes instead of in uniform, that meant no bodycam. If I'd started the audio recorder on my phone, this would all have been cleared up easily. But it was too late for woulda, coulda, shoulda. The hard evidence would have to sort itself out later. And *later* already meant after my reputation had been thoroughly trashed in the papers and online.

The Constitution said you got the benefit of the doubt, but as far as the asinine press was concerned, that didn't apply to me because I was a cop.

I'd gotten the side-eye treatment from Mrs. Butternut next door when I loaded up my car. She'd already gossiped about me to a half dozen nearby residents and was probably checking out the price of pitchforks on Amazon so they could get rid of me and clean up the neighborhood.

After folding the envelope in two, I stuffed it in my purse so it wouldn't be a constant reminder of my poor judgment. Instead, rest and recuperation away from my city was the plan—a damned good plan. The recuperation, I needed. The rest, I deserved, and the peace I was due.

Ivan and the rest of those fuckers in Internal Affairs would have to wait until I was back on active duty.

The car behind me honked twice.

The light had turned green. I buckled up before shifting back into drive. That earned me another honk from the asshole behind me.

I stuck my left hand out the window and gave the jerkwad in the white pickup a middle-finger salute as I hit the gas. Maybe not a good idea in a town as small as Clear Lake since I planned on being here for two months.

The pickup roared from behind me and pulled alongside.

*Good job, Vonn. One fucking minute in Clear Lake and already making enemies.*

Feeling pretty stupid, I smiled and waved at the driver to deescalate the situation. Maybe he'd forgive me. My tiny Prius wasn't going to outrun him, or do well if we played bumper cars.

The driver returned my wave before pulling ahead and back into my lane. All I could make out through the dirty window was that he was a man. The truck roared like it didn't have a muffler. Typical—a guy driving a big, loud truck to compensate for some other deficiency, no doubt.

I also noticed a gun rack on the back window of his pickup as he pulled in front of me. Without my service weapon, I was probably the only one around here not armed.

"In two-tenths of a mile, turn right onto Miller Avenue," the lady in my phone told me.

Mr. Gun Rack in the white pickup made the same turn onto Miller.

Pulling off to the shoulder short of the intersection, I waited for a solid minute. Seeming like I was following the guy I'd just flipped off wouldn't be smart. When my hand went instinctively to my hip and confirmed I was unarmed, I decided to find a store tomorrow to buy a gun.

Administrative leave meant I couldn't carry my badge or service weapon, but I still had my second-amendment right to bear arms. My weapon had always been my equalizer. With it on my hip, it didn't matter how big or mean the man in front of me was. Since I'd started packing heat, no man scared me anymore.

I turned down the gravel drive at the number that mirrored my rental reservation. The cottage at the end looked just as it had online. Another trait of small-town America: the rental listing had been honest about what it was and what it wasn't.

Shutting down the engine, I had to wonder—why was I so paranoid? I could handle things, and none of the bad actors back in Richmond knew I was here. I took a deep breath. My relaxation in this place needed to be mental as well as physical.

*This is small-town America, Vonn. A peaceful place where people look out for one another, unlike the almost nightly shootings in the big city.*

I sighed. Strapping a gun to my hip while not carrying a badge didn't sound like the right way to blend in with a small town like this. Anonymity was my friend, so no running out to buy a gun.

After a mental pat on the back for unfolding myself from the car without the aid of a single swear word, I closed my eyes. Breathing in air that was all country and no city eased my pain and lightened my mood. I pulled out my ponytail and shook my hair. This would be two months or so of hair-down relaxation and recuperation from my wounds—the physical ones at least.

I turned toward next door, the Cleaver house we'd stayed in four summers in a row when I was a kid. It looked just as it always had. Behind the house, the dock still protruded from the beach into the still waters of the lake. I could almost see my younger self arriving here for a languid summer of fun.

Those summers had been the happiest times of my life.

This little cabin I'd booked was as close as I could get to replicating the experience. The bigger house next door wasn't a rental any longer.

As promised, I found the key under the mat. The carved sign above the door read *Raccoon*. Family names out here were weird. Why couldn't it have been Smith or Harris or something normal? It was the same lake, but something felt different.

I realized it was the scent. I'd loved the honeysuckle that climbed the trellis next door. If this were my cottage, I'd add that.

I let myself into the Raccoon cabin.

The room facing the lake had a nice view, and the property had a dock of its own. A canoe tied to the dock came into view when I walked to the window, and there were two carved wooden raccoons on the back deck. The message light blinked on the phone.

"Ms. Vonn, Priscilla here. I hope y'all have a nice stay at Clear Lake. Paddleboard is under the deck, and the canoe is at the dock. If any ol' thing needs fixin', just give a holler at five-five-five twenty-six twenty-six."

Priscilla, who I understood was also the town's real estate agent, had rented me this cabin by the lake, and her greeting was a nice touch.

The next surprise was on the counter: a bottle with a red bow and a sticky note.

The Peanut Barrel stocks all the flavors

It was Flatfoot butterscotch whiskey. I hadn't had a flavored whiskey like this before. It had to be better than the Fireball I'd mistakenly guzzled once.

I'd never been old enough to set foot in The Peanut Barrel, Clear Lake's bar, before, but that was going on tonight's itinerary. I'd keep my bottle of rum in reserve.

Hobbling through the pain, I schlepped my junk into the cabin. I didn't see any lights on in the Cleaver house, and I mentally planned a walk by the lake side of the place for a peek inside to see how much it had changed since we'd rented it.

I stopped for one more deep lungful of country air before bringing in the last bag.

The only sound was the birds—quite a change.

~

WHEN I PULLED INTO THE PEANUT BARREL'S PARKING LOT A LITTLE LATER, I noticed three white pickups.

*Get a grip, Vonn. Everybody in this burg probably has a pickup or two. You don't need to be so damned paranoid.*

I resisted the temptation to check for gun racks. Back in Richmond, one would have stood out like a beacon. But in this part of the state, they were probably as common as fishing poles. That would also explain the lower crime statistics in this county. A lot of criminals were idiots, but it took a special kind of stupid to burglarize a house where you knew the owner was armed.

I heard the arguing as soon as I opened the car door.

"I warned you to stay away from him." The angry shout came from a big man, who had a tiny redhead pinned against a car a few spaces over. His hairy arms caged her in place.

"We was just talkin'," she protested in a voice laced with fear.

I slammed the door to my car and started over. I'd seen this play out badly way too many times on the job. "Hey."

"How many times do I have to tell you?" he screeched as he slammed her against the car.

I heard her head hit the glass of the window and hop-skipped my way to the fracas. "Hey, asshole."

The hairy brute momentarily shifted his focus to me. "Stay out of this,

## SNEAK PEEK: TEMPTATION AT THE LAKE

bitch." With a monster beer belly, he was in serious need of a diet, but no one who carried around nearly three hundred pounds was weak.

When my gun hand came back empty from my belt, I had to make a new plan.

He grabbed her shoulders, pulled her away from the car, and slammed her into it again with a sickening thud. "When will you fucking learn?" His scream was feral.

I reached him in a few unsteady skips. A quick kick to the back of his near-side knee buckled him just enough. Jumping on his back, I got a chokehold in place. "Let go of her," I yelled into his ear.

A few onlookers from the patio glanced over, and one put his phone to his ear.

Bigfoot growled angrily as he released the redhead, who slumped to the ground. He clawed at my arm barred across his throat, and when that didn't work, he slammed us back against the car behind me.

The blow knocked all the air out of me. He repeated it, and after the third time, he pried my arms loose. The dynamics of this takedown then shifted in his favor.

A siren sounded in the distance. Help was on the way. I just had to avoid him until then.

I stayed upright and dodged the first punch he threw my way.

A kick with my good leg aimed at his balls missed when my bad leg folded under the strain. I caught the gut overhanging his belt.

Dancing sideways as best I could, I dodged another swing.

The siren was close now.

I hadn't backed up far enough, and the next blow caught me in the right boob, launching me back against a car. It stung like a mother, but I slid sideways off the car, to not be boxed in.

"You should have stayed out of this, bitch." He lunged and swung again.

The police car skidded to a stop on the gravel.

I didn't look back at Bigfoot fast enough. Pain bloomed in my cheek, and I went down.

A kick to the ribs followed. I closed my eyes and covered my face for the next blow.

# CHAPTER 2

*Casey*

THE SOUND OF THE SIREN FILTERED IN FROM OUTSIDE AND BECAME LOUD WHEN Rusty opened the door.

"Fight in the parking lot," he yelled. "It's Gibs again."

Gibson Pollock was responsible for more than his share of fights in town, and not many of them fair.

I didn't move fast enough and ended up behind ten potential spectators crowding through the door.

Gibson's on-and-off girlfriend, Loretta Sands, was on the ground, holding her head.

Gibs had a woman on his back, choking him. All I could make out was her long, blond mane.

Good for her. The asshole deserved it.

I laughed at Gibson's plight and stood on the patio with the rest. Eleven months and thirteen days—that's how long I had left to stay out of trouble.

It turned ugly when Gibs slammed Blondie into the car behind them with a sickening thud.

That turned it for me. Screw the Pollocks and the consequences, I raced for the stairs. The siren grew louder as I squeezed by the looky-loos. I took the steps two at a time. Too many people in this town were too afraid of the Pollocks to get involved.

Gibs had dislodged Blondie when I made it to the pavement. She dodged his hasty swing. He missed a second time, telegraphing his swing too early. But Blondie made the mistake of looking over when the cop car skidded to a stop five yards from them. Gibson's next fist found its mark, and the girl went down hard.

The grunt Gibs made when I drove him to the ground a few seconds later was the best sound I'd heard all day. I raised my fist to finish the job. Breaking his nose would even out only a portion of what I owed him.

The painful jolt hit me in the back. I shuddered as the searing heat wracked through me, and I fell to the side, shaking uncontrollably.

Fucking Devlin held the trigger down on his Taser for another second and smiled. The deep blue of his uniform almost matched the darkness of his soul.

"What the fuck?" Pris yelled at him.

Like the asshole he was, Devlin shifted the Taser to his other hand, and pulled his gun on her.

My sister backed up. She was impulsive as shit, but not crazy.

Devlin waved his gun in my direction. "Rusty, you and the guys carry this dirtbag inside."

With the continuing spasms, I couldn't work my mouth—or any other part of my body—to complain as they carried me back inside The Peanut Barrel.

It had happened again.

---

## JORDAN

I PUSHED MYSELF UP, BUT HADN'T EVEN MANAGED TO GET TO MY KNEES WHEN the stupid cop Tased my protector.

After the yelling, I squinted and made out his nameplate: *D. Pollock*.

Several men carried my protector off.

Bigfoot groaned. "Aren't you going to arrest him for violating the order?"

"Shut up," the cop spat.

Bigfoot pointed at me as he sat up. "She started it. She almost choked me to death." His shirt had split open from the tackle, and a mass of dark chest hair spilled out.

Officer Pollock trained his weapon on me. "Get up and face the car."

Arguing with an armed idiot was not a good play. I struggled to my feet, turned toward the car, and put my hands on the roof. I knew better than to resist. "He was beating up that girl." I tossed my head toward the redhead who'd gotten up and backed away.

Bigfoot huffed. "We was just talkin' when *she* jumped me for no reason. Arrest the bitch."

"That's a lie," a short brunette shot back.

"Shut up, Pris," Officer Pollock said as he started to pat me down. "You go with your brother before I arrest your ass for interfering with a police officer."

She walked away. "You mean *sorry excuse* for a police officer."

The girl had a mouth on her.

I winced when Pollock moved down to my legs.

"What's this?" he asked, patting my wound.

"Bandage."

He shifted to the other leg. "Loretta, what happened?"

Bigfoot scowled.

"Gibs and me was just talking loud is all," said the girl who'd been beaten up by the big moron.

"That's a lie. She's just scared," I mumbled softly to the officer. I'd seen this countless times. The battered woman was too afraid to speak up.

"You're not from around here, are you?" he asked me.

"She choked me—damn near killed me," Bigfoot protested again.

"Shut up, Gibs," Pollock said.

I ignored the big man and answered the cop's question. "Richmond."

"Well, Richmond, we got a law against strangling people in this part of the state. Put your hands behind your back."

I put my hands behind my back as instructed and couldn't believe nobody in the crowd was speaking up. "That law requires I either wound him or cause bodily injury," I noted.

"What? You a lawyer?" Pollock asked as he secured the cuffs on one hand.

"A cop."

That stopped him. "I don't see a badge."

"ID back left pocket."

In any other situation, I'd have laid him flat on the ground for the way he felt my ass up finding my business cards. I couldn't carry my full ID while on administrative leave.

"Detective Vonn. Richmond Police, huh? This doesn't prove anything. Anybody can print up one of these."

"It's real. Call the number and talk to my captain."

He was quiet for a second. "Your name is familiar. Do I know you?"

"No."

He scratched his chin. "You the Vonn in the news?"

Even here in the backwoods, I couldn't escape the news stories.

I nodded. "Yeah."

Instead of securing my other wrist, he unlocked the first one. "That was a righteous shoot."

For once the media scrutiny had worked in my favor. "Damned straight, it was." An attack on one cop was an attack on us all, and that put Pollock in my corner.

Gibson erupted. "What the fuck, Devlin? You just letting her go after what she did to me?"

It figured that bruiser had enough run-ins with the law to be on a first-name basis with them. I turned around and leveled him with a glare.

"Gibs, she's right about the law," Pollock told him as he handed me his card. "Call me. We can catch dinner."

*Fat chance.*

A blonde with a short bob took my elbow. "Why don't you come inside, honey, and let's get you cleaned up."

I went with her and left Idiot Cop behind. My cheek was on fire from the punch, and my hand came back with blood when I touched my temple where I'd hit the ground.

*Good going, Vonn. Come here to heal, and inside of an hour you've got more injuries than you came with.*

"I'm Sonya, by the way," she said. "And dear, everything's on the house for you tonight."

"Thanks... I'm Jordan."

Loretta followed us toward the door as the rest of the silent crowd disbursed.

"Go home, Gibs, and cool off," Idiot Cop told the brute.

Inside there were baskets of peanuts everywhere, and shells crunched under my feet.

A round of applause from the customers surprised me.

Sonya stopped. "You've got fans." She put her arms up for quiet. "This here is Jordan," she announced to the crowd.

I waved meekly, feeling like I was back in middle school. They raised their glasses toward me.

"Treat her nice. Or else." Sonya pulled me by the elbow toward the ladies' room.

I hobbled behind her into the larger-than-expected restroom. In the mirror, I could see the results of not ducking fast enough. The large, red splotch where my cheek burned would be blue by tomorrow, and no amount of makeup could hide it. Blood from a cut ran down the other side of my face.

"I've got ice behind the bar, but let's clean up that cut." Sonya pulled a first aid kit from the cabinet under the sink.

"What's the story with Bigfoot?"

"This will sting a little." She wet a gauze pad with alcohol, and it *did* sting as she patted and wiped my cut. "Gibson Pollock is a first-rate asshole." She changed pads after the first one turned red with my blood.

"And he knows the cop?"

"Devlin is his brother."

I winced as she rubbed harder. "That explains a lot."

A moment later, she opened up a Band-Aid. "I know this looks ugly, but leave it on tonight." She added some ointment before applying it.

"Thanks. Who was the guy who tackled him?"

"That would be Case Benson."

I took a stab at the small-town dynamics. "Let me guess—the cop and he don't get along."

"That's putting it mildly. The problems between the Bensons and the Pollocks go back a ways, and especially between those two. Now, let's get you some ice."

I could go for that, and a drink. After she put things away, I followed her out.

Sonya went behind the bar, and I took a stool, happy to get the weight off my bad leg.

She returned with crushed ice in a bag, which I gladly put to my hot cheek.

"You should be more careful about who you tangle with." The voice came from behind me.

"And he shouldn't beat up women." I turned.

"Case," he said. "May I?" He pointed to the stool next to me.

## SNEAK PEEK: TEMPTATION AT THE LAKE

*Please,* my hormones shouted.

I clamped my eyelids closed for a second to reset my brain.

He wasn't Hollywood-pretty-boy gorgeous. Instead he had a ruggedly handsome action-star look, with broad shoulders, dusty blond hair, stubble over a square jaw, and deep blue eyes that looked right through me. He had my full attention.

I didn't normally go for tattoos, but the ones that disappeared under his shirt sleeve I liked. I hadn't dated much since joining the force, and I certainly hadn't come here looking for company, but that didn't mean I couldn't ogle a good-looking man, and this one defined *ogle-worthy.*

He took the seat next to me and leaned closer. "This is the part where you tell me your name," he whispered.

The man had me tongue-tied. The twinkle in his eye as he looked me up and down screamed *beware, too hot to handle.* He was the kind of guy who probably had something like *Welcome aboard* or *free rides* or *Caution: choking hazard* stenciled on his underwear. If he even wore underwear.

He tapped his chest and said, "Case." He pointed at me.

"Jordan," I squeaked. "Thanks for out there," I managed a few seconds later.

The dimples that appeared with his broad smile were to die for. I could barely breathe. The man sucked all the oxygen out of the air around him. That had to be it. I didn't get this way around guys. I had self-control.

He cocked his head. "Nachos."

My brain was so busy cataloging everything about him that I didn't understand.

"Would you like some nachos?" he repeated.

∾

To continue reading, get **Temptation at the Lake** on Amazon.

Printed in Dunstable, United Kingdom